Dictionary of Film
Quotations

The Wordsworth
Dictionary of Film
Quotations

—

Compiled and edited by
Tony Crawley

Wordsworth Reference

First published as *Chambers Film Quotes* by W&R Chambers Ltd,
43-45 Annandale Street, Edinburgh, 1991.

This edition published 1994 by Wordsworth Editions Ltd,
Cumberland House, Crib Street, Ware, Hertfordshire SG12 9ET.

ISBN 1-85326-329-X

Printed and bound in Denmark by Nørhaven.

The paper in this book is produced from pure wood
pulp, without the use of chlorine or any other substance
harmful to the environment. The energy used in its
production consists almost entirely of hydroelectricity
and heat generated from waste materials, thereby
conserving fossil fuels and contributing little to the
greenhouse effect.

CONTENTS

	page
Introduction	vii
List of Topics	xi
QUOTATIONS	1
Index of Authors	287

INTRODUCTION

'You must not quote to me what I once said. I am wiser now.'
Romy Schneider (1938–82), *Sunday Express*, 25 June 1966

They *all* say that. In every film-world interview I've made in 30 years. Brando goes further (of course) and suggests most celebrities hang themselves by their own talk. Welcome to the games people say . . .

Steven Spielberg says 'There's only seven genuine movie stars in the world today' (*Sunday Times* magazine, 5 November 1989). This compilation of the sayings of film people stems from more than 360 movie stars – W.C. Fields, Mae West to Kevin Costner, Julia Roberts – including Spielberg's coda: 'and Sean Connery is one of them'. Spielberg, of course, is another.

Directors are here, producers, screen and book writers, three or four critics, a few film technicians, a couple of film stars' parents, an assistant director, an MP and even a few anonymous folk. The range is (I hope) as broad as the appeal of cinema, covering not merely the Holy Grail of Hollywood but most of the global film world (Depardieu, Kieslowski, Konchalovsky, Makavejev, Mastroianni).

The idea is to match their mission in life – to inform and amuse. Easy – as they love talking about any and everything, mainly themselves, their acting, careers, their favourite stars (Woody Allen, Marlon Brando), their money, drugs and, of course, their shrinks.

Topics and quotations are in alphabetical order – except the James Bond section (chronological) and Marriages (numerical). Certain categories, Acting, Directors, Nudity, Self-Portraits, Sex, Stars, etc, have been split asunder – into sexes, *not* sexism – merely to avoid a huge wedge of 30 to 50 quotations on one subject. Others like Celebrity/Fame/ Success, Criticism/Critics/Reviews, Hollywood, Media/Press, are divided for similar reasons.

Each quotation is as fully sourced as possible; those bearing date-lines only (Cannes, 23 May 1976, Deauville, September 1984, Munich, 5 February 1987, etc) are from my own tape-scripts of interviews either published (who can trace *all* the cuttings anymore?), utilized in a non-quotable manner (reported speech) or, quite simply, never writtten for all manner of reasons. In all such cases, my choice, like life itself, is arbitrary.

In studying the stars – and, thereby, the editor – it is best to recall one of the sayings of Chairman John Cleese: 'The great mistake most people make is the assumption that most people are sane. I know very few people who are sane – and only one man in my life who was really grown up. All the other people are terribly recognizable as kids who have learned grown-up ways of behaving.' (*The Times*, 12 December 1982).

Flaunting tradition, there are no libraries to thank – except my own cuttings-filled archives. However, I do thank my editors: Alastair Fyfe Holmes, the first editor I've dealt with solely by Fax (the next message reads: 'What do I do with the 1000 quotes that never made the final cut?') and the eagle-eyed Ann Vinnicombe, and two good friends in Britain: Graham Spiers, for kindly supplying me with cuttings over the decade I've lived in France; and Peter Cargin, answering an 11th-hour plea for vital research. Plus my international journalist colleagues for their interviews across the ages; essentially, the best of the breed at *Playboy*, *Rolling Stone*, *Premiere*, the sadly defunct *Films Illustrated*, *Evening Standard*, *Daily Mail*, *Photoplay* (now *Film Monthly*) and the Virgin (later Pan) *Film Yearbook*.

Apart from a few rare instances, none of the quotations derive from the plethora of filmland auto/biographies, rather the average, workaday interview-go-round of film folk. 'Actors', said Glenn Ford (*TV Times*, 1972), 'feel they must act when they're interviewed – compelled to give an answer, pose as experts on things they know nothing about. It's a better policy to keep your mouth shut.'

This book, therefore, is dedicated, to those that didn't – in particular, to the best interviewees in my career: Michael Caine, John Cleese, Joan Collins, Gérard Depardieu, Clint Eastwood, Sir Alfred Hitchcock, Jessica Lange, Robert Mitchum, Meryl Streep, Jean-Louis Trintignant and Roger Vadim.

And John Huston – in fighting form to his last words, according to his son, Danny, on American television: 'How many rifles you got?' '28, John.' 'Plenty of ammo?' 'Yes, John.' 'Then, knock 'em dead, kid!'

Tony Crawley

LIST OF TOPICS

1 Accents
2 Acting by Actors
3 Acting by Actresses
4 Acting Advice
5 Actor-Directors
6 Actors
7 Actresses
8 Adultery
9 Age
10 Agents
11 Alcohol
12 Woody Allen
13 Ambition
14 America
15 American Actors
16 American Dream
17 Animals
18 Anti-Image
19 Army
20 Art
21 Artists
22 Audience
23 Auteur
24 Authors
25 Autographs
26 Awards
27 Bad Movies
28 Bad Taste
29 Beauty
30 Bernardo Bertolucci
31 Billing
32 Bitches
33 Black
34 Bodies
35 Bond. James Bond.
36 Bond Girls
37 Boredom
38 Marlon Brando
39 Breasts
40 British Films
41 Budgets
42 California
43 Camera
44 Cannes Festival
45 Cannes Winners
46 Career
47 *Casablanca*
48 Casting
49 Casting Couch
50 Catchphrases
51 Causes
52 Celebrity
53 Celibacy
54 Censorship
55 Characters
56 Character Actors
57 Childhood
58 Choices
59 Cinema
60 Classics
61 Cocaine
62 Comedians
63 Comedies
64 Comedy

65 Commercials
66 Confidence
67 Credo
68 Criticism
69 Critics
70 Cults
71 Cynicism
72 Dating
73 Dead
74 James Dean
75 Death
76 Diets
77 Difficulties
78 Directing
79 Directing Advice
80 Directors
81 Directors by Actors
82 Directors by Actresses
83 Directors by Directors
84 Directors by Producers
85 Directors by Sisters
86 Directors' Debuts
87 Directors on Their
   Films
88 Directors on
   Themselves
89 Divorce
90 Drugs
91 Drugs in Films
92 Dying
93 Early Days
94 Early Roles
95 Editing
96 Ego

97 Entertainment
98 European Films
99 Extras
100 Eyes
101 Faces
102 Failure
103 Fame
104 Family
105 Fan Mail
106 Fans
107 Fashion
108 Fatherhood in Three
    Stages
109 Favourite Roles
110 Feminism
111 Feminity
112 Film Acting
113 Film Business
114 Film Festivals
115 Film-Making
116 Films
117 First Time
118 Friends
119 Future
120 Genius
121 Gossip
122 God
123 Guilt
124 Happiness
125 Hates
126 Hedonism
127 Height
128 Heroes
129 History

130 Sir Alfred Hitchcock
131 Hollywood by the
    Home Team
132 Hollywood by Visiting
    Players
133 Hollywoodians
134 Homosexuality
135 Horror
136 Humour
137 Hype
138 Image
139 Improvisation
140 Influences
141 Interviewees
142 Interviewers
143 Kissing
144 Stanley Kubrick
145 Legends
146 Life
147 Locations
148 Looks
149 Los Angeles
150 Love
151 Lovers
152 Love Scenes
153 Love Stories
154 Macho
155 Make-Up
156 Marriage
157 Marriages
158 Media
159 Meetings
160 Meetings – Hollywood
    Style

161 Memorable Roles
162 Memorable Scenes
163 Men and Women
164 Men by Men
165 Men by Women
166 The Method
167 Money
168 Marilyn Monroe
169 Morality
170 Movies
171 Myths
172 Names
173 Nicknames
174 Nudity by Men
175 Nudity by Women
176 Old Movies
177 Oscar Night
178 Oscars
179 Oscar Winners
180 Personality
181 Philosophy
182 Plastic Surgery
183 Political Office
184 Politicians
185 Politics
186 Pornography
187 Power
188 Press
189 Privacy
190 Producers
191 Producers by Stars
192 Producers on Stars
193 Producing
194 Psychoanalysis

195 Public
196 Public Recognition
197 Publicity
198 Quality
199 Q & A
200 Race
201 *Rambo*
202 Religion
203 Reputations
204 Retirement
205 Reviews
206 Rock 'n' Roll
207 Roles by Actors
208 Roles by Actresses
209 Roots
210 Rumours
211 Salaries
212 Schooldays
213 Science Fiction
214 Scripts
215 Second Generation
216 Self-Portraits (Female)
217 Self-Portraits (Male)
218 Sequels
219 Sex Appeal
220 Sex by Men
221 Sex by Women
222 Sex Films
223 Sex Scenes
224 Sex Symbols
225 Sexuality
226 Shakespeare
227 Smiles
228 Sobriety
229 Song and Dance
230 Special Effects
231 Stardom
232 Stars
233 Stars by Directors
234 Stars on Directors
235 Stars on Female Stars
236 Stars on Male Stars
237 Meryl Streep
238 Studios
239 Studio System
240 Success
241 Superstars
242 Swearing
243 Talent
244 Television
245 Truth
246 Typecasting
247 Unemployment
248 Villains
249 Violence
250 War
251 Weight
252 Orson Welles
253 Westerns
254 Wives
255 Women by Men
256 Women by Women
257 Women Directors
258 Work
259 World
260 Writers

261 Writers by Stars

262 Writers on Stars

263 Writing

264 Youth

QUOTATIONS

1 ACCENTS

1 I'd always had a terrible fight to get work in Britain on account of my Edinburgh accent. And I still haven't lost it completely. I won't – I don't think it's right to lose it.

Sean Connery
Films & Filming, March 1974

2 Our [Canadian] accents are almost like American accents – but not quite. It's slightly off, which makes it dream-like.

David Cronenberg
International Herald Tribune, 14 November 1990

3 Spencer [Tracy] had to play a Portuguese fisherman in *Captains Courageous* and MGM were worried about how'd he speak. For God's sake who knows how a Portuguese fisherman speaks English? Of course, MGM found a Portuguese fisherman . . . 'How would you say fish?' Spencer asks him. 'Would you say: *feesh*?' 'No,' said the guy, 'I'd say fish.' End of that!

Katharine Hepburn
Evening Standard, 1969

4 I can do Irish, Welsh, Manchester, Liverpool, Birmingham, Cockney and New York Jewish lesbian.

Julie Walters
International Herald Tribune, 13 May 1983

2 ACTING BY ACTORS

1 Acting is experience with something sweet behind it.

Humphrey Bogart (1899–1957)
Quoted by Anthony Hopkins, *Films Illustrated*, December 1980

2 Acting is just hustling. Some people are hustling money, some power. I don't put it down. But I resent people putting it up.

Marlon Brando
Playboy, January 1979

3   Timing! My mother gave me that. I was born with it. I don't think you can teach a person to act.

Sir Charles Chaplin (1889–1977)
Radio Times, March 1979

4   Acting has always been holy to me. When I act I don't get caught lying very often.

Kevin Costner
Time, 7 September 1987

5   Acting isn't really respected enough as an art.

Robert De Niro
Newsweek, 16 May 1977

6   I appreciate teamwork. I don't like a one-man show. I'm an interpreter, a sort of tool – I don't mean an object. The right tool is quite essential. Try pounding a nail in with screwdriver.

Gérard Depardieu
Cyrano de Bergerac publicity release, 1990

7   Here I am, a grown man pretending to shoot it out with Burt Lancaster. It's a childish quality. Something that most of us lose as we grow older.

Kirk Douglas
Photoplay, July 1987

8   This is so silly, I'm in my 40s now, playing make-believe.

Michael Douglas
Playboy, February 1986

9   Acting isn't an intellectual art, at all. Strictly animalistic – it comes out of the animal part of the brain.

Clint Eastwood
Newsweek, 23 September 1985

10   You work hard for very many years to learn a technique which you then have the audacity to forget.

William Hurt
Film Yearbook, 1986

11   Acting is like making love. It's better if your partner is good but it's probably possible if your partner isn't.

Jeremy Irons
Cinéma, Cinémas, Antenne 2 (French TV), 15 January 1991

12   Acting is like letting your pants down: you're exposed.

Paul Newman
Time, 6 December 1982

13   What is acting but lying and what is good acting but convincing lying?

Lord Laurence Olivier (1907–89)
Confessions of an Actor: An Autobiography, 1982

14   Acting has been described as farting about in disguise.

Peter O'Toole
Scene, 12 December 1962

15   My acting is a bit like basketball. Most females in my films come off very well. I give great assist. And if I'm lucky, I even score.

Burt Reynolds
Photoplay, May 1981

16   There's not much to acting as far as I'm concerned.

Roy Rogers
Photoplay, January 1976

17   It sounds pompous but it's the nearest thing I can do to being God. I'm trying to create human beings and so does He.

Rod Steiger
London, 10 October 1970

---

3   ACTING BY ACTRESSES

---

1   Acting has never done anything for me except encourage my vanity and provoke my arrogance.

Candice Bergen
Sunday Mirror, 1967

2   You don't have to be smart to act – look at the outgoing president of the United States.

Cher
Playboy, December 1988

3   Very self-indulgent. I get a walloping satisfaction out of it.

Julie Christie
Newsweek, 20 December 1965

4   Acting should be bigger than life. Scripts should be bigger than life. It should *all* be bigger than life.

Bette Davis (1908–89)
Playboy, July 1982

5   Acting engenders and habours qualities that are best left way behind in adolescence. People-pleasing, going on those interviews and jamming your whole personality into getting the job, ingratiating yourself to people you wouldn't fucking spit on if they were on fire.

Carrie Fisher
Vanity Fair, August 1990

6   Acting is frivolous. But frivolity is a big part of our society. So we might as well relax and enjoy it.

Jane Fonda
Photoplay, 1976

7   Acting is a nice childish profession – pretending you're someone else and, at the same time, selling yourself.

Katharine Hepburn
Time, 16 November 1981

8   Acting is a way of living out one's insanity.

Isabelle Huppert
Unifrance news bulletin, 1979

9   You'd think it something one would grow out of. But you grow *into* it. The more you do, the more you realize how painfully easy it is to be lousy and how very difficult to be good.

Glenda Jackson
People, 18 March 1985

10   I don't understand acting except when I'm doing it. And, sometimes, not even then.

Nastassja Kinski
Time, 2 May 1983

11   Acting is just a natural thing in my family. Other boys and girls go into the family business. So do we.

Hayley Mills
Weekend, 6 February 1963

12   You're continually in the position of the woman about to experience the great love of her life. All your woman's wiles are put to use.

Jeanne Moreau
Show, March 1963

13   I give myself to my parts as a lover. It's the only way.

Vanessa Redgrave
Time, 17 March 1967

14   It's a willingness to be naked, whether you have your clothes on or not, to strip away those parts of you that stand in the way of the truth of any individual – fascinating!

Helen Shaver
Photoplay, March 1987

15   When you're asked to explain it, words become inadequate. You shouldn't try to explain this mystery inside you. You have it or you haven't.

Simone Signoret (1921–85)
Films & Filming, 1962

16   I do a job. I get paid. I go home.

Maureen Stapleton
People, 3 May 1982

17   Some of the most intense affairs are between actors and characters. There's a fire in the human heart and we jump into it with the same obsession as we have with our lovers.

Sigourney Weaver
Playboy, August 1986

18   Acting is like sex. You should do it, not talk about it.

Joanne Woodward
You: Mail on Sunday magazine, 1987

4   ACTING ADVICE

1   Keep it simple. Make a blank face and the music and the story will fill it in.

Ingrid Bergman (1915–82) to daughter Isabella Rossellini
Time, 2 May 1983

2   Acting, in general, is something most people think they're incapable of but they do it from morning to night. The subtlest acting I've ever seen is by ordinary people trying to show they feel something they don't or trying to hide something. It's something everyone learns at an early age.

Marlon Brando
Newsweek, 13 March 1972

3   If you're obsessed with your destination, you miss 80% of the point of acting: the ride there, the people you meet along the way.
Kevin Costner
Time, 26 June 1989

4   What acting really is, is pretending – while you're pretending you're not pretending.
Ted Danson
Film Yearbook, 1986

5   What's the difference how you do it? You've just got to do it as long as it's right within the nature of the situation.
Robert De Niro
American Film, March 1981

6   Concentration does not mean inhibition. One can and should be attentive yet appear nonchalant.
Gérard Depardieu
Cyrano de Bergerac publicity release, 1990

7   Forget the ego, you'll get there. Be real or get out.
Bruce Dern
Films Illustrated, October 1978

8   My old drama coach used to say: 'Don't just do something, stand there.' Gary Cooper wasn't afraid to do nothing.
Clint Eastwood
Newsweek, 23 September 1985

9   Baby it out. That's an old marble shooter's expression for approaching your target cautiously instead of trying to take it out with one shot.
Henry Fonda (1905–82)
Evening Standard, 26 April 1974

10   Honesty isn't enough for me. That becomes very boring. If you can convince people what you're doing is real and it's also bigger than life – that's exciting.
Gene Hackman
Show, 1972

11   Blank face is fine. The computer works faster than the brain, don't forget. The art of acting is not to act. Once you show them more, what you show them, in fact, is bad acting.
Anthony Hopkins
Knave, November 1980

12 When I have to cry, I think about my love life. When I have to laugh, I think about my love life.

Glenda Jackson
Quoted by Kim Basinger, *Playboy*, May 1986

13 I don't have a tendency to discuss what I do – before, during or even after.

John Malkovich
Paris, 14 November 1990

14 The less you do, the better you do it.

Marcello Mastroianni
Il Corriere Della Sera, 3 August 1985.

15 If you get an impulse in a scene, no matter how wrong it seems, follow the impulse. It might be something and if it ain't – take two!

Jack Nicholson
Rolling Stone, 14 August 1986

16 You must have – besides intuition and sensitivity – a cutting edge that allows you to reach what you need. Also, you have to know know life – bastards, included – and it takes a bit of one to know one, don't you think?

Lord Laurence Olivier (1907–89)
Daily Mail, 28 March 1979

17 Learn your lines, don't bump into the furniture – and in kissing scenes, keep your mouth closed.

Ronald Reagan
Film Yearbook, 1988

18 Come to work on time, know your lines and don't bump into the other actors.

Spencer Tracy (1900–67)
Quoted by Charlton Heston, Deauville, September 1982

19 The actor must have no personality at all. He must strip the layers away, arriving like a blank page. Very difficult, like having childhood innocence back again. You must give the impression that the scenario was never written. That you're inventing it at the precise moment you act it – an elaborate kind of improvisation.

Jean-Louis Trintignant
Films Illustrated, July 1979

5   ACTOR-DIRECTORS

1   It's impossible to direct yourself in a movie.

Sir Stanley Baker (1927–76)
Denham village, 15 February 1969

2   There is an aphorism, well regarded by Freudian analysts and talent agents alike, that all people are half-actors. We can expand that wisdom a bit and posit the following: all actors are half-directors.

Bob Balaban
Premiere, April 1988

3   I did it once. It was an ass breaker.

Marlon Brando
Rolling Stone, 20 May 1976

4   You direct yourself in most films, anyway.

Marlon Brando
Playboy, January 1979

5   I want to be where the light is – and direct a home run. [And he did.]

Kevin Costner
Ritz, No. 134, 1989

6   Everybody wants to direct. [And he will.]

Robert De Niro
American Film, March 1981

7   Every actor should direct at least once. It gives you a tolerance, an understanding of the problems involved in making a film. In fact, every director should act.

Clint Eastwood
Playboy, February 1974

8   I don't want to be a director. I want to direct. There's a difference.

Marty Feldman (1938–82)
Guardian, 15 September 1976

9   Actors who are in it for any length of time either evolve into directors or drunks.

Gene Hackman
Film Yearbook, 1985

10   I might direct again. But I ain't giving up my day job.

Bob Hoskins
Screen International, 13 May 1988

11   It's better directing myself than working with most of the assholes I've made films with.

Klaus Kinski
Screen International, 1988

12   I feel talented as a director. I don't feel *desired* as a director.

Jack Nicholson
American Film, January–February 1984

13   As a director, I wouldn't like me as an actor. As an actor, I wouldn't like me as a director.

Robert Redford
Premiere, March 1988

14   I want to direct two times a year. You can only hold your stomach in for so many years.

Burt Reynolds
Time, 9 January 1978

6   ACTORS

1   He's an actor but he doesn't look at himself in mirrors all the time like most of them.

Ann-Margret (on husband Roger Smith)
Sunday Express, 1966

2   When I fly into Europe, it's embarrassing for me to put 'actor' on my landing card.

Warren Beatty
Time, 3 July 1978

3   There's something wrong with actors, we've always been a suspect breed. Socially, I find myself more admissable now in England because I've written books.

Dirk Bogarde
Ritz, April 1983

4 Teeth are a vitally important part of an actor's equipment. I have over 30 toothbrushes at home and always keep a good supply at the studio.

Peter Cushing
Scream and Scream Again publicity release, 1969

5 As a person, I'm not very interesting. As an actor, I hope I'm riveting.

Willem Dafoe
Film Monthly, June 1989

6 To be an actor, it's not sufficient to make gestures, recite texts. It's also to provoke, to molest, to forget yourself, risk everything. One must see, listen, live – and go! And be good, bad or bloody ridiculous.

Gérard Depardieu
Mulhouse (France), 9 September 1972

7 Actors have a universal language, like athletes and musicians. They're good ambassadors for their countries – they transcend political lines.

Kirk Douglas
Photoplay, September 1978

8 Actors are paid to be selfish and self-involved.

Michael Douglas
Photoplay, August 1986

9 Actors are often thought of as talking props.

Emilio Estevez
Film Yearbook, 1986

10 You become an actor, maybe, because there are these complexes about you that aren't average or normal and aren't the easiest things to live with.

Henry Fonda (1905–82)
Time, 16 February 1970

11 Essentially what actors do is put colours on a palette for directors to paint with.

Scott Glenn
Photoplay, January 1986

12   The plight of the actor, even if he's a star, is the plight of the women's movement. They're saying the same thing to us: get into bed, give me a good time, then give me something to eat, go get the laundry, be a good girl and behave yourself and let us men get on with what counts.

Dustin Hoffman
Films Illustrated, May–June 1980

13   Only difference between me and other actors is I've spent more time in jail.

Robert Mitchum
Paris Passion, June 1990

14   The only shot I had was either to become a crook, a dope dealer – or an actor.

Joe Pantoliano
Premiere, December 1989

15   There are two types: toupee actors and non-toupee actors.

Donald Pleasance
Daily Mail, 1965

16   Someone called actors: 'sculptors in snow'. Very apt. In the end, it's all nothing.

Vincent Price
Sunday Express, 1964

17   Hey, don't call me an actor, man. Call me somethin' else. Put down animal on my passport. Or, businessman because I'm in the business of living and surviving. But don't call me an actor – that's somethin' I don't have a lot of respect for now.

Mickey Rourke
You: Mail on Sunday magazine, 1987

18   During *Double Indemnity* Fred MacMurray would go to rushes. I remember asking Fred: 'How was I?' 'I don't know about you – but I was wonderful!' Such a true remark. Actors only look at themselves.

Barbara Stanwyck (1907–90)
Los Angeles Times, 5 April 1987

7 ACTRESSES

1 The fact that I don't like working with women so much is a professional, not a personal thing. The hair and make-up become the obsessive thing. You're ready to go and suddenly it's 'Stop! My hair's come down.' I mean, who cares?

Tom Berenger
7 Days, 19 November 1989

2 I've a soft spot for actresses. When I was poor, they were the only people who were nice to me.

Michael Caine
Showtime, 1965

3 I never felt scandal and confession were necessary to be an actress. I've never revealed my real self or even my body in my films. Mystery is very important.

Claudia Cardinale
Telegraph Sunday magazine, 11 April 1982

4 My mother was against me being an actress – until I introduced her to Frank Sinatra.

Angie Dickinson
Cinéma Cinémas, No. 40, Antenne 2 (French TV), February 1986

5 I had no desire to be a film actress, to always play somebody else, to be always beautiful with somebody constantly straightening out your every eyelash. It was always a big bother to me.

Marlene Dietrich
Sunday Times, 22 September 1964

6 An actress is being paid a lot of money to be sexy, attractive, charming and intelligent. It's almost a Western example of a geisha.

Michael Douglas
Playboy, November 1980

7 Actually, I hold a degree in speech therapy. I was going to get my doctorate but acting got in the way. Pity, I always thought I'd like to do something dignified.

Madeline Kahn
Sunday Times, July 1975

8   I always wanted to be an actress. My mother told me to get a job as an elevator operator – because Dorothy Lamour was discovered that way.

Sally Kellerman
Daily Mail, 14 August 1972

9   I try to tell myself I'm not schizophrenic. But when I'm not acting, I'm not alive. Everyday life is just not heightened enough for me. I'm more focused, more interesting when I'm working.

Swoosie Kurtz
The Daily Breeze (sic), America, 6 November 1987

10   Uncomplicated girls can't act.

Producer Joe Pasternak
Photoplay, November 1961

11   When I was about eight, I happened to mention to my father that I wanted to be an actress and he gave me a wallop in the face.

Greta Scacchi
The Times, 7 December 1984

12   I was a better actress the first day I auditioned for Otto Preminger than all the time we worked together.

Jean Seberg (1938–79)
Show, August 1963

13   There are two sorts: the ones who cheat and the ones who feel more confident as they get older. I think I'm one of the latter.

Simone Signoret (1921–85)
Unifrance news bulletin, 1978

14   An actress is someone with no ability who sits around waiting to go on alimony.

Jackie Stallone, mother of Sylvester
Film Yearbook, 1990

15   I'm an *actor*. An *actress* is someone who wears boa feathers.

Sigourney Weaver
American Film, October 1983

8   ADULTERY

1   If you were married to Marilyn Monroe – you'd cheat with some ugly girl.

George Burns
Playboy, June 1978

2   The minute you start fiddling around outside the idea of monogamy, nothing satisfies anymore.

Richard Burton (1925–84)
Playboy, 1963

3   I've never been out with a married woman, never. I respect others' properties.

Michael Caine
Look, 30 May 1967

4   I enjoyed being an adultress ... taking a certain vengeance for the fact that my husband was not being faithful.

Joan Collins
Playboy, April 1984

5   I said to this priest: 'Am I expected to believe that if I went out and had an affair that God was really going to be uspet? OK, thou shalt not kill ... steal ... but thou shalt not commit adultery? If no one is any the wiser, what the hell difference does it make?' He was lovely. He told me the Commandments were laid down for a lot of guys living in the desert.

Diana Dors (1931–84)
Sunday Times, 1976

6   People who commit adultery must die. Everyone knows that. Any movie tells you that!

Richard Dreyfuss
Game, June 1976

7   Monogamy is impossible these days for both sexes. I don't know anyone who's faithful or wants to be.

Goldie Hawn
Daily Mail, 8 August 1977

8   It's a game I never play.

Sophia Loren
Sunday Mirror, 1 September 1964

9   Why fool around with hamburger when you have steak at home?

Paul Newman
Radio Times, 24 June 1971

10   Cheating has such a negative connotation. What I was doing, basically, was following my heart, not my mind. Temptation is presented in spades. It's there so much that one doesn't even consider it temptation, it becomes almost a rite of spring.

Sylvester Stallone
Rolling Stone, December 1985

11   I couldn't stand that my husband was unfaithful. I am Raquel Welch – understand?

Raquel Welch
Vogue, 1973

9   AGE

1   In the morning I feel about 50; then, depending on how the day goes, I might get down to about 22. When I'm directing on stage, I'm 43 and 32 when making a film because I feel less in control. Acting? Oh, then I'm 24. And when I'm on my own, I feel about 17 and think the world is all before me.

Lindsay Anderson at 61
Film Yearbook, 1985

2   I was brought up to respect my elders and now I don't have to respect *anybody*.

George Burns at 87
Playboy, June 1978

3   Suddenly you start to get these roles as the mother of the ingenue you'd have been playing five years ago – it happens in a very swift moment.

Julie Christie
Independent, 16 September 1987

4   When I started in films, they used to sign on girls for a seven-year contract at 17 or so, because studio doctors and people who were supposed to know thought women had passed their peak by the age of 26.

Joan Collins at 53
The Observer, 6 October 1985

5   I've honestly not been too aware of my age until I went to the doctor for a full check-up. He said I had the heart of a young man – 'but you're not young, you're 40'.

Sean Connery
Evening Standard, 1971

6   An actress I knew – when I filmed with her, I was 31 and she was 36. Today, I'm 40 and she's still only 37.

Tony Curtis
Sunday Express, 10 October 1965

7   At 50, I thought proudly: Here we are, half century! Being 60 was fairly frightening. You want to know how I spent my 70th birthday? I put on a completely black face, a fuzzy black Afro wig, wore black clothes and hung a black wreath on my door.

Bette Davis (1908–89)
Films Illustrated, December 1979

8   If I mention my age, my agent will kill me. The thinking is if I say I'm 30 they might not let me play a part that calls for 35. They'll say I'm too young. Or, too old for some other part. Crazy!

Brad Davis
Los Angeles Times, 6 April 1980

9   Females get hired along procreative lines. After 40, we're kind of cooked.

Carrie Fisher
Time, 18 February 1991

10   I was terrified when I turned 30. I was pregnant and had the mumps and Faye Dunaway was just coming out in *Bonnie and Clyde*. I thought: Oh my God, I'll never work again. I'm old!

Jane Fonda
Time, 3 October 1977

11   When you're my age, you just never risk being ill – because then everyone says: Oh, he's done for.

Sir John Gielgud at 84
Sunday Express magazine, 17 July 1988

12   Lionel Barrymore first played my grandfather, later my father, and finally, he played my husband. If he'd lived, I'm sure I'd have played his mother. That's the way it is in Hollywood. The men get younger and the women get older.

Lillian Gish
Film Yearbook, 1984

13   I absolutely refuse to reveal my age. What am I – a car?

Cyndie Lauper
Film Yearbook, 1991

14   I'm in pretty good shape for the shape I'm in.

Mickey Rooney at 58
Films Illustrated, July 1979

15   No one is 22. I've got shoes older that that.

Sylvester Stallone
Rolling Stone, December 1985

16   I think I'm finally growing up – and about time.

Liz Taylor at 53
Film Yearbook, 1987

17   Professionally, I have no age.

Kathleen Turner
Newsweek, 27 February 1989

18   Who wants to be 100?

Estelle Winwood (1883–1984) on reaching her century
International Herald Tribune, January 1983

10   AGENTS

1   I was in the process of throwing two guys out of the bar, when a Hollywood agent walked in. He watched me throw these guys in the street and asked me if I'd ever thought about becoming an actor. Six months later, I was in my first film.

Reb Brown
Howling II publicity release, 1985

2   If he can't get through the door, he goes through the window. If the window is bolted, he breaks down the wall.

Red Buttons (on his agent Martin Baum)
Variety, 21 February 1984

3   I have an agent I trust professionally more than anybody else, but with the best intentions he could put me in the shithouse just as fast as somebody who wanted to ruin me.

James Caan
Playboy, February 1976

4   An actor friend introduced me to my agent, Susan Smith. We met and had a couple of drinks and she got shit-faced. Really, really shit-faced! I said: 'That's the agent for me.'

Brian Dennehy
Knave, 1988

5   Being a star is an agent's dream, not an actor's.

Robert Duvall
Film Yearbook, 1985

6   My agent said: 'You aren't good enough for movies.' I said: 'You're fired.'

Sally Field
Playboy, March 1986

7   Only agents last for ever.

William Goldman
Adventures in the Screen Trade, 1983

8   There was a period when I didn't have an agent and I called William Morris. I said: 'I'm looking for an agent.' She [the telephonist] said: 'What's your name?' I said: 'Al Pacino.' She said: 'Are you *sure*?'

Al Pacino
Playboy, December 1979

11   ALCOHOL

1   The trouble with the world is that it's always one drink behind.

Humphrey Bogart (1899–1957)
Time, 14 April 1986

2   My father considered that anyone who went to chapel and didn't drink alcohol was not to be tolerated. I grew up in that belief.

Richard Burton (1925-84)
Playboy, 1963

3   I'd rather get sloshed than stoned.

James Caan
Playboy, February 1976

4 Drinking removes warts and pimples. Not from me. But from those I look at.

Jackie Gleason (1916–87)
Playboy, 1962

5 Lady Booze is a very cruel mistress.

John Hurt
Film Yearbook, 1986

6 Tequila. Straight. There's a real polite drink. You keep drinking until you finally take one more and it just won't go down. Then, you know you've reached your limit.

Lee Marvin (1924–87)
Sunday Express, 27 March 1966

7 I try not to drink too much because when I'm drunk, I bite.

Bette Midler
Films Illustrated, 1981

8 I had a hollow leg. I could drink everyone under the table and not get drunk. My capacity was terrifying.

Elizabeth Taylor
Los Angeles Times, May 1987

9 Hell, I used to take two-week lunch hours!

Spencer Tracy (1900–67)
Bill Davidson, *Spencer Tracy: Tragic Idol*, 1988

10 I never trust a man that doesn't drink.

John Wayne (1907–79)
Game, 1974

12 WOODY ALLEN

1 Woody has good navigational instincts in this writing mass of egos and good and bad advice. He's not afraid to engage, even though the world perceives him as a reclusive. He's a very good friend. He's dependable, helpful. He works hard, he's ethical. He saves string.

Marshall Brickman, co-scenarist *Annie Hall, Manhattan*
Newsweek, 24 April 1978

2   There's no question that the Woody Allen character that appears on the screen is a Greek god version of what he's like in real life. I met him once and he tried to hide behind Mia Farrow.

John Cleese
The Observer magazine, 23 February 1986

3   I went up to Woody Allen. 'Oh Mr Allen, I really admire your work. I think you're terrific. And I read somewhere that you're very shy, so I feel we've something in common. I'm very shy, too.' He just looked at me and said: 'Well, you could've fooled me.'

Joan Collins
Playboy, April 1984

4   I've been the luckiest actress alive. Where else could I enjoy that kind of variety.

Mia Farrow
Crimes and Misdemeanours publicity release, 1989

5   He's one of the few people who can really write roles for women.

Barbara Hershey
Photoplay, August 1987

6   Woody Allen makes movies like I do. Movies that don't try to hustle every 14-year-old in the country.

Henry Jaglom (Who?)
Film Yearbook, 1985

7   My work on Woody's films can be phoned in. I'm useless. That's the God's honest truth. Woody uses the same crews for all his pictures, the same actors. They know what they're gonna get paid – what do I have to show up for? What can I contribute? I'm not gonna tell him what's funny, that's for sure.

Charles Joffe, co-producer all of Allen-directed films since 1969
Cannes, 16 May 1987

8   He's smashing! I can't make head or tail out of half of what he says.

Diane Keaton
Time, 26 September 1977

9   I'm certainly not going to promote this 'black Woody Allen' line. Don't get me wrong, I like Woody Allen but you could ask him why there are no blacks in his films. Hey – that's his world. Half of Neuva York is black. I'm showing my half.

Spike Lee
Knave, April 1987

10   He's the one who does what he really wants.

Louis Malle
Films Illustrated, March 1981

11   They say Woody Allen got something from the Marx Brothers.
He didn't. He's an original. The best. The funniest.

Groucho Marx (1890–1977)
Time, 3 July 1972

12   A casting session with Woody, it's hysterically funny – if you're
not involved. He can't look an actor in the face. He goes off and
hides. So shy, it's incredible.

Martin Ritt (1920–91)
Films Illustrated, February 1980

13   The 'new Woody Allen'? That I don't buy. He's made some
masterpieces and some films where I wanna burn the negative – as
everybody has. Now he's just into intellectual exercises, sexual
relationships in a drawing-room fashion. They never get sweaty. I just
wish sometimes he'd get *primal!*

Steven Soderbergh
Knave, October 1989

14   My first meeting with Woody Allen lasted 30 seconds. He looked
at me, said hello, asked someone to take a Polaroid, thanked me very
much and I was shown the door. When I came out, the woman due
after me was still doing the same thing as when I went in. She was
shocked – 'What *happened*?' But that's how it is. My agent had
forewarned me. Not hers. She was stunned.

Dianne Wiest
Cannes, 16 May 1987

15   Woody makes a movie as if he were lighting 10 000 safety matches
to illuminate a city. Each one is a little epiphany: topical, ethnic or
political.

Gene Wilder
New Yorker, 1978

13 AMBITION

1 To tell you the truth, I even think there's room for a singin'
cowboy today.

Gene Autry at 81
The Forbes 400 magazine, 24 October 1988

2 I've played the lot, a homosexual, a sadistic gangster, kings,
princes, a saint, the lot. All that's left is a *Carry On* film. My last
ambition.

Richard Burton (1925–84)
Evening Standard, February 1972

3 I always wanted to do *Peter Pan*. I've always resented that only
women get to do it. It's about a boy who refused to grow up, not a girl.

Brad Davis
Los Angeles Times, 6 April 1980

4 I want everything. Not that I want everything right now, but I do
want everything.

Nastassja Kinski
Film Yearbook, 1983

5 My aim is to make one great film, just one that is truely great –
even if I have to make a hundred to do it.

Claude Lelouch
French TV, 1984

6 To play Tarzan – at my age, with a big belly; even Cheetah with
white hair. We've had enough beautiful and strong Tarzans!

Marcello Mastroianni at 60
Gente, 23 August 1985

7 It was always my ambition to be a barbarian when I grew up.

John Milius
Film Yearbook, 1984

8 I'd like to produce, direct, write, score and star in a film in exactly
the way that Chaplin did. I'll do that before I'm 30.

Eddie Murphy
Photoplay, May 1985

9 I've been lucky enough to win an Oscar, write a best-seller – my
other dream would be to have a painting in the Louvre. The only way
that's going to happen is if I paint a dirty one on the wall of the
gentlemen's lavatory.

David Niven (1909–83)
Evening Standard, 1975

10   I'd like to to be able to use all my acting muscles before I'm finished.

Burt Reynolds
Photoplay, May 1981

11   I want this film, so badly, I'd stab *myself* in the back to to get it.

Producer Joel Silver
Vanity Fair, August 1990

12   I'd like to make Steven Spielberg my slave and have him make any movie I wanted.

Sean Young
Film Yearbook, 1991

14   AMERICA

1   There's no culture in this country.

Marlon Brando
Playboy, January 1979

2   I've spent two years of my life in America and I've married Americans twice. But I still feel insecure about making jokes there.

John Cleese
Playboy, November 1988

3   *Robin and Marian* was supposed to be called *The Death of Robin Hood* but Americans don't like heroes who die or anything that might smack of not being a victory.

Sean Connery
International Herald Tribune, 3 December 1983

4   America is where I belong. This is where it has to happen.

Jane Fonda
Time, 16 February 1970

5   When I first went to America is 1928, there were spittoons everywhere. I remember avoiding spit at it flew past me in Times Square. Very unattractive.

Sir John Gielgud
Time, 15 August 1983

6 America only makes children's pictures. I only go if I'm invited. I certainly wouldn't go there to grub for work.
John Hurt
Ritz, summer 1984

7 Either you're bored to death or else someone tries to kill you.
Marthe Keller
Unifrance news bulletin, 1977
(*See also* 133.3)

8 America may be violent, greedy and colonialist but my God, it's interesting.
Paul Newman
Today, 6 January 1973

9 Americans fascinate me -- like science fiction fascinates me. I feel as strange among them as I would among Martians.
Jean-Louis Trintignant
Films Illustrated, July 1979

15 AMERICAN ACTORS

1 English actors are purists about acting. They'll do smaller parts, smaller pictures, if they find it an exercise for them. We don't do that. Like Caruso said: 'Only birds sing for nothing.'
John Derek
Films Illustrated, March 1980

2 American actors examine the implication of every line. They imagine the character's past -- when they're just made up for the hour you see them on film. They ask: 'What does Malcolm do for a living?' You have to think of something: 'Oh, well, he's a, uh, an out of work saxaphone player.' They go: 'Really? Oh, I didn't think of that.'
Neil Jordan
In Dublin magazine, 8 December 1988

3 Generally somewhat mad. They're very good actors but they suffer too much -- getting fat, skinny. They're upset by an interior battle.
Marcello Mastroianni
Il Corriere Della Sera, 3 August 1985

16 AMERICAN DREAM

1   There is disillusionment wafting through the heady winds of the American Dream.

David Puttnam
Film Yearbook, 1989

2   How could Puttnam say the American dream is dead? He spent one year here and left with millions of dollars. Only in America!

Ray Stark
Film Yearbook, 1989

17 ANIMALS

1   I gave my youth and beauty to men. Now I'm giving my wisdom and my experience, the better part of me, to the animals.

Brigitte Bardot
Paris, 17 June 1987

2   I had so many complaints about the horse's head [in *The Godfather*]. There were 30 or so people killed in the film but everyone said: 'You killed a living animal to get the horse's head?' Not I. The horse was killed by the dog food companies to feed your little poodles.

Francis Coppola
Films Illustrated, October 1979

3   I got this image of [*Taxi Driver*] Travis as a crab. To prepare for that, I swam around underwater and looked at the sea life. I've used a cat, a wolf, a rabbit, a snake, an owl. Certain animals give you certain feelings.

Robert De Niro
Playboy, January 1989

4   An audience will be much more shocked by the death of a pig than by the death of a human being – even if told that it's a real human being.

Jean-Luc Godard
Rolling Stone, 14 June 1969

5   Difficult acting with a chimp? No, no. The emotions were the same. In a way it was like playing opposite Paul Newman. The chimpanzee reacted differently, that's all.

Charlotte Rampling
Max, Mon Amour publicity release, 1986

6   That horse, Pie, I've used him in all the Westerns for the last 15 years. He's 27, which is a lot of age for a horse. He's getting grey at the nose and has this tendency to fall asleep. While we're waiting for a short, he'll start nodding off – then pull himself together with a jerk.

James Stewart
London, January 1966

7   The first time I saw the gorillas was a miracle to me – like turning a corner and seeing a unicorn. The group started manoeuvring around me. I just can't describe the joy. When you crawl into a group that is all sunning and resting, the babies will come over. Their mothers trusted me – they knew their children well enough to know it was not my choice that they were swinging on my pigtail.

Sigourney Weaver (on *Gorillas in the Mist*)
Premiere, October 1988

18   ANTI-IMAGE

1   It would sort of relieve the anxiety and the ambivalence I have about it, if someone would say: 'That's it. It's over. You cannot make another film.' I'd suddenly heave a huge sigh of relief.

Woody Allen
Time Out, 1 November 1989

2   Politics? I'm much more middle of the road than most people think.

Jane Fonda
Photoplay, February 1986

3   I'm getting so fond of the characters in this story, I'd like to keep them alive.

Sam Peckinpah (1925–84) (on *The Osterman Weekend*)
Los Angeles Times, December 1982

19 ARMY

1   Join the army, see the world, meet interesting people – and kill
'em.

Woody Allen
Screen International, 8 December 1990

2   I beat the army by being declared psychoneurotic. They thought
I was crazy. When I filled in their forms, under 'Race', I wrote:
'Human.' Under 'Colour': 'It varies.'

Marlon Brando
Playboy, January 1979

3   Except for the 16 weeks of basic training, I spent all my military
career in the swimming pool at Fort Ord.

Clint Eastwood
Playboy, February 1974

4   They took me out of jail into the infantry at Fort McArthur, San
Pedro, California. I found myself assigned, after a difference with a
senior medical officer, to the Keester Police. The Rectal Inspectal! I
lined up 900 characters a day and said: 'Bend over and spread your
cheeks . . . Oh, you've still got your 1942 licence tags on you . . .
D'you think you can smuggle that bunch of grapes out of the army?'

Robert Mitchum
Deauville, September 1989

5   The Army Selection Board told me I had the voice of a
gentleman and the spelling of a clown. What spelling had to do with
winning wars is beyond me.

Oliver Reed
Playdate (New Zealand), 1971

20 ART

1   When I was doing *Love and Death* in Paris, the art director was a
veteran of World War II who had spied, been caught, tortured and
sent to a concentration camp. It made me feel so utterly trivial. It
confronted a prejudice I've always had that, as Oscar Wilde said, art
is useless.

Woody Allen
Newsweek, 24 April 1978

2   Lucifer is the patron saint of the visuals arts. Colour, form – all these are the work of Lucifer.

Kenneth Anger
Independent, 18 January 1990

3   There aren't too many original American art forms – other than the Western and jazz or blues.

Clint Eastwood
Cannes, 12 May 1985

4   Everything is dying of art-attacks. Everyone is so busy being artistic – especially directors. They dehydrate the simplicity of it. I just like to get on with it. Do it! Rehearse it! Shoot the damned thing! Don't talk about it, stumbling round for a needle in the haystack when it's right there under his butt end. Shoot it!

Anthony Hopkins
Films Illustrated, December 1980

5   My first art teacher said art is one thing: a stimulating point of departure. That's it!

Jack Nicholson
American Film, January–February 1984

6   During a shot, I concentrate totally upon the actor's face. If the conditions are propitious and the actor explodes, his entire subjectivity expresses itself and we then reach the best that art can offer.

Martin Ritt (1920–91)
Films Illustrated, February 1980

7   I don't make art, I buy it.

Producer Joel Silver
Vanity Fair, August 1990

8   I don't know where the world would be without art.

Sylvester Stallone
Antenne 2 (French TV), 1989

21   ARTISTS

1   The last great artists died maybe a hundred years ago. In *any* field.

Marlon Brando
Playboy, January 1979

2   The artist must be free. He can't be tied by rules. He leads. He leads the way up the mountain. He strives to reach the top. But others hold him back.

Anthony Quinn
Daily Sketch, 3 September 1963

3   It was very contagious, this feeling that in order to be a true, honest, heroic artist you had to do yourself in or go bananas, so that your insanity became a badge of honour. I knew guys who walked off roofs.

Sam Shepard
Film Yearbook, 1987

4   I believe, to the marrow of my bones, that, as far as America is concerned, the respect for the artist is about the level of respect for the waste matter of a dog last Monday in Hyde Park.

Rod Steiger
London, 10 October 1970

5   I wish there were a way to get what you need as an artist without having to appear strident.

Raquel Welch
Playboy, December 1979

22   AUDIENCE

1   I owe the public nothing more than good entertainment. That's all they're paying me for. I don't think they should know if I use Johnson's Polish on my loo floor or if I sleep with Chinese women.

Dirk Bogarde
Penthouse, 1965

2   The relationship between the artist and the audience is rather like a courtship.

Albert Brooks
Los Angeles Times, 1985

3   America is the audience. It's the tiger. I'll feed the hungry tiger. But I don't wanna live in the same cage.

Tommy Chong
Film Yearbook, 1984

4   When young people don't want to kiss their girl in the living-room because their parents are looking, the best place to go is a movie theatre. So, the movie's not important. We think we're such great film-makers when in reality our audience just wants to be alone.

Tony Curtis
Deauville, 7 September 1986

5   I've always had the ability to say to the audience: 'Watch this if you like it and if you don't – take a hike.'

Clint Eastwood
Newsweek, 23 September 1985

6   I'd like to be able to stop the picture between reels so the audience could discuss the points made.

Jean-Luc Godard
Sunday Times, 1968

7   Don't confuse them. An audience in confusion, an audience not understanding, an audience asking questions is *not* emoting.

Sir Alfred Hitchcock (1899–1980)
London, 21 April 1966
(*See also* 22.12)

8   You've got to keep attacking the audience's values. If you pander to them, you lose your vitality.

Jack Nicholson
Newsweek, 7 December 1970

9   If you can reveal to an audience what lies within them, you can be as important as a philosopher, a psychiatrist, a doctor, a minister or whatever. You have to feel and love not only your own role – or some element in it – but also feel and love the audience. Sounds sentimental, I'm afraid, but there you have it.

Lord Laurence Olivier (1907–89)
Daily Mail, 28 March 1979

10 You can never give the public enough. They always want more.

Burt Reynolds.
Sylvia Safran Resnick, *Burt Reynolds*, 1985

11 The audience and I are friends. They allowed me to grow up with them. I've let them down several times. They've let me down several times. But we're all family.

Mickey Rooney
Time, 29 October 1979

12 I learned a long while back that an audience would rather be confused than bored.

Paul Schrader
Film Yearbook, 1984
(*See also* 22.7)

13 I always think of the audience when I'm directing – because I am the audience.

Steven Spielberg
Film Yearbook, 1988

14 The audience is the best judge of anything. They cannot be lied to. Truth brings them closer. A moment that lags – they're gonna cough.

Barbra Streisand
Newsweek, 5 January 1970

15 I've dealt with most of the stars and almost all the directors in Hollywood and I've met very, very few who have *any* perception of an audience.

Ned Tanen, ex-Universal Pictures chief
Film Yearbook, 1985

23 AUTEUR

1 He is wonderfully subversive and wickedly funny. Half of what he says, I am sure, is designed to mislead younger film-makers.

John Boorman (on *l'auteur suprême* Jean-Luc Godard)
Money Into Light, 1985

2   Henri-Georges Clouzot: 'Don't you think films should have a beginning, a middle and an end?' Jean-Luc Godard: 'Certainly. But not necessarily in that order.'

Cannes, May 1965

3   I once told Godard that he had something I wanted – freedom. He said: 'You have something I want – money.'

Don Siegel (1912–91)
Film Yearbook, 1988

24   AUTHORS

1   *Underworld* was my first filmed book. I think there's about seven of my lines left in it.

Clive Barker
Knave, 1987

2   It isn't what they put in that bothers me but what they left out. It's as if they took the family to the laundry. Still, I expected worse.

John Irving (on the film of his *World According To Garp*)
International Herald Tribune, 22 October 1982

3   It's remarkable how quickly things which seemed vital to the novel can be forfeited in the film. You've got to shoot your own dog. Maybe it's more tough if I say you have to shoot your own horse.

Norman Mailer
Deauville, 6 September 1982

25   AUTOGRAPHS

1   People think they have the right to be offended if someone asks for an autograph. What right . . .? They have made you! I spent 30 years working to become important enough for people to want my autograph.

Sammy Davis Jr
Evening Standard, 13 March 1964

2   They all say the same thing: 'My wife will never believe I've met you unless you sign.' What kind of wives think their husbands are all liars?

Cary Grant (1904-86)
Sunday Express, 7 June 1964

3   Once a crowd chased me for an autograph. 'Beat it,' I said, 'go sit on a tack!' 'We made you,' they said. 'Like hell you did,' I told them.

Katharine Hepburn
Newsweek, 10 November 1969

4   I don't mind autograph hunters when I go down to the fish and chip shop. As long as I get my chips.

David Hemmings
London, 29 June 1966

5   I always used to sign Kirk Douglas or Gary Cooper.

Robert Mitchum
Ritz, No. 143, 1989

6   I stopped signing autographs when I was standing at a urinal at Sardi's and a guy came up with a pen and paper. I wondered: Do I wash first and then shake hands?

Paul Newman
Playboy, April 1983

7   I love collecting autographs! I just met Rich Little and he gave me *his* – isn't that *great*?

Brooke Shields at 16
Photoplay, November 1981

8   Signing autographs is just silly.

Joanne Woodward
Daily Mail, 25 May 1979

9   I was fascinated by the intimacy with which autograph hunters spoke of these people they didn't know. Like 'Barbra's very tough to work with.' Which means Barbra Streisand told them to shove it up their ass. That's what 'very tough to work with' means, actually.

Scenarist Paul Zimmerman
Cannes, 7 May 1983

26 AWARDS

1   I don't believe in awards of any kind. I don't believe in the Noble Peace Prize.

Marlon Brando
Playboy, January 1979

2   They don't mean anything to me. Until I win one. [He did. They do.]

Keith Carradine
Cannes, 23 May 1978

3   Contrary to the Americans who do it so well, I wouldn't know how to collect my prize. The role of a prizewinner may very well be the only one in which I wouldn't be comfortable.

Gérard Depardieu
Unifrance news bulletin, May 1980

4   I'm actually sick of accepting awards for Jack Nicholson. I was thinking of starting a cottage industry accepting awards for actors who're too busy working – unlike me. Jack is thrilled to get this award – and he'll be even more thrilled when his secretary tells him about it.

Louise Fletcher
Variety, 28 February 1984

5   I can't say I believe in prizes. I was a whizz in the three-legged race – that's something you *can* win.

Katharine Hepburn
The Times, 28 April 1969

6   I'm not out to win prizes – that's for horses.

Werner Herzog
The Business of Film, 14 May 1984

7   Actors are the world's oldest, underprivileged minority – looked upon as nothing but buffoons, one step above thieves and charlatans. These award ceremonies simply compound the image for me.

George C. Scott
Time, 22 March 1971

8   You always have to remind yourself that Delacroix never won a prize, that Cézanne never sold a picture.

Cybill Shepherd
Rolling Stone, 9 October 1986

9   Most awards, y'know, they don't give you unless you go and get
them – didja know that? Terribly discouraging.
Barbra Streisand
Sunday Times, 1968

10   You can get too easily seduced by Hollywood. The sun fries
your brain, you get a couple awards – then you want a Rolls-
Royce.
James Woods
Films Illustrated, April 1980

27   BAD MOVIES

1   You can't be good in a bad movie.
James Caan
Los Angeles Times, 31 May 1987

2   It's just as hard to make a bad movie as it is to make a good
movie.
Robert De Niro
French TV, 6 November 1990

3   You learn something from seeing a bad movie as much as you do
from seeing a good movie.
Clint Eastwood
Playboy, February 1974

4   God knows I've done enough crap in my life to grow a few
flowers.
Dustin Hoffman
American Film, April 1983

5   John Huston told me early on: 'I don't change anything. If that's
the way they want it, that's the way they got it. They want bad
pictures, we can make 'em bad, too. Cost a little more.'
Robert Mitchum
Ritz, No. 143, 1989

6   I can truthfully say I will never make a bad film.
Eddie Murphy
Photoplay, July 1987

7   They criticize me: 'Why's he's doing such muck?' To pay for three children in school, for my family and their future.

Lord Laurence Olivier (1907–89)
Daily Mail, 28 March 1979

8   I wouldn't be honest with you if I said I wasn't ashamed of some of the movies, and the songs I've had to sing in them.

Elvis Presley (1935–77)
Evening Standard, 5 August 1969

9   I've made a lot of *shlock*. But my wife [the late Coral Browne] waited five years for the right script – which won her the British Academy award. Then, she waited three years for the next right part. Somebody's got to pay the rent.

Vincent Price
Film Yearbook, 1989

10   I can't believe I did all those bad films in a row. I went to the well one too many times.

Burt Reynolds
Los Angeles Times, 4 January 1987

11   I'd rather be playing bridge than making a bad movie.

Omar Sharif
Film Yearbook, 1990

12   I collect all the reviews of the films I turned down. And when they're bad – I have to smile.

Simone Signoret (1921–85)
Unifrance news bulletin, 1977

28   BAD TASTE

1   There's not enough bad taste! I LOVE bad taste! I live for bad taste! I am the spokesman for bad taste! People come to me to explain bad taste. It's a lot of hypocrites denouncing what's bad, saying what you musn't do. But when the lights are out, they're doing all those things. We know. 'Cos we do them, too.

Mel Brooks
Films Illustrated, January 1982

2   Perhaps my taste is bad. But I find it good. That's more than you can say for most ministers and politicians' remarks. A great number of official gatherings are really in bad taste – in my terms.

Jean Yanne
Unifrance news bulletin, 1975

---

29   BEAUTY

1   God forbid that an actress in London has a pretty face. The critic will never forgive her. But let her have cross-eyes and green teeth and they'll laud her to the skies.

Sir Noël Coward (1899–1973)
Los Angeles Times, 3 March 1985

2   Beautiful? Of course not! That's the whole point about me.

Jeanne Moreau
Time, 5 March 1975

3   The most important quality is that she doesn't know she's beautiful, or if she does, she doesn't believe it. There's nothing more unattractive – for me – and less sexual than a woman who *knows* she's a beauty, who *knows* men are looking at her.

Roger Vadim
Game, March 1975

4   It's necessary, at some point, to destroy your beauty.

Raquel Welch
Newsweek, 4 March 1968

---

30   BERNARDO BERTOLUCCI

1   Bertolucci is very sensitive but he's taken with success. He likes being on the cover.

Marlon Brando
Playboy, January 1979

2   Bertolucci is more of a gangster than a movie director. He's one of my enemies.

Maria Schneider
Film Yearbook, 1986

3   For me, Bernardo is The Function. The only way I can explain it is in the analogy with mathematics and the word 'function' – addition, subtraction, multiplication, anything that numbers go through and change because of it. And when the function is a function of love, the drapes on the windows, the doors that are hung, the characters, the clothes, everything goes through this function and comes out touched and inspired by it. There are a lot of numbers but what really matters is the function.

Debra Winger
Paris, 14 November 1990

31   BILLING

1   I will never be below the title.

Bette Davis (1908–89)
Playboy, July 1982

2   How can it be 'A Marty Ritt Film'? It's not. If I ever write one, direct one and star in it, then you can call it a Marty Ritt Film.

Martin Ritt (1920–90)
Film Yearbook, 1987

3   I have trouble with star billing. I remember thinking on *Cannery Row*: How can I put my name ahead of Steinbeck's?

Debra Winger
Playboy, June 1983

32   BITCHES

1   It's easy to play a bitch.

Joan Collins
Playboy, April 1984

2   I love playing bitches. There's a lot of bitch in every woman – a lot in every man.

Joan Crawford (1904–77)
Variety, April 1973

3   Isn't that what Joan Collins' success is based on? People love bitches. The more dreadful they are, the more awful things they say, the more heavenly they are.

Stephen Frears
You: Mail on Sunday magazine, February 1989

4   It's a very male-chauvinist word. I resent it deeply. A person who's a bitch would seem to be mean for no reason. I'm not a mean person. Maybe I'm rude without being aware of it – that's possible.

Barbra Streisand
Playboy, October 1977

33   BLACK

1   Whoopi Goldberg is blazing a trail for black women – for just black anything to be successful. Still, I often ask myself if I have to be a 30-year-old ex-junkie who lived in Berkeley and did stand-up comedy in Germany, before I can get some respect.

Rae Dawn Chong
Playboy, April 1987

2   You can see I'm black. It's not something I consciously think about. It just is. It's like having a dick. You don't think about having a dick. You just have one.

Whoopi Goldberg
Playboy, June 1987

3   Richard Pryor is really, genuinely black – a black comedian speaking to black people on the street that white people happen to overhear. Whereas Eddie Murphy is playing the street black for the white audience. He comes from a middle-class family on Long Island. He hasn't really got anything to say. He's just got a posture.

Tony Hendra
Paris, 1984

4   Being black has never been a hindrance to me. I've been called nigger only once in my life.

Eddie Murphy
Time, 11 July 1983

5   I'm black and I've decided I like my colour. Anyone that doesn't, that's their worry.

Sidney Poitier
Evening Standard, 1966

6   You come out of an office where they've been talking millions of dollars and you feel all pumped up – and you can't get a cab. It's one hell of a burden being black in this country.

Richard Pryor
Photoplay, October 1983

34   BODIES

1   My body is my business and I work on it every day.

Marilyn Chambers
Cannes, May 1984

2   My body is an asset and that's all. It's not something I made, it's something I was born with.

Jamie Lee Curtis
Clothes Show, November 1988

3   I'm perfect. The areas that I need help on are not negotiable. They have to do with gravity.

Jane Fonda
People, 12 November 1990

4   Jane Fonda didn't get that terrific body from exercise. She got it from lifting all that money.

Joan Rivers
Sunday Express magazine, November 1987

5   I see a body as a classy chassis to carry your mind around in.

Sylvester Stallone
Film Yearbook, 1988

6 You have the best shoulders – gee!

Andy Warhol (1921–87) to Raquel Welch
Interview, January 1975
(*See also* 34.7)

7 There is beauty in every part of the body: delicate fingers, slender arms, gracefully curving shoulders, well-formed rib-cage, a flat, firm tummy, a supple back with the smooth valley that runs down the middle of it, the shape of the buttocks and the way it moves, the softness of the pubic area, the thighs tapering to the knees, the calf, the ankle – all of that to me is tremendously sensual. Combine these things with the tilt and roundness of the eyes, the fullness of the lips and the way the hair is worn and how can anyone doubt that boobs are just a small part of it?

Raquel Welch
Playboy, 1970

35   BOND. JAMES BOND.

1 With his clothing and his cars and his wines and his women, Bond is a kind of present day survival kit. Men would like to imitate him – or, at least, his success – and women are excited by him.

Sean Connery
Playboy, 1965

2 Bond is not identifiable with the public. He can shoot anybody on sight. My kind of men can't. They're average men involved in bizarre situations.

Sir Alfred Hitchcock (1899–1980)
London, 21 April 1966

3 If you go out of a James Bond film and I ask you if you can tell me what you've seen, you can't. There are 20 000 things in James Bond. You can't describe a mixed salad. Too many things in it.

Jean-Luc Godard
Rolling Stone, 14 June 1969

4 I don't think a single other role changes a man quite so much as Bond. It's a cross, a privilege, a joke, a challenge. And it's as bloody intrusive as a nightmare.

Sean Connery
Sunday Mirror, 2 May 1971

5   I didn't see Sean in any of the first script, except when I had to
say: 'My name is Bond, James Bond.'

Roger Moore
Game, April 1975

6   Everyone knows Sean's the real James Bond. Kids think I'm his
stand-in.

Roger Moore
Photoplay, 1979

7   I like Bond. But it's silly to take it seriously. It's just a great big
comic strip.

Roger Moore
Daily Mail, 3 January 1975

8   Roger comes in the humour door and I go out it.

Sean Connery
Time, 1 November 1982

9   Sometimes I wear a white dinner jacket, sometimes a black one.

Roger Moore
Time, 1 November 1982

10   I've never made up my mind who Bond is. Sometimes I think
it's very dramatic, but mostly it's comedy. One thing I know for
certain – it's entertainment.

Producer Cubby Broccoli
International Herald Tribune, 28 January 1983

11   By analyzing the Bond films one can see what's happening to
the film industry over the last 20 years. The first Bond film cost $1
million. The current one [*Octopussy*] is nearly $39 million.

Producer Michael Wilson
International Herald Tribune, 28 January 1983

12   When *Dr No* went to Japan, they translated it as *No Need For
Any Doctors*.

Sean Connery
International Herald Tribune, 3 December 1983

13   I knew if it [*The Living Daylights*] was a failure, I'd be a world-
famous failure. You think about it very hard in a way you would not
think about any other project.

Timothy Dalton
Premiere, January 1989

36 BOND GIRLS

1 It's a mystery. All I did was wear this bikini in *Dr No* – not even a small one – and *whoosh*! Overnight I've made it.

Ursula Andress
Sunday Express, 9 August 1964

2 Bond is not my type at all. I like quiet, intelligent, sensitive men.

Barbara Bach (*The Spy Who Loved Me*)
Photoplay, November 1976

3 I'm amazed at how fit Timothy Dalton is. His big sport is . . . fishing!

Maryam d'Abo (*The Living Daylights*)
Cannes, 1987

4 There was a stigma attached to the Bond girls. Because a woman was good-looking and had a good body, the feminists assumed it was trash. I was a single mother with two kids to support! In order for there to be a Jane Fonda or a Vanessa Redgrave, there have to be people like me. That's the way it is.

Britt Ekland (*The Man With The Golden Gun*)
Film Yearbook, 1988

5 A lot of 007's appeal, let's face it, stems from his doings with the ladies. So, find the ladies and we've won half the battle.

Director Guy Hamilton
Sunday Mirror, 2 May 1972

6 It's a champagne life. On and off the set. Very funny scene: James Bond comes into my bathroom and I say, 'Pass me something to slip on.' And he passes my slippers.

Luciana Paluzzi (on *Thunderball*)
Evening Standard, 25 June 1965

37 BOREDOM

1 I get bored easily. I've been bored most of my life.

John Cleese
Today, 20 September 1988

2   It's a bore – B-O-R-E – when you find you've begun to rot.
Katharine Hepburn
People, 5 November 1990

3   Threatened with boredom, I'll run like a hare.
John Huston (1906–87)
Time Out, 18 April 1980

4   There's no force more powerful in film-making than the fear of an audience's boredom.
Norman Mailer
Cannes, May 1987

5   I do get bored easily. So, I'd rather do a short, interesting stint than a long, dreary one.
Jack Nicholson
Photoplay, April 1984

6   You can kill, you can maim people, but to be boring is truely a sin. And God will punish you for that.
Burt Reynolds
Playboy, October 1979

38   MARLON BRANDO

1   I'd trade everything to be Marlon Brando. I so envied his talent – so thrilling to me.
Woody Allen
Time Out, 1 November 1989

2   Marlon is not here tonight because – he's Marlon.
Ellen Burstyn at a New York tribute to Elia Kazan
Variety, 28 January 1987

3   Anyone of my generation who tells you he hasn't 'done' Brando is lying.
James Caan
Time, 7 April 1975

4 Fascinating and scary. Not somebody I'd want to get involved with for one second.

Joan Collins
Playboy, April 1984

5 I was the Marlon Brando of my generation.

Bette Davis (1908–89)
Daily Telegraph obituary, 9 October 1989

6 The actor who made a lot of scratch out of one itch.

Peter Evans
Daily Express, 3 February 1964

7 *On The Waterfront* came out and there were 150 guys [at RADA] all doing Brando impressions.

Albert Finney
Ritz, No. 127, July 1988

8 I don't think there's anybody better when he wants to be good.

Henry Fonda (1905–82) (Brando's mother got Fonda started as an actor in 1926)
Playboy, December 1981

9 When you see Brando in the famous cab scene in *On The Waterfront*, it's still breathtaking.

Anthony Hopkins
Knave, October 1980

10 Did you see *Julius Caesar*? Christ! I'll never forget that. It was like a furnace door opening -- the heat came off the screen. I don't know another actor who could do that.

John Huston (1906–87)
Playboy, September 1985

11 I didn't have to do any directing there. The [*Waterfront*] cab scene was written so well and [Brando, Rod Steiger] understood it. But *Brando*? He was smart, he knew everything. He was smarter than you – really clever. He made my films good. I helped him, but he helped me, too.

Elia Kazan
Photoplay, August 1983

12 I love Marlon Brando. Never seen him bad, just less good.

Lee Marvin (1924–87)
Photoplay, November 1981

13   Marlon's focus is eruptability – always in the potential of the masses-type hero.

Paul Newman
Rolling Stone, 5 July 1975

14   He's got it all. That's why he's endured. When I first saw *On The Waterfront* I couldn't move. I couldn't leave the theatre. I'd never seen the like of it. I couldn't believe it.

Al Pacino
Playboy, December 1979

15   We forget how this man revolutionized acting. Look at the chances he takes – think of all the stars who just drift along playing themselves.

Anthony Quinn
Sunday Express, 13 October 1963

16   A woman mistook me for Brando. I dissuaded her but she kept coming back, insisting I was Brando. Finally, I blew my top: 'Listen lady, can't you get it through your thick head that I am not Marlon Brando!' A broad smile crossed her face. She turned to her husband: 'See, I told you it was him.'

Burt Reynolds
Superman publicity release, 1978

17   Now *there's* a strange animal. Marlon is such a pure piece of animal flesh. He's pansexual, beyond normalcy of any kind. Once in a while, he'll give you a few minutes of his special genius – magic time.

Roy Scheider
Playboy, September 1980

18   I used to criticize Brando for his judgment and selection of roles. Not any more. He couldn't find any good scripts, either.

Robert Shaw (1927–78)
Daily Mail, 29 August 1978

19   He's an authentic genius in his field. No question in my mind about that. The thing about his genius is the originality, the freshness he brought to acting. Just overwhelming. Nobody had ever seen anything like that before. I wouldn't want to do an entire film with the little darling – he'd drive you crazy. He's dreadfully slow, does it over and over and over. Marlon would improve *all* the time. I'm not sure about the rest of us.

George C. Scott
Playboy, December 1980

20   The finest actor who ever lived. He was my idol when I was 13. He's done enough work to last two lifetimes. Everything I do, I think: Can Brando play this [with me]?

Barbra Streisand
Playboy, October 1977

21   Brando is one of the finest actors we've had. I'm sorry he didn't have the benefit of older, more established friends – as I did – to help him choose the proper material in which to use his talent.

John Wayne (1907–79)
Daily Mail, 18 January 1974

Footnote: I think there's a well-known contest in the acting profession to see who can say the best stuff about Marlon.

Jack Nicholson
Rolling Stone, 2 May 1976

39   BREASTS

1   If you don't want someone to see your breasts – don't take your shirt off.

Ellen Barkin
Film Yearbook, 1991

2   Topless is just topless. That's nothing. Why is it OK for men to go around topless when some of them have bigger boobs than many women?

Jill Clayburgh
Photoplay, 1981

3   When I was 18 in Hollywood, the wardrobe lady had to measure my cleavage. Only 1½ or 2 inches were permissable exposure. If too much was showing, in went a disgusting flower.

Joan Collins
Photoplay, 1978

4   I don't think all I have going for me is a great pair of breasts.

Jamie Lee Curtis
Clothes Show, November 1988

5   Men have always been hung up on breasts.
Diana Dors (1931–84)
Daily Mail, 11 February 1978

6   I'm very proud of my breasts as every woman should be. It's not
cellular obesity. It's womanliness.
Anita Ekberg
Daily Mail, 2 September 1972

7   For *Star Wars*, they had me tape down my breasts because there
are no breasts in space. I have some. I have two.
Carrie Fisher
Playboy, July 1983

8   At Warner Brothers for my first screentest, I had to wear falsies.
Jack Warner told me: 'You'll never become a movie star if you're
flat chested.'
Jane Fonda
Sunday Times, 17 October 1976

9   I was barechested in quite a few *Picnic* scenes, so I had to shave
my chest every day. The censor said hairy chests weren't nice. Do
you think it's fun standing in front of a mirror running a razor all the
way down to your navel at 6 am every morning?
William Holden (1918–81)
Photoplay, May 1977

10   I was five months pregnant when I made that nude scene in
Women In Love. I'd never had such a marvellous bosom.
Glenda Jackson
Reveille, 20 February 1971

11   I'd rather play cards if I can't have a lady with big tits.
Russ Meyer
Film Yearbook, 1984

12   People make jokes about my bosoms, why don't they look
underneath the breasts at the heart? It's obvious I've got big ones
and if people want to assume they're not mine, then let them.
Dolly Parton
Playboy, October 1978

13   Yes, Howard Hughes invented a bra for me. Or, he tried to. And one of the seamless ones like they have now. He was way ahead of his time. But I never wore it in *The Outlaw*. And he never knew. He wasn't going to take my clothes off to check if I had it on. I just told him I did.

Jane Russell
Cinéma, Cinémas, No. 37, Antenne 2 (French TV), November 1985

14   You have the kind of breasts I could take home to my mother.

American fan letter to Susan Sarandon. (Her comment: 'There are so many great breasts around. I think my breasts are highly over-rated.')
Playboy, May 1989

15   We tried foam appliances that fit over Daryl Hannah's breasts which made them look like breasts without nipples. But at the last minute everyone decided that we'd never get the audience *not* to look at her breasts, *especially* if they didn't have nipples.

Splash film special-effects man Robert Short
Film Yearbook, 1986

16   When you have a bosom like mine, there's a very narrow margin between being sexy and ridiculous. Many men told me, in no uncertain terms, they didn't like big bosoms. I don't think I would if I were a man. I can't stand the word boobs – not too keen on bosom, either. I've always called mine: 'snokes'.

Madeline Smith
Daily Mirror, 15 September 1976

17   I'd never 'made love' to a woman on screen or off before. But I'm glad I did it. I made a discovery. I didn't know how guys felt fondling a woman's breasts. I didn't realize that when a woman lays on her back, they go sideways and they've got to be gathered up. And they move around, slide out of your hands. They're floppies.

Angel Tompkins (on *The Naked Cage*)
Prevue, May 1986

18   Just mention Brigitte Bardot to most men and the first thing that pops into their head is boobs. Marilyn Monroe and boobs. Raquel Welch and boobs. Ridiculous! Who knows, someday men may come to appreciate, say, the teeth and the lips and the back of the neck as erogenous zones, too. That's what they are, at least to me.

Raquel Welch
Playboy, 1970

19 I massage my breasts – you should do it, yourself, 'cos the muscle under the arm doin' the massagin' holds the bust up an' keeps the breasts firm. Breast exercises stimulate the whole body an' glands an' everythin' else, ya know.

Mae West (1893–1980)
Playboy, 1970

20 I asked Dylan Thomas why he'd come to Hollywood and very solemnly he said: 'To touch a starlet's tits.' 'OK,' I said, 'but only one finger.'

Shelley Winters
Sunday Times, 2 May 1971

40 BRITISH FILMS

1 The modern perception of British cinema has nothing to do with British *films* – merely with the business of getting more money through the box-office.

Lindsay Anderson
Sunday Times, 16 March 1986

2 British films are box-office poison.

Michael Caine
Screen International, 29 July 1978

3 If you're not English, you're a foreigner – so you must be sexy. It's an old British film cliché.

Claudia Cardinale
Venice, 1981

4 Every so often Britain turns out a good film – that doesn't mean a comeback. I know they say it is – for a whole two weeks! America makes films all the time and suddenly Britain thinks it's going to corner the world market in movies – it's fanciful nonsense.

Tom Conti
Cannes, 15 May 1983

5 There's nothing original in British cinema today. It's the bastardization of any other cinema you like to name. Instead of speaking English, it speaks American.

Hugh Hudson
Film Yearbook, 1987

6   Ideally, one would like to work in England. But if no one in England is going to take their courage in both hands and dig into their pockets and finance films – then, you're going to have to work abroad.

Glenda Jackson
Evening Standard, 3 April 1974

7   I love British cinema like a doctor loves his dying patient.

Ben Kingsley
Dinard (France), 29 September 1990

8   I did a picture in England one winter and it was so cold I almost got married.

Shelley Winters (in her original line, *Sunday Times*, 2 May 1971, she'd been so cold on a winter sports holiday she almost got married.)
Ritz, March 1983

41 BUDGETS

1   If a picture costs $6 million, I hope it looks like $10 million on the screen. If it costs $5 million and looks $3 million – that's a failure to me. There's an awful lot of pictures that cost $20/30 million that look to me like $6/7 million.

Clint Eastwood
Film Comment, October 1984

2   Whenever I think about the budgetary problems, I think about the problems of Errol Flynn . . . reconciling net income with gross habits.

British government minister Malcolm Rifkind
Film Yearbook, 1986

3   You read a lot about movies with budgets of $25–30 million. Hell, if a studio can piss away that kind of money, why not let 'em piss on me?

Roy Scheider
Playboy, September 1980

4   My first film will be a very simple one. I'll need only $10 million. The film will be about a boy, his dog and his budget.

Robin Williams
Playboy, October 1982

42 CALIFORNIA

1 California is a great place – if you happen to be an orange.
Fred Allen (1894–1956) (often attributed to Orson Welles)
Leslie Halliwell, *The Filmgoer's Book of Quotes*, 1973

2 In California, they should make the interiors of cars out of teflon.
You've got to get in and out of them so often – you might as well just
slide in and out.
Mel Brooks
American Premiere, September 1981.

3 In California, people don't tell each other anything . . . they're
afraid it will end up as a *Love Boat* episode.
Allan Carr
Film Yearbook, 1985

4 The silly state.
Harrison Ford
Deauville, September 1982

5 I spent two miserable years in California. But it was Barbara
Stanwyck who said: 'The best place to be miserable is California.'
Russian director Andrei Konchalovsky
Knave, October 1986

43 CAMERA

1 I simply love the camera and it loves me. But the amount of
concentration you have to use to feed that camera is so enormous
that you're absolutely ragged at the end of a day after doing
something simple – like a look.
Dirk Bogarde
Show, 1969

2 I was born in front of a camera and really don't know anything
else.
Joan Crawford (1904–77)
Variety, April 1973

3   Not a very nice-looking instrument. Very much like an X-ray machine. It's all black metal and has a lot of similarities to a gun. They ought to cover it with a cloth or something.

Michael Douglas
Films Illustrated, September 1979

4   Change camera angles a lot. When you're looking at a film, you're looking at a flat piece projected on a flat surface. The only way you can approach a 3-D feeling is to get the camera right in there – so the audience can feel part of a group rather than just observers *of* a group.

Clint Eastwood
Hollywood Reporter (Kodak advertisement), 10 May 1983

5   The most beautiful woman in the world can look like dog shit on camera. Fortunately for me, it also works the other way around.

Mel Gibson
Rolling Stone, 29 August 1985

6   In front of a camera, I have to be careful what I think – it all shows.

Shirley MacLaine
Look, 1960

7   You can't fool that 70 mm lens. It's terrifying what it picks up. You can see what time someone hobbled to bed. You can see the germs having a party in his eyeballs.

Peter O'Toole
Sunday Express, 12 April 1964

44   CANNES FESTIVAL

1   My idea of hell. You see all the people you thought were dead and all the people who *deserve* to be dead. After a while, you start to think you might be dead, too.

Dirk Bogarde
Films Illustrated, July 1975

2   Butlins on acid.

Screenwriter Frank Clarke
1988

3   I'm here for the ... um ... er ... um ... experience.
Robert De Niro
1983

4   I enjoy Cannes. I come for the event, not prizes.
Clint Eastwood
1990

5   Where are we going? Do I need tickets?
Jerry Lewis
1983

6   Being on the Cannes jury is like being a Mormon. We can't talk. They swear us to secrecy – not only now but hereafter. For 60 years, I've been seeing movies and coming out and talking about them. A basic reflex. A habit. A real addiction. Now I have to give it up. My throat gets dry. My tongue hurts. I really want to talk!
Norman Mailer
Screen International, 16 May 1987

7   Has anybody got a tea-bag for the hot water in my glass?
Paul Newman (at a packed press conference)
1987

8   Every time I've been to Cannes, I've made up my mind never to return. Every time, my vanity wins over.
Alan Parker
Film Yearbook, 1984

9   It's like a fire in a brothel during a fire.
Russian director Eldar Riazanov
1983

10   I didn't really want to come to Cannes with *Max Mon Amour*. I've gone through enough exams in my life.
Producer Serge Silberman
1986

11   It was *my* idea to pose but *their* idea for my clothes to come off – to the point where they *tore* them off.
Edy Williams
Adult Cinema, March 1984

45 CANNES WINNERS

1 *Ma chère* Cher – sorry you have to share.
John Boorman (presenting shared Best Actress award)
1985

2 Thank you – your money's behind the wash basin.
Terry Jones (accepting jury prize for *Monty Python's Meaning of Life*)
1983

3 If you don't like me – I don't like you!
Maurice Pialat (being booed while winning top prize for *Sous Le Soleil de Satan*)
1987

4 It's all downhill from here.
Steven Soderbergh (winning top prize with his first first feature, *sex, lies and videotape* at age 26)
1989

46 CAREER

1 With me, a career was the simple matter of putting groceries on the table.
James Cagney (1899–1986)
Cagney By Cagney, 1976

2 I've turned myself inside out. I've played murderers, transvestites, drunks, everything. I just thought: I'm 50 now, it might be nice to have a quiet life. Romantic comedies are usually set in glamorous places, you don't have to turn up in the Philippines jungle.
Michael Caine
Toronto Star, 16 September 1983

3 I've made some of the greatest films ever made – and a lot of crap, too.
John Carradine (1906–88)
Film Yearbook, 1990

4 Whatever I want, I get. But how my career has gone is a mystery to people.

Kevin Costner
Ritz, No. 134, 1989

5 You keep thinking you've reached a level where it's going to be bliss, where people start giving you all these wonderful things and how can you choose between all this brilliance – and it just ain't so.

Sally Field
Films Illustrated, August 1979

6 I don't know which was the greatest disaster: my career or my wives.

Stewart Granger
Radio Times, 5 October 1972

7 Yes, I was competitive but not in a way I thought dishonourable.

Cary Grant (1904–86)
Photoplay, February 1983

8 I started near the top and worked my way down.

Sterling Hayden (1916–86)
Cinéma, Cinémas, No. 20, Antenne 2 (French TV), January 1984

9 I was asked to act when I couldn't act. I was asked to sing *Funny Face* when I couldn't sing and dance with Fred Astaire when I couldn't dance – and do all kinds of things I wasn't prepared for. Then, I tried like mad to cope with it.

Audrey Hepburn
Daily Mail, 22 April 1976

10 With all the opportunities I had, I could have done more. And if I'd done more, I could have been quite remarkable.

Katharine Hepburn
Time, 16 November 1981

11 My life has taken off – my life, my career – everything. I can honestly say I've never been happier. I'm walking around thinking: any minute how, 25 tons of horseshit is going to fall on my head.

Bob Hoskins
Film Yearbook, 1988

12 Two of the greatest turnin' points in my career: first, meetin' Jerry Lewis; second, leavin' Jerry Lewis.

Dean Martin
Look, 26 December 1967

13　I haven't changed anything but my underwear. I had a certain amount of luck – and instinct. Largely being in the right place at the right time. Sometimes, I've been in the wrong place at the right time. Every two or three years I knock off for a while. That way I'm constantly the new girl in the whorehouse. I'm a whore with a heart of gold. I just show up and do it.

Robert Mitchum
Paris Passion, June 1990

14　There are three stages in an actor's career. The first is when he shows up on the set and says: 'You should've seen the girl I was with last night. God! I didn't sleep. She was *amazing*!' In the second stage, he's a leading man and says: 'You know, I found the most wonderful restaurant – you wouldn't believe the fish.' By the third stage, he's a character actor. Now he says: 'Oh, I had the most lovely bowel movement last night.'

Paul Newman to Tom Cruise
Film Yearbook, 1988

15　I'm not a Catholic, I'm a Jew – but I made *The Cardinal*. I'm not a senator – but I made *Advise and Consent*. I'm not a dope fiend – but I directed *The Man with the Golden Arm*. And I'm not a virgin – but I produced *The Moon Is Blue*.

Otto Preminger (1906–86)
Variety, 1963

16　Had I been brighter, the ladies been gentler, the Scotch weaker, the gods kinder, the dice hotter – it might have all ended up in a one-sentence story.

Mickey Rooney
Evening Standard, 1971

17　I've been really serious about this as a career since I was 12 years old.

Steven Spielberg
Los Angeles Times, 3 December 1989

47   CASABLANCA

1   I never knew how the picture was going to end, if I was really in love with my husband or Bogart. So I had no idea how I should play the character. I kept begging them to give me the ending but they'd say: 'We haven't made up our minds. We'll shoot it both ways.' We did the first ending and they said: 'That's good, we won't bother with the other.'

Ingrid Bergman (1915–82)
Radio Times, 18 January 1973

2   Paul Henreid told me about Michael Curtiz making *Casablanca*. Curtiz suddenly decided he needed a poodle for a scene. The prop man and assistant directors ran in all directions, searching and making calls. Meanwhile, Curtiz and Bogart played chess. Eventually, an animal wrangler arrived with a selection of poodles for the director to choose from. 'Not a poodle!' he screamed. 'A *poodel*! With water.'

John Boorman
Film Yearbook, 1986

3   Just a routine assignment. Frankly, I can't understand its staying power. If it were made today, line for line, each performance as good, it'd be laughed off the screen. It's such a phoney picture. Not a word of truth in it. It's camp, kitsch. It's just . . . slick shit!

Co-scenarist Julius J. Epstein
Deauville, 8 September 1984

48   CASTING

1   I called Jack and said: 'I need someone to play Eugene O'Neill and it's got to be somebody who leaves no doubt that he could take Diane Keaton away from me.' He said: 'Well, you have no choice!'

Warren Beatty (on *Reds*)
Radio Times, 14 July 1990

2   I got the job because I could belch on cue.

Charles Bronson (on his first film *You're In The Navy Now*)
Photoplay, January 1987

3 I'd walk out of offices with my fingers in my ears so I wouldn't hear someone who didn't know as much as I did telling me what to do.

Kevin Costner
Time, 7 September 1987

4 I could tell I got the part immediately because Blake Edwards took his sunglasses off.

Bo Derek (on *10*)
Films Illustrated, March 1980

5 Cubby Broccoli thought Raquel Welch was closer to Rhett Butler than Scarlet O'Hara.

Guy Hamilton (on casting *Diamonds Are Forever*)
Sunday Mirror, 30 May 1971

6 You start with the compromise of casting. They say: 'What about Julie Andrews?' I say: 'Fine, if you want her.' 'Well, she's the hottest thing there is.' And that's how she came into *Torn Curtain*. Then, you start fixing things up to accommodate Julie Andrews.

Sir Alfred Hitchcock (1899–1980)
London, 21 April 1966

7 They tested more than 100 actors for [*Golden Boy*] and I got it. I had to play a violinist-turned-prizefighter which wasn't easy considering I couldn't fight or play the violin. I wasn't even sure I could act.

William Holden (1918–81)
Photoplay, May 1977

8 I knew I'd got [*Scarface*] when I cut Al Pacino's finger in the test. I had to throw some dishes at him. Suddenly, there was all this blood. And I thought: Oh my God, did I cut Al Pacino. I'll never get this movie now. But it was *my* hand. They must have thought: Hey! If she can cut herself and not know it – a real actress!

Michele Pfeiffer
Knave, July 1989

9 When Buñuel was casting *Viridina*, he wanted me: 'I saw him as a corpse in a film and he was wonderful.' So Buñuellian!

Fernando Rey
Knave, August 1986

10   I did two tests for *The Graduate*. One with Dustin Hoffman – a *disaster*. We were nervous, nothing seemed to be working. He kept saying: 'This is terrible.' He didn't use that word. 'This is the worst thing I've ever done.' He didn't use those words, either.

Katharine Ross
London, 6 August 1968

11   I wasn't a very good actor. I wouldn't have cast myself if I'd come to see myself.

John Schlesinger
Film Yearbook, 1988

12   I was up for a wonderful part but I was told: 'Sorry, you're the best actor for the role but this calls for a guy-next-door type. You don't look like you've ever lived next door to *anyone*.'

Donald Sutherland
Playboy, October 1981

49   CASTING COUCH

1   I had to go and see this guy, very important man, and everyone said: 'Watch out. Shelley, the second you get into his office, he'll tear your dress off.' 'I'll remember,' I said, 'I'll wear an old dress.'

Shelley Winters
Sunday Times, 2 May 1971

50   CATCHPHRASES

1   I start *Bette Davis In Person* shows with film clips ending with the 'Fasten your seat-belts' line from *All About Eve*. Then, I come on stage, light a cigarette, look around and say 'What – a – *dump*!' Really breaks the ice – people laugh and relax instead of having to *revere* me.

Bette Davis (1908–89)
Playboy, July 1982

2 'Make my day' came from the screenwriter Joe Stinson. Only thing I did, I reprised it at the end – that's my contribution. I saw the line as a goodie.

Clint Eastwood
Film Comment, October 1984

3 I never meant 'Come up and see me sometime' to be sexy.

Mae West (1893–1980)
Playboy, 1970

51 CAUSES

1 Today I'd be a dyed blonde, a numb and dumb pill-popping star, if I hadn't taken up a cause. I could very well be dead like Marilyn. Not through drugs but dead just the same.

Jane Fonda
Daily Mail, 14 April 1980

2 I remember as a child going around with Votes For Women balloons. I learnt early what it is to be snubbed for a good cause.

Katharine Hepburn
The Times, 28 April 1969

52 CELEBRITY

See also 103 Fame
240 Success

1 I was born into big celebrity. It could only diminish.

Carrie Fisher, daughter of Debbie Reynolds and Eddie Fisher
Vanity Fair, 1990

2 Whatever comes at you, comes at you. There's no training ground. *There's no classes in celebrity.*

William Hurt
Rolling Stone, 26 November 1981

3 People can be very cruel. They don't mean to be. They just don't regard celebrities as real. And I guess, in some ways, we're not.

Don Johnson
Film Yearbook, 1990

4 There's a good point to celebrity – I can get a table in a restaurant. The bad point is that fans start videotaping me while I'm eating.

Steve Martin
Blitz, 1987

53   CELIBACY

1 The doc once suggested as an experimental cure for emotional problems, I should try being celibate for six months – as all the creative juices expended in sex can give a man great power and energy in other directions. He was right. That six months was the most productive and sexually exciting time of my life. What power it gives one to say: '*No!*'

Anthony Quinn
Sunday Mirror, 1974

2 My writing partner and I had a sign above a map of the Florida Keys we were writing about. 'D.O.D.' Discipline Our Dicks. No female distraction.

Charlie Sheen
US magazine, 25 January 1988

3 You've gotta conserve your sex energy in order to *do* things. Through this knowledge, I started to really write. When I started a picture, I'd stop all my sex activities and put that energy into my work – get absorbed in the sexiness of *that*.

Mae West (1893–1980)
Playboy, 1970

4 I abstain from sex a lot so I can keep on schedule with exercising, dieting, studying. All this pent-up sexual energy needs a release – and maybe it's coming out of my eyes. It has to spill out somewhere.

Edy Williams
Erotic X-Film Guide, 1984

54 CENSORSHIP

1 Vulgarity is in the hand of the beholder.

Mel Brooks
Films Illustrated, January 1982

2 Twenty-some states in the United States have statutes that say showing the nipples to children is obscene. That's the first thing we come into contact with when we arrive on this planet: a woman's breasts. Why should that be considered obscene?

Clint Eastwood
Playboy, February 1974

3 I do not see any solution to film censorship other than its abolition.

Kirk Douglas
Today's Cinema, 2 April 1969

4 Oh, I get it. It's simple. PG means the hero gets the girl, 15 means that the villain gets the girl and 18 means everybody gets the girl.

Michael Douglas (on UK censor ratings)
Film Yearbook, 1989

5 This isn't an X-rated body. This is a PG body.

Mariel Hemingway
Film Yearbook, 1983

6 Life is full of censorship. I can't spit in your eye.

Katharine Hepburn
American CBS TV, 13 January 1979

7 In *Sunset Boulevard*, I had to sit on Gloria Swanson's bed with one foot firmly on the floor – and my overcoat on! Hell, I was living off her in the film. Everybody in the audience knew I was a kept man so why did they have to be so modest?

William Holden (1918–81)
Photoplay, May 1977

8 Censorship hurts pictures, it damages them. The only form of censorship that's at all significant is what the French do – burn the theatre down.

John Huston (1906–87)
Rolling Stone, 19 February 1981

9 If you suck a tit, you're an X – cut it off with a sword, you're a GP.

Jack Nicholson
Playboy, 1971

10   I'd be *insulted* if a picture I was in didn't get an X-rating. Don't forget, dear, I *invented* censorship.

Mae West (1893–1980)
Playboy, 1970

55   CHARACTERS

1   I never really like the characters I play. I only come to love them afterwards.

Gérard Depardieu
Sous Le Soleil de Satan publicity release, 1987

2   The public dictates whether you retire a character. Everytime I do one, I say it's the final one but Dirty Harry is like an old friend. Every once in a while you like to just drop in on him, see what kind of shenanigans he's up to.

Clint Eastwood
Knave, April 1989

3   The characters I play have a need to be cuddled.

Dudley Moore
Photoplay, May 1983

4   I'm at least 75% of every character I play. For the rest, you have to search out and adopt the character's own justfication and rationalization.

Jack Nicholson
Time, 21 August 1974

5   You can be true to the character all you want but you've got to go home with yourself.

Julia Roberts
New York Times, 18 March 1990

56 CHARACTER ACTORS

1 If I become a supporting actor, it would cut my money by three-quarters.

Michael Caine
Screen International, 29 July 1978

2 I don't think of myself as a character actress – that's become a phrase which means you've had it.

Bette Davis (1908–89)
Photoplay, January 1976

3 I've always thought of myself as a character actor rather than a leading man.

Clint Eastwood
TV Times, August 1988

4 Lee Strasberg would say over and over again: 'There's no such thing as a juvenile or an ingenue or a villain or a hero or a leading man – we're all characters.'

Dustin Hoffman
American Film, April 1983

5 I'm a character actor in a leading man's body.

William Hurt
Ritz, 1989

57 CHILDHOOD

1 We were so poor, my mother couldn't afford to have me. The lady next door gave birth to me.

Mel Brooks
Playboy, December 1974

2 I was seven years old before I used a toilet that flushed. We had the kind of toilet where when it was full, you covered it over and dug a new one.

Tommy Chong
Rolling Stone, 14 December 1978

3 As a child, my most vivid yearning was to persuade Walt Disney to put me into movies like *Old Yeller*.

Glenn Close
Photoplay, February 1988

4 Early childhood is a melodramatic situation. Learning and being scolded is melodrama.

Gérard Depardieu
Cyrano de Bergerac publicity release, 1990

5 The 30s: my parents and my sister and myself just had to move around to get jobs. People were actually living in chicken houses.

Clint Eastwood
Film Comment, October 1984

6 My stepmother was a bitch. She made us cut willow switches with which she'd beat us . . . and made me wear a dress and called me Louise.

James Garner
Photoplay, July 1986

7 I had three mothers, five grammar schools and ten houses by the time I was ten.

Tom Hanks
Photoplay, November 1988

8 I was the archetypal spotty teenager who suffered the tortures of the damned because I wasn't like those girls in the magazines. I had lank, greasy hair and I was fat and spotty.

Glenda Jackson
Evening Standard, 3 April 1974

9 I was so skinny, they gave me the nickname *stechetto* – the stick. I was tall, thin, ugly and dark like an Arab girl. I looked strange. All eyes. No flesh on my bones.

Sophia Loren
Sunday Mirror, 30 August 1964

10 I sorta grew up at MGM, it was a fantastic playground – all the underground passages to the sound-stages. Terrific! And Daddy would let me ride on the camera boom with him. But what I *really* dug was the dance rehearsals: Fred Astaire, Gene Kelly, my mother.

Liza Minnelli
Rolling Stone, 14 May 1973

11 We made our own soap and in the summertime we'd go to the river – it was like a big bath. In the wintertime we just had a pan of water and we'd wash *down* as far as possible and we'd wash *up* as far as possible. Then, when somebody'd cleared the room, we'd wash *possible*.

Dolly Parton
Playboy, October 1978

12   I never saw a lavatory until I was 10. I spent the first 20 years of my life almost continually hungry.

Anthony Quinn
A Star For Two publicity release, 1990

58   CHOICES

1   I choose films with the shortest schedule and the most money.

Klaus Kinski
Club International, 1981

2   Either you decide to stay in the shallow end of the pool or you go out in the ocean.

Christopher Reeve
Films Illustrated, December 1978

3   If it's interesting material but a weak director or if I don't like his personality, I won't do it. If it's a really great director I like and the cast isn't right, then I won't do it. It gets a little complicated.

Mickey Rourke
Deauville, September 1989

4   Some people just skim through films, saying: 'I don't really want to do this but I need the money.' Well, fuck that. I'd live on the streets, first.

Tuesday Weld
Show, January 1972

59   CINEMA

1   Cinema is just a form of masturbation. Sexual relief for disappointed people. Women write and say: 'I let my husband do it because I think it's you lying on top of me.'

Dirk Bogarde
Penthouse, 1965

2 The cinema was my eduation – my child-minder. I fell asleep at *Hell on Frisco Bay* and again in *Giant* – woke up at 4 am and was picked up by the police thinking I was breaking *into* the cinema when, in fact, I was breaking *out*.

Brian Cox
Kaleidoscope, BBC Radio 4, 31 January 1991

3 Cinema is there for eternity and that's incredible.

Gérard Depardieu
Time, 6 February 1984

4 The medium is too powerful and important an influence on the way we live – the way we see ourselves – to be left solely to the tyranny of the box-office or reduced to the sum of the lowest common denominator of public taste.

David Puttnam
Film Yearbook, 1989

60 CLASSICS

1 If my film makes one more person feel miserable, I'll feel I've done my job.

Woody Allen (on *Manhattan*)
Time, 30 April 1979

2 I don't think Bertolucci knew what *Last Tango In Paris* was about. And *I* didn't know what it was about. He went around telling everybody it was about his prick.

Marlon Brando
Rolling Stone, 20 May 1976

3 On alternate days, *Annie Hall* would appeal to us. Then, we'd get disgusted – who wants to see another love story about New York City? When I saw the rough-cut, I thought it terrible, completely unsalvagable. It rambled and was tangential and just . . . endless.

Marshall Brickman (Woody Allen's co-scenarist)
Films Illustrated, November 1980

4 *Apocalypse Now* is not *about* Vietnam, it *is* Vietnam. We were in the jungle; there were too many of us; we had access to too much money, too much equipment; and, little by little, we went insane.

Francis Coppola
Films Illustrated, October 1979

5   Orson Welles lists *Citizen Kane* as his best film, Alfred Hitchcock opts for *Shadow of a Doubt* and Sir Carol Reed chose *The Third Man* – and I'm in all of them.

Joseph Cotton
London, December 1977

6   On *The Blue Angel*, I thought everything we were doing was awful. They kept a camera pointed here [groin]. I was so young and dumb.

Marlene Dietrich
Time, 15 January 1973

7   In 1964 my agent came up and said how would I like to go to Spain to make an Italian-Spanish-German remake of a Japanese samurai film? Yeah, well, I told *him*. Then, I read it and recognized it as Kurosawa's *Yojimbo*. Seemed a way-out idea to have the hero as the protagonist.

Clint Eastwood (on *A Fistful of Dollars*)
Elstree Studios, 9 April 1968

8   Certainly, *Room At The Top* was the first British film in which a man and a woman went to bed without one of them having one foot on the floor.

Laurence Harvey (1928–73)
Premiere (UK), 1970

9   A significant role for me? Seems to be – *now*! Charles [Laughton] called me up: 'I've a book here about a thoroughly unredeemable shit.' And I said: 'Present!'

Robert Mitchum (on *The Night of the Hunter*)
Ritz, No. 143, 1989

10   When I read *Last Tango In Paris*, I didn't see anything that worried me. I was 20. I didn't want to be a star, much less a scandalous actress – simply to be in cinema. Later, I realized I'd been competely manipulated by Bertolucci and Brando.

Maria Schneider
VSD magazine (France), 12 November 1980

11   Oh, torture. Torture. My pubic hairs went grey.

Steven Spielberg (on shooting *E.T.*)
Rolling Stone, 24 October 1985

12   *It's A Wonderful Life* is such a *pure* movie. It wasn't taken from a novel or play. It was developed from one little paragraph. Simple story, no message, no violence, no mob scenes. When the movies have a story like this they do it better than any medium there is.

James Stewart
Evening Standard, 24 January 1975

13   I really don't remember much about *Cleopatra*. There were a lot of other things going on.

Elizabeth Taylor
Film Yearbook, 1987

61   COCAINE

1   My friend asked the producer what the budget was. The producer said: 'I'll tell you what the cocaine budget was – $750 000.' My friend thought for a second and said: 'Well, it's all up there on the screen.'

Michael Caine
Los Angeles Times, 23 October 1984

2   A director friend – I won't name him – was obliged to have a special $750 000 cocaine budget for his actors. I saw the film and said: 'All the money's on the screen.' [No inflation in seven years?]

John Cleese
Liberation (France), 12 February 1991

3   Any movie I've ever made, the minute you walk on the set they tell you who's the person to buy it from. Cher said they're going to make two monuments to us – the two girls who lived through Hollywood and never had cocaine.

Teri Garr
Playboy, October 1981

4   It's made people numb and I think it's made them angry under the numbness.

Anjelica Huston
Vanity Fair, 1990

5   Ten million mothers freebase – and I blow up!

Richard Pryor
Time, 29 March 1982

6 I was doing a lot of coke at the time. I understood the meglomania, the delight, the paranoia of cocaine. I was near the top of the film business and nearly blew it away. *Scarface* was my farewell to coke. *Salvador* was my comeback.

Oliver Stone
Los Angeles Times, 17 December 1989

7 Cocaine is God's way of saying you're making too much money.

Robin Williams
Screen International, 15 December 1990

62 COMEDIANS

1 Comics are famously tragic people.

Marlon Brando
Playboy, January 1979

2 Most great comedians were great athletes. Physical humour demands rhythm and timing. I love making people think I've just killed myself.

Chevy Chase
Playboy, July 1976

3 Peter Sellers crossed into his work. He was a great master. Unfortunately, it mastered him.

Goldie Hawn
Playboy, January 1985

4 I despise Chaplin. I think he was a faggot. So prissy. So English – I mean that in the worst sense. I just want to reach into the screen and punch the little fucker. Keaton's just brilliant, one of the funniest people ever on the screen.

Tony Hendra
Paris, 1984

5 It's acceptable for men to act the fool. When women try, they're considered aggressive and opinionated.

Madeline Kahn
Photoplay, September 1975

6 Making *yourself* look stupid seems much more human. Making other people look stupid just seems cheap.

Steve Martin
Blitz, 1987

7 A lot of us have a lot of hatred and pain in us – all the things that make good actors.

Eddie Murphy
Los Angeles Times, 3 November 1985

8 I'm a classic example of all humorists – only funny when I'm working.

Peter Sellers (1925–80)
Sunday Mirror, 19 August 1973

63   COMEDIES

1 I always wanted to do comedies but nobody discovered this until my old age. They think all Swedes are like Garbo.

Ingrid Bergman (1915–82)
The Times, 18 January 1971

2 I've been offered so few comedies I could count them on one finger.

Peter O'Toole
Photoplay, April 1988

3 I've been making movies from scripts that didn't make me laugh. The producers would say: 'It'll be funny because you're in it.' I'm not going to do that anymore.

Richard Pryor
Photoplay, October 1983

4 That's the secret of *Cannonball* and *Smokey and the Bandit* – and *Police Academy*. They're laughing so much they didn't hear the words. If you listened to the words – you'd throw up.

Burt Reynolds
Film Yearbook, 1989

64 COMEDY

1 When you do comedy, you're not sitting at the grown-ups' table, you're sitting at the children's table.

Woody Allen
Newsweek, 24 April 1978

2 I can't do comedy.

Marlon Brando
Playboy, January 1979

3 Comedy is serious – deadly serious. Never, never try to be funny! The actors must be serious. Only the situation must be absurd.

Mel Brooks
Playboy, December 1974

4 Serious? Serious closes on Saturday!

Tommy Chong
Rolling Stone, 14 December 1978

5 Tension is wonderful for making people laugh.

John Cleese
Film Yearbook, 1990

6 Comedy is the most honest way for an actor to earn his living. People would rather laugh than cry. The quickest way to change drama into comedy is simply to speed up the film.

Tony Curtis
Photoplay, May 1967

7 Comedy, like sodomy, is an unnatural act.

Marty Feldman (1938–82)
Screen International, 25 January 1991

8 It's like a soufflé. If it gets overdone, the soufflé crashes. That's how delicate comedy is. Like music – it's as if I hear the beat in my head.

Goldie Hawn
Playboy, January 1985

9 The secret to all comedy writing is – write Jewish and cast Gentile.

Writer-producer Robert Kaufman
Film Yearbook, 1984

10 Comedy is the only way I know of being serious.

Sir Peter Ustinov
Time, 8 August 1983

11   My comedy is like emotional hang-gliding.
Robin Williams
Playboy, October 1982

65   COMMERCIALS

1   I never will consent to having my name or my face used in any merchandizing context beyond advertising the actual artistic work I've done. I have said no even when I was tempted with regular earnings for Ziggy Stardust dolls.
David Bowie
Variety, 17 May 1983

2   I had a whole career saying 'Ring around the *collar*, honey' and 'Sa-aay, *this* fried chicken is *really* good!' People would come up to me on the street and say 'I know you – Alka-Seltzer, right?' You get tried of being known as Alka-Seltzer.
Peter Boyle
Playboy, December 1973

3   I've done commercials in Australia I'd pay you not to see – pretzels, fish fingers . . .
John Cleese
The Times, 12 December 1987

4   I'm an actor and not into that kinda stuff.
Tom Cruise
Playboy, July 1986.

5   They've brought me more publicity than any film I've done. I'm recognized on every street corner in New York.
Catherine Deneuve (on her Chanel ads)
Newsweek, 8 October 1973

6   I've always had this American-pie face that would get work in commericals . . . I'd say things like 'Hi Marge, how's your laundry?' and 'Hi, I'm a real nice Georgia peach.' Sometimes this work is one step above being a cocktail waitress.
Teri Garr
Washington Post, April 1983

7 It's better to appear in a good commercial in Japan than a bad movie in America.

Valerie Kaprisky
Screen International, May 1990

8 To be asked to do a commercial in Japan is considered a great honour, especially if you're a foreigner. To be asked to do a commercial in this country [America] is a sign that you're on the take or on the skids.

Paul Newman
Playboy, April 1983

9 I did it as a favour to my first fiançé's father's pharmaceutical laboratories. I got paid very well – and that set the price for the others. Now everybody's doing it and I can't get in again.

Joanna Shimkus
London, August 1969

10 I was the all-American face. You name it, honey – American Dairy Milk, Metropolitan Life Insurance, McDonald's, Burger King. The Face That Didn't Matter – that's what I called my face.

Debra Winger
Washington Post, December 1983

66 CONFIDENCE

1 I think I'm getting a little confidence now.

Sir John Gielgud at 71
Sunday Times, December 1975

2 I grew up with a lot of brothers and sisters. I did all I could do to really stand out and that nutured a lot of confidence and drive and ambition.

Madonna
Rolling Stone, 9 May 1985

67   CREDO

1   All films are subversive.
David Cronenberg
French TV, 1989

2   I like it, I do it. That's my code.
Alain Delon
Cinema & TV (South Africa), 1973

3   I hate imitation. I've a reverence for individuality. I got where I am by coming off the wall.
Clint Eastwood
Newsweek, 23 September 1985

4   I'll work anywhere, any time, any price.
Mel Gibson
Photoplay, July 1983

5   If it isn't happening, *make* it happen.
David Hemmings
Films Illustrated, November 1981

6   In 40 years, I've never been late. They pay me enough – so the least I can do is arrive sober, be on time and know all the jokes.
David Niven (1909–83)
TV Times, 1974

7   I just don't want to be hampered by my own limitations.
Barbra Streisand
Playboy, October 1977

68   CRITICISM

See also 205 Reviews

1   One critic wrote: 'I've now found someone to replace Tony Curtis as the world's worst actor -- Elvis Presley.'
Tony Curtis
Sunday Express, 10 December 1965

2   There's a woman reviewer in LA who doesn't like me. She reviewed *Dillinger* and said: 'Richard Dreyfuss draws extra attention to himself by overdoing it, as usual, playing Baby Face Nelson like a rabid pug dog.' The words that leapt off the pages were 'as usual'.

That was the first film I'd done. I wanted to call her up and say: 'Did I offend you in some way when we were infants? Have I hurt your family? Was this something to do with before we emigrated? Is this blood that goes back to Sicily?'

Richard Dreyfuss
Rolling Stone, 31 July 1975

3   I was once described by one of my critics as an aesthetic fascist.

Alan Parker
Film Yearbook, 1990

4   Critics are no longer able to judge my performances. My looks seem to get in the way.

Robert Redford
Photoplay, August 1976

5   There are three lovely critical expressions: pretentious, gratuitous, profound. None of which I truly understand.

Nicolas Roeg
Game, August 1976

6   Pauline Kael reviews *The Day of the Locust*: 'There's nothing specifically wrong with Donald Sutherland's performance. It's just awful.' That was the most destructive, stupid piece of criticism I've ever received. I stopped reading reviews after that.

Donald Sutherland
Playboy, October 1981

69   CRITICS

See also 205 Reviews

1   There's a lot of pear-shaped critics, like that Jay Cocks, who think if an actor's in shape, he can't be any good. One way or another I'll get that man. Not physically, but I'll get him.

Charles Bronson
Playboy, 1975

2   Some critics are emotionally dessicated, personally about as attractive as a year-old peach in a single girl's refrigerator.

Mel Brooks
Playboy, December 1974

3   They're like bouncers. In order to break up a fight, they have to start one first.

Tommy Chong
Playboy, September 1982

4   I know of two cases where critics writing on *The Stud* delivered their reviews before they'd seen the film.

Joan Collins
Screen International, 19 May 1979

5   Listening to critics is like letting Muhammad Ali decide which astronaut goes to the moon.

Robert Duvall
Film Yearbook, 1984

6   Judith Crist hasn't been knocked out over everything I've done – or *anything* I've done. I think she liked *The Devil In Miss Jones* but she thought *Beguiled* was obscene.

Clint Eastwood
Playboy, February 1974

7   My job is to make people laugh. The critics' job is to stop me.

Paul Hogan
Film Yearbook, 1989

8   The bunch of critics we have now in London couldn't write decent *advertising* copy let alone journalism. They're blind and deaf.

Glenda Jackson
People, 18 March 1985

9   I've got nothing against Rex Reed. I understand he's been very kind to me. But do you really want to let yourself be influenced by someone who's been in the same *building* as *The Gong Show* – let alone been on it.

Kevin Kline
Toronto Star, 28 August 1983

10   Pauline Kael is the *Rambo* of film critics . . . a demented bag-lady.

Alan Parker
Film Yearbook, 1990

11   Critics are fuelled by their own failed ambitions. I can't *tell* you the number of critics who slip me script on the side. Then, they rip you apart as an actor because you haven't responded to their screenplay.

Robert Redford
Premiere, March 1988

12 I've not read *one* review of *Mahler*. I know it's a good film. The critics who recognize it as such are good critics. Those who do not are bad critics.

Ken Russell
Films Illustrated, April 1974

13 You wouldn't believe some of the things they've said about me. Like Rex Reed saying my career is more mysterious than cot death!

Sylvester Stallone
Film Yearbook, 1988

14 New York critics – I hear when one of them watched *A Star Is Born*, he talked back to the screen.

Barbra Streisand
Playboy, October 1977

70 CULTS

1 In 1975 I started to wonder what this David Cronenberg cult could've looked like: thick glasses, runny noses, celibate since birth and probably Communists for all we knew.

Martin Scorsese
Toronto Festival programme, 1983

2 You can't live off being a cult.

Barbara Steele, ex-horror queen turned producer
London, 1 February 1968

71 CYNICISM

1 I have a very low regard for cynics. I think it's the beginning of dying.

Robert Redford
Time, 29 March 1976

2 If you're not cynical, you're stupid.

Screenwriter Paul Zimmerman
Cannes, 7 May 1983

72 DATING

1 I'd go out with women my age. But there *are* no women my age.
George Burns at 87
Playboy, June 1978

2 I will not date a depressed woman. I want to have fun.
George Hamilton
Playboy, July 1980

73 DEAD

1 Bogie said himself that dead is dead and life is for the living and you've got to move on – and if you don't, it's self-indulgent and does the dead no good. He said it dishonoured them because if they gave you so little care for your own life, then they didn't leave you with very much.
Lauren Bacall
Guardian, 18 October 1972

2 The Pythons are all dead. Apart from me. And except for Terry Jones. And he's suffering from a terminal illness and has lost control of his bodily functions. So, if you go to see him – wear protective clothing.
John Cleese
Today, 20 September 1988

3 They announced on US TV that Patrick Magee, star of *The Avengers*, had died. So they rang up my daughter in Palm Springs. 'Sorry to hear that your father's dead.' She said: 'But I was talking to him 12 minutes ago in Australia.' They said, 'No, he's dead – it's just the time difference.'
Patrick MacNee
Knave, October 1984

4 In Hollywood sometimes you're even dead *before* you're dead.
Spencer Tracy (1900–67)
Sunday Express, 1960

5   I don't believe people die. They just go uptown. To Blooming-
dales. They just take longer to get back.

Andy Warhol (1927–87)
Film Yearbook, 1984

6   I wouldn't mind being dead – it would be something new.

Estelle Winwood (1887–1984) at 100 (she died 18 months later)
International Herald Tribune, January 1983

74   JAMES DEAN

1   James Dean epitomized the very thing that's so campily res-
pectable today – the male hustler. He had quite a sordid little
reputation. I admire him immensely.

David Bowie
Playboy, September 1976

2   Intense, moody, incredible charisma. Short, myopic, not good-
looking. You know who he was like? A young Woody Allen.

Joan Collins
Playboy, April 1984

3   I caught all James Dean's films within a six-month period. I was
very, very affected by the fact that he was communicating to me and
the audience. And I said: 'That's it. That's what I want to do.' Dean
was so real. I believed he was the real person – that he wasn't acting.

Bruce Dern
Films Illustrated, October 1978

4   I thought Dean was *fantastic*! Maybe he's lucky he died when he
did. His [*East of Eden*] performance now is so stereotyped. All the
bad imitations have destroyed James Dean.

Anthony Hopkins
Films Illustrated, December 1980

5   It blew my mind when he died. Still does . . . He woulda been a
great director. On *Giant*, I was 18, he was 24. I watched him act, he
watched me and told me when he thought I was good; like he was a
sorta teacher and I was a student. I learned a lot from the guy – and
it sure got me into trouble!

Dennis Hopper
Cannes, 26 May 1976

6　What I disliked was the Dean legend. He was a hero to the people who saw him only as a little waif, when actually he was a pudding of hatred.

Elia Kazan
Sunday Times, 1969

7　The person I really related to was James Dean. I grew up with the Dean thing. *Rebel Without A Cause* had a very great effect on me.

Al Pacino
Playboy, December 1979

8　James Dean was the strongest influence on any actor that ever stepped in front of the camera. Ever.

Martin Sheen
David Dalton and Ron Cayen, *James Dean: An American Icon*, 1985

9　In James Dean, today's youth discovers itelf. Less for the reasons usually advanced: violence, sadism, hysteria, pessimism, cruelty and filth than for others more infinitely simple and commonplace: modesty of feeling, continual fantasy life, moral purity but all the more rigorous, eternal adolescent love of tests and trials, intoxication, pride and regret at feeling oneself outside society, refusal and desire to become integrated and, finally, acceptance – or refusal – of the world as it is.

François Truffaut (1932–84)
Arts, 26 September 1956

75　DEATH

1　It's not that I'm afraid of death, I just don't want to be there when it happens.

Woody Allen
Today, 23 July 1989

2　For a long time, I focused on the disposal of my body. It'd be a relief to die in an explosion – *that* would take care of the problem.

Candice Bergen
American Film, October 1981

3　I'm getting very curious about what I'm going to be doing *after* I'm dead.

John Cleese
Playboy, November 1988

4 My Scots accent was stronger in this new Bond film [*Never Say Never Again*] than in the others. I suppose you get more relaxed the nearer you get to the grave.

Sean Connery
Film Yearbook, 1985

5 Death is what makes life an event.

Francis Coppola
Film 91, BBC TV, 5 March 1991

6 Death is the only thing left to respect. Everything else can be questioned. But death is truth. In it lies the only nobility for man and beyond it the only hope.

James Dean (1931–56)
Photoplay, September 1985

7 I don't like death. I find it's an uninteresting anecdote, unfortunately final. I never like final things.

Gérard Depardieu
Sous Le Soleil de Satan publicity release, 1987

8 I often wonder how I'm going to die. You don't want to embarrass friends.

Cary Grant (1904–86)
Variety, 6 December 1983

9 Afraid of death? Not at all. Be a great relief. Then I wouldn't have to talk to you.

Katharine Hepburn
People, 5 November 1990

10 I'd like to die by turbine. See, if you're sucked into a turbine, you get whipped into instantaneous ether.

William Hurt
Rolling Stone, 26 November 1981

11 You do not die, you just change form. You are divine, as is everything.

Shirley MacLaine
Playboy, September 1984

12 I sense an incredible feeling of searing agony from being burned. I've never liked the idea of being dead, of short-circuiting.

Jack Nicholson
Playboy, 1971

13   Best way to go is like one of the furry creatures in the forest, crawling underneath the bramble bush. It's rather more noble than wishing your family around you, feeling your pulse ... fussing about.

Lord Laurence Olivier (1907–89)
Daily Mail, 27 March 1970

14   Few people understand it and live it when it comes.

Terence Stamp
Time Out, 30 August 1984

15   You must not wait until someone comes and steals your death. You must decide on it, yourself.

Jean-Louis Trintignant
Telegraph Sunday magazine, 1 April 1979

76   DIETS

1   The putting on [weight for *Educating Rita*] was simple and delightful. The taking off took longer. I live in Beverly Hills, so I took the Beverly Hills diet. I ate a lot of pineapple. It made me spotty – so I ate a lot of Nivea cream.

Michael Caine
Ottawa Citizen, 17 September 1983

2   I was on a diet, so I asked the waiter if he had any mineral water. He replied: 'Not as such.' What a marvellously evasive reply!

John Cleese
Daily Mail, 17 February 1979

3   Sex is good for slimming.

Julie Newmar
Evening Standard, 1967

4   A lot of diets aren't healthy. They're too radical.

Elizabeth Taylor
Los Angeles magazine, 1987

77 DIFFICULTIES

1 Robin was in the script almost until we were shooting *Batman*.
It's kinda hard to give a psychological profile to a guy in a yellow
cape and green boots.

Tim Burton
Deauville, September 1989

2 One of the major problems of developing a property for yourself
is that it tends to be made for *you* – when who *you* are is what you
want to change.

Harrison Ford
Deauville, September 1982

3 It wasn't the easiest thing for a man called Goering to persuade
Jewish businessmen to back a film called *Hitler's Son*.

Producer Dr Gerd Goering
Variety, 11 April 1978

78 DIRECTING

1 If you don't get it right, what's the point?

Michael Cimino, director of *Heaven's Gate*
Variety (Kodak advertisement), 23 July 1980

2 Even if you see a film which you think is terrible and you say, 'Oh,
that man can't direct'; there's one thing he did: he finished the film!
And if you can finish a feature film, go all the way to the end without
killing someone or taking 3000 aspirins, you *have* to have something
going for you. Because it's a crazy mountain to try and climb.

Tom Conti
Cannes, 15 May 1983

3 The worst is a director that tells someone to do something. You
say: 'I've never been in this situation. What do you mean I go over
there and smile?' They don't understand you could do it another
way – better for you, give you more confidence, more joy. It might
not be the way the director imagined it. But in the long run it'll have
the same effect. You have to have give and take. If it's out of
balance, it won't work.

Robert De Niro
American Film, March 1981

4 I like to work on a director's second film, when you learn if he's going to go on for six or 10 more films. Or not.

Gérard Depardieu
American Film, October 1983

5 I discovered early on – get a tough director.

Katharine Hepburn
Panorama (USA), March 1981

6 I can write. I think I edit quite well. I know, I could direct – but I'd be mediocre.

David Puttnam
Film Yearbook, 1986

7 Directors are supposed to help the audience. Good directors don't direct actors.

George C. Scott
Playboy, December 1980

8 I prefer a kind of one-word direction. One word – and I can do it good. Shy. Tense. Sex. Fear. I'm not being very exotic with the words – but things.

Tuesday Weld
Films Illustrated, September 1978

79 DIRECTING ADVICE

1 Best piece of advice came from Steven Spielberg: 'Wear comfortable shoes.'

Bob Balaban
Premiere, April 1988

2 My professor told me when I started in the 40s that a director should listen and keep his mouth shut. Took me a long time to understand I talked too much. Now I know you should listen with your ears – and your heart.

Ingmar Bergman
Paris Passion, December 1989

3 Don't be afraid of anything.

John Cassavetes (1929–86)
Los Angeles Times, 6 May 1989

4 Concentrate on the story, leave the details to others – and sit whenever you can.

John Huston (1906–87)
Cap d'Antibes, 23 May 1979

5 If you can drive a car, you can direct a movie.

John Landis
Film Yearbook, 1990

6 It takes a long time to learn simplicity.

Louis Malle
Films Illustrated, March 1981

7 Have a go. Anybody can do it.

Alan Parker
Paris Passion, December 1989

8 I asked other directors for advice. Bob Aldrich told me always to listen to everybody. Mel Brooks told me to remember to fire someone the first day.

Burt Reynolds
Nancy Streebeck, *The Films of Burt Reynolds*, 1983

9 Most of the so-called new techniques were tried out 30 or 40 years ago and abandoned because they distracted from the essential. The best direction is that which is least visible.

Martin Ritt (1920–91)
Films Illustrated, February 1980

10 Time and speed are desperate shackles and terribly difficult to fight. But it's worth having a go.

Nicolas Roeg
Films Illustrated, July 1980

80 DIRECTORS

1 We'd have better films if directors controlled them completely.

Woody Allen
Time Out, 1 November 1989

2 Everyone should do everything they can to achieve my point of view – not because I'm annointed by God but because it's my picture.

John Berry
Los Angeles Times, 8 July 1990

3   After a director is fired, it's like he's got AIDS. Nobody will touch him. Nobody wants to come too close.

Martin Brest
Knave, May 1985

4   As an actor, I feel we need them, maybe much more than they need us.

Alain Delon
Films & Filming, 1964

5   The relationship between an actor and a director is like a love story between a man and a woman. I'm sure sometimes I'm the woman.

Gérard Depardieu
American Film, October 1983

6   Directors are never in short supply of girlfriends.

Bob Fosse (1927–87)
Film Yearbook, 1985

7   A great many directors don't even like actors. They think we're in the way.

Ben Gazzara
Films Illustrated, December 1979

8   There are two kinds of directors – allies and judges.

John Hurt
Radio Times, 1971

9   A novelist sits over his work like a god, but he knows he's a particularly minor god. Whereas a director making a small movie is a bone-fide general of a small army.

Norman Mailer
Tough Guys Don't Dance publicity release, 1987

10   A lot of directors don't realize the hardest thing to do is to make chicken salad out of chicken shit. I've done that a lot.

Burt Reynolds
Playboy, October 1979

11   I don't believe I ever worked for two directors who knew anything about acting. They're usually technicians, editors – or, should be.

Mickey Rooney
Pinewood Studios, 29 September 1978

12   When you're working for a good director, you become subjective and submissive. You become his concubine. All that you're seeking is his pleasure.

Donald Sutherland
Film Yearbook, 1986

81 DIRECTORS BY ACTORS

1 Nicolas Roeg – an old warlock. There's a very strong alchemy in his movies. You come out winded from the experience of working with him.

David Bowie
Ritz, October 1983

2 What he did 20 years ago seems natural. Now he's involved in psychotherapy – he pushes his actors to the limit to see when they'll crack.

Claude Brasseur (on Jean-Luc Godard)
Screen International, 10 May 1985

3 I wasn't worried about working with a non-English-speaking director like [Japanese] Nagisa Oshima. Having worked with so many English-speaking directors who didn't know what the fuck they were talking about, I thought it wasn't going to make any difference.

Tom Conti
Cannes, 15 May 1983

4 De Mille was a caricature of himself – a god in his own cloud. He built the cloud, got on it and lived there.

John Derek
London, 17 December 1979

5 Steven Spielberg doesn't know anything about actors, that's obvious.

Bruce Dern
Films Illustrated, October 1978

6 With Robert Altman, it's as if he's not on the set. He leaves you alone as opposed to Henry Hathaway who says: 'When I say action – tense up, Goddammit!' Coppola is like a kid with an all-day sucker. Anything he wants, he gets.

Robert Duvall
Hollywood Reporter, 28 September 1983

7 Robert Altman knows what, he doesn't know how. Irvin Kershner knows how, he doesn't know what.

Elliott Gould
International Herald Tribune, 4 August 1973

8 Coppola is extraordinary, sort of from another planet.

Bob Hoskins
Photoplay, May 1988

9   Ken Russell *accentuates*. He gives everything an exclamation mark – the mark of an honest, artistic man.

Oliver Reed
Playdate (New Zealand), 1971

10   You see Buñuel's films, you think of a complicated mentality, maybe twisted with *beaucoup* complexes about religion and sex. No! He was clean. Like a baby. So clever, so clean – *fresh!* Everything I do reminds me of him because he *surprised* me. So did Orson Welles. They *still* surprise me. Even after their deaths and my 150 films.

Fernando Rey
Knave, August 1986

11   My idea of a director is a chap who puts me in the middle of a stage and shines a bright light on me.

Sir Ralph Richardson (1903–83)
Quoted by Simon Callow, *Los Angeles Times*, 11 February 1990

12   Sergio Leone taught me: less is more. Working with him was a once-in-a-lifetime experience for eight solid months. It's like your first time – it'll never quite be the same. Maybe, it'll be better. But it'll never be the same.

James Woods
Deauville, 9 September 1983

82   DIRECTORS BY ACTRESSES

1   It's rare to find a director who really likes and knows how to look at a woman through a camera.

Isabelle Adjani
Rolling Stone, 26 August 1976

2   Really exciting working with Ken Russell. But it's a strange movie when you don't hear 'Cut!'

Ann-Margret
Guardian, September 1974

3 Marty Scorsese's never negative. He said: 'Do you think you should laugh in this scene?' 'Oh, no Marty, I can't see where she'd laugh.' 'Oh, yeah, you're right. Forget I ever said anything.' That's what he does, very subtly: like he planted the seed, watered it and split. As I was doing the scene, I don't know where it came from, but I just started laughing.

Rosanna Arquette
Rolling Stone, 9 May 1985

4 Bob Altman is a great guy. For him, life comes first, movies second.

Kim Basinger
Film Yearbook, 1987

5 I'd never make another film rather than work with [Otto] Preminger again. I don't think he could direct his little nephew to the bathroom.

Dyan Cannon
Time, 17 January 1972

6 Milos Forman doesn't want to discuss anything with his actors.

Louise Fletcher
Time, 12 April 1976
(*See also* 234.12)

7 Mel Brooks is sensual with me. He treats me like an uncle. A dirty uncle.

Madeline Kahn
Newsweek, 17 February 1975

8 If Fassbinder found someone who liked to suffer, he made them suffer – and enjoyed it. He was like a cat coming at you with his paws. You never knew whether he'd stroke or claw you.

Hanna Schygulla
Time, 4 March 1985

83 DIRECTORS BY DIRECTORS

1 Ingmar Bergman amazes me in part because he tells intellectual stories and they move forward for endless amounts of time with no dialogue.

Woody Allen
Time, 30 April 1979

2 Eisenstein seems to be all form and no content. Chaplin is all content and little form. Nobody could've shot a film in a more pedestrian way than Chaplin. Nobody could've paid less attention to story than Eisenstein. But both are great film-makers.

Stanley Kubrick
Newsweek, 26 May 1980

3 If he heard his best friend was dying while he was on the set, I doubt if he'd take it in. Once he's started a film, there's really nothing else in his life.

Ronald Neame (on Sir David Lean)
Film Yearbook, 1986

4 Oliver Stone, I don't like. But then nobody likes Oliver. He's just an aggressive man like me. But he hasn't my sense of humour.

Alan Parker
Film Yearbook, 1990

5 He reminded me a little bit of Walt Disney's version of a mad scientist.

Steven Spielberg (on George Lucas)
Film Yearbook, 1985

6 The film director is rather like a cabinet minister: it's a vague profession. Anybody who sets out to be a film director must start somewhere else.

Sir Peter Ustinov
Cinema Papers (Australia), April 1982

7 Like him? We're getting married!

John Waters (on Pedro Almodovar)
Cannes, May 1990

8   The man's as fascinating and as variable as his films. A Mephistopheles, an outrageously seductive, unfrocked cardinal, an amiable Count Dracula who drank only the best vintages of burgundy and never bared his teeth except to smile. He lives up to his living legend – and he lives it up.

Orson Welles (1915–85) (on John Huston)
Variety, 8 March 1983

9   I'm not bitter about Hollywood's treatment of me – but of its treatment of Griffith, von Sternberg, Buster Keaton and a hundred others.

Orson Welles (1915–85)
French TV, 1985

10   I hear Otto Preminger's on holiday. In Auschwitz.

Billy Wilder
Films Illustrated, January 1980

---

84   DIRECTORS BY PRODUCERS

1   Steven must be making a movie, physically shooting something at some point during the course of the year – or he'd go mad.

Kathleen Kennedy (on Steven Spielberg)
Deauville, 14 September 1985

---

85   DIRECTORS BY SISTERS

1   He's the best director in the world – period.

Talia Shire (on Francis Coppola)
MTV, 19 January 1991

2   I always write boys. Maybe I'm always writing about Steve.

Anne Spielberg, co-scenarist of *Big*
Premiere, January 1988

86 DIRECTORS' DEBUTS

1 When I felt unsure of my abilities and terrified of the whole enterprise, I said to myself: You're an actor, right? So act like a director.

Bob Balaban
Premiere, April 1988

2 I did dumb things. First day on the set, first scene, sound men are ready, cameras are rolling, the director's supposed to say: 'Action!' Being a little nervous, I said: 'Cut!'

Mel Brooks
Playboy, December 1974

3 *Slow Motion* is my second first film – which is rare. *Breathless* is the first film. This is the second first.

Jean-Luc Godard (20 years and 37 films separated the debuts)
Cannes, May 1980

4 Like being pecked to death by a thousand pigeons. Everybody's got questions. You get out of the car in the morning. All you want is a bacon sandwich and there they are. 'What do you want me to do about this? How are we going to do that?' Even when I'd go to the loo, they'd be banging on the door.

Bob Hoskins
Screen International, 13 May 1988

5 The actors were all in their places – looking at me expectantly. I'd no idea what was required. Finally, my assistant, the splendid Jack Sullivan, whispered: 'Say action!' I did so and *The Maltese Falcon* was underway.

John Huston (1906–87)
Variety, 8 March 1983

6 The Godfather of Aussie TV, Hector Crawford, called me back from location one Tuesday. 'You're going to be a director.' Oh, OK! It'd be a nice, easy six months' training. 'When do you want me to start?' Monday! I had four days and the weekend to get ready.

George (*Neverending Story II*) Miller
Munich, 1989

7 I got my first assignment as a director in 1927. I was slim, arrogant, intelligent, foolish, shy, cocksure, dreamy and irritating. Today, I'm no longer slim.

Michael Powell (1905–90)
Film Yearbook, 1988

8   I responded with the message that [*Gator*] was possibly the worst screenplay I'd ever read. Asked to direct it, I replied I'd welcome the opportunity to direct such fine material.

Burt Reynolds
Film, May 1982

9   My own start in movies was a lucky one, thanks to a contract that for almost 30 years remained unique in Hollywood history. That contract shattered all precedents and challenged for a brief moment the basic premise of the whole studio system. Quite simply, I was left alone.

Orson Welles (1915–85) (on *Citizen Kane*)
Look, 11 March 1970

---

87   DIRECTORS ON THEIR FILMS

1   I've never made a film that could remotely be considered a masterpiece. Not even remotely.

Woody Allen
Time Out, 1 November 1989

2   I made mistakes in drama. I thought drama was when actors cried. But drama is when the audience cries.

Frank Capra
Cinéma, Cinémas, No. 12, Antenne 2 (French TV), February 1983

3   In some ways, this is *Death Of A Salesman, Italian Style* – with my family.

Francis Coppola (on *Godfather III*)
MTV, 19 January 1991

4   In all my films, there's three or maybe four minutes of real cinema.

Akira Kurosawa
Film Yearbook, 1987

5   No one caught on that *Ryan's Daughter* was actually an adaptation of *Madame Bovary*.

Sir David Lean (1908–91)
Film Yearbook, 1986

6   Halfway through shooting [*Performance*], they'd already started to hate it. Do you recall the scene in the bath with Mick, Anita and Michele? Someone from Hollywood complained the bath water was too dirty. I mean . . .!

Nicolas Roeg
Game, August 1976

7   Unfortunately, directors never see their films for the first time.

Jerry Schatzberg
Paris Passion, December 1989

88   DIRECTORS ON THEMSELVES

1   I've always been a self-confessed opportunist.

Peter Bogdanovich
Films Illustrated, April 1972

2   I only direct in self-defence.

Mel Brooks
Newsweek, 17 February 1975

3   I may show actors too much by mimicry but I'm a damn fine director.

Sir Charles Chaplin (1889–1977)
Show, June 1972

4   I like a lot of takes. I just go on until the actors get it right.

Stephen Frears
Paris Passion, December 1989

5   I consider myself just another member of the crew, the highest-paid member of the crew.

William Friedkin
Los Angeles Times, 19 November 1989

6   Most directors don't like to go to films very much. I go to see if I can steal something that's good.

George Roy Hill
Paris Passion, December 1989

7   I direct as little as possible. I relieve myself of the ardours of direction, simply by casting it right.

John Huston (1906–87)
Cannes, 18 May 1984

8   My dream was to be a journalist. Then, I realized you can make films and stay a journalist. You can make films and stay anything else.

Dusan Makavejev
Films Illustrated, December 1981

9   I've a lot of admiration for mercenary directors who can take anything and make it work. But if it's not my material, if I don't care tremendously about it, I don't do a good job.

Louis Malle
Today, 28 January 1990

10   I never listen. I watch. And if I believe it, I print it.

Martin Ritt (1920–91)
Films Illustrated, February 1980

11   I hate shooting – getting up at 5.30 am. I prefer noon to midnight. I'm not awake until 3 pm.

Martin Scorsese
Antenne 2 (French TV), 10 January 1991

12   When I grow up I still want to be a director.

Steven Spielberg
Time, 15 July 1985

13   It's about a bastard director who's full of himself, who catches people, creates and then destroys them. It's about us, John!

Orson Welles (1915–85) to John Huston acting in the never seen *Other Side of the Wind*
Time Out, 18 April 1990

89   DIVORCE

1   For a while we pondered whether to take a vacation or get a divorce. We decided that a trip to Bermuda is over in two weeks but a divorce is something you always have.

Woody Allen
Time, 3 July 1972

2   The only fight Elizabeth and I had over the divorce was when I said 'You take everything' and she replied 'No, you take it all.'
Richard Burton
Daily Mail, 2 August 1974

3   I don't see any reason for marriage when there is divorce.
Catherine Deneuve
Los Angeles Times, 13 April 1975

4   I've been divorced four times. Every marriage started for bad reasons – and ended for good.
Producer Robert Evans
Film Yearbook, 1991

90   DRUGS

1   I don't do more drugs than any other schmuck out there in the public. And, uh ... I liked doing it. I'm just noticed more than anyone else. [He overdosed two months later.]
John Belushi (1949–82)
Rolling Stone 21, January 1982

2   When I was a drummer, I smoked reefers. Then, we called it 'tea'. By the time it was called 'shit', non-musicians were smoking grass. Wasn't sharp anymore.
Mel Brooks
American Premiere, September 1981

3   I get worried if I have to take an aspirin.
Michael Caine
Playboy, 1966

4   Just a phase I went through. When you see friends of yours dying, you realize it just isn't worth it.
Chevy Chase
Rolling Stone, 13 October 1983

5   If I'd wanted to do drugs, I'd have *done* them. I just don't like them. They're stupid.
Cher
Playboy, December 1988

6   The ruination of civilization – the worst thing that has happened to modern man.

Joan Collins
The Observer, 6 October 1985

7   I was very sick. I was dying. I was either going to stop or die. I stopped.

Peter Coyote
Cannes, 8 May 1987

8   It's very good to get through them while you're still young and then talk about how great or bad it was for the rest of your life.

Carrie Fisher
Film Yearbook, 1986

9   I met this chick in New York and she saw a strung-out paranoid Pisces. And she said: 'Here, smoke a little of this instead.' And I did. And I got ripped. And I stopped wearing a gun. And I stopped drinking. And I got less and less violent.

Peter Fonda
Rolling Stone, 6 September 1969

10   I get high staring at posters in the street.

Jean-Luc Godard
IT, 6 September 1968

11   My intention in taking LSD was to make myself happy, A man would be a fool to take something that *didn't* make him happy.

Cary Grant (1904–86)
Daily Mail, 6 September 1973

12   The worst drug today is not smack or pot, it's refined sugar. Sugar kills!

George Hamilton
Playboy, July 1980

13   Of course, drugs were fun. And that's what's so stupid about anti-drug campaigns – they don't admit that.

Anjelica Huston
Vanity Fair, July 1990

14   I don't take pills. I drink herbal tea.

Madonna
Time, 27 May 1985

15   Once, it gave me an orgasm that lasted for three days. But then, I don't need pot. My orgasms normally last that long anwyay.

Dudley Moore
Playboy, 1984

16   I've said – for ever – that I smoke marijuana. I missed no acting classes during 12 years. I haven't missed a day's work from illness in 30 years. I'll put my medical charts, my sanity charts up against anybody's.

Jack Nicholson
Rolling Stone, 29 March 1984

17   They become a crutch. It just . . . gets you. Ten years go by and you don't even know it. Before you can do anything about it, you have to admit it has got you. Some people never can.

Richard Pryor
Photoplay, October 1983

18   I was on different drugs – crystal Methedrine, which had more of an edge. When you walked down the streets, your heels made sparks.

Sam Shepard
Playboy, March 1984

19   The most expensive habit in the world is celluloid not heroin and I need a fix every two years.

Steven Spielberg
OM, December 1984

20   I don't like drugs. Drugs kill.

Andy Warhol (1927–87)
Rolling Stone, 15 April 1971

---

91   DRUGS IN FILMS

1   The real trick was in snorting all those drugs and making it look convincing. Al Pacino told me to use powdered milk. What he didn't tell me was that the day after you've snorted a lot of this stuff, milk starts running down your nose . . . dripping all over the place.

Michael J. Fox
Sunday Express magazine, 29 May 1988

2   In *Panic In Needle Park*, I was playing someone dealing drugs on a street corner – and there was a guy actually dealing heroin right there. I looked at him, he looked at me and I got real confused.
Al Pacino
Playboy, December 1979

92   DYING

1   I was dead. I had eight heart attacks. After six, they didn't think I could take any more. Nobody ever had. When I thought I was just falling asleep, I was really dying. If that's dying, I'll never fear it again.
Peter Sellers (1925–80) (on his Hollywood heart attacks)
Sunday Express, 24 May 1964

2   It was a bit close, I admit. Eight times my heart stopped. I was dead, clinically, for close on two minutes. I went right to the limit.
Peter Sellers (1925–80)
Daily Mirror, 26 September 1977

3   I was frightened. I was angry. I was fierce. I didn't want to die ... I died four times. You feel yourself going, falling into a horrible black pit. You hear a screaming jet. Your skin is falling off ... I felt I touched God.
Elizabeth Taylor (on her equally famous brush with death)
Look, 15 August 1961

93   EARLY DAYS

1   I thought I'd never be an actor but then I saw Van Johnson had freckles just like me.
Michael Caine
Showtime, 1965

2   I was skating by with charm and American ingenuity in a marketing job. A white rat could've done it . . . If I had to get a job taking the trash out, it was gonna be Hollywood trash.

Kevin Costner
Ritz, No. 134, 1989

3   I worked for a while as a doorman at a Howard Johnson restaurant in Times Square. I wore one of those white uniforms with green braid – like something from an American high school band. My former Marine Corps captain came by, recognized me, looked me up and down and said: 'Hackman, you're a sorry-looking sunuvabitch.'

Gene Hackman
Films Illustrated, September 1978

4   I lived below the official American poverty line until I was 31.

Dustin Hoffman
Film Monthly, May 1989

5   I was a total loner, not by self-design. I just didn't know what the hell to say to people. I was so shy. I used to stammer and lisp and dribble at the mouth.

Anthony Hopkins
Films Illustrated, December 1980

6   I used to empty ashtrays for the cigarette butts, re-roll them and make myself a fag. I used to live on a pound of sausages and a cooking apple.

Glenda Jackson
Evening Standard, 29 October 1976

7   My father was a milkman. So, I delivered milk.

Karl Malden
Film Yearbook, 1985

8   I packed pineapples at a local cannery in Honolulu, but you got very little applause. I typed student records at Columbia University, sold gloves at a Manhattan department store and worked briefly as a go-go dancer. Guys kept trying to dance with me and I had to fight them off with a club. Loved every minute of it!

Bette Midler
Photoplay, March 1980

9   When I was 15, I had my own comedy act – even played a strip joint once until my mother found out. I remember a girl took off her clothes to the theme of *Romeo and Juliet*.

Dennis Quaid
Munich, 12 February 1985

10   By 21, I'd studied to be a priest, been a preacher with Aimee Semple McPherson, worked with Mae West and boxed with Primo Carnera.

Anthony Quinn
Cinema TV Today, 28 April 1973

11   I'd work in the summer for four weeks moving props. When that ended, I'd go and work the lights for a week. If they wanted someone to fall off a horse, I'd do that, too, or work on a dress set as an extra for while. In those days you'd work in every department [to find your] true place in the business.

John Wayne (1907–79)
Photoplay, June 1968

94   EARLY ROLES

1   In *This Is Spinal Tap*, I played the drummer who died in a bizarre gardening accident. My arm was yanked off in *Cat People*. I was killed by a frying pan in *Eating Raoul*. Oh, and let's not forget my Disney years. I don't know if they wanted me as much as my geeky-looking glasses – 'You're bringing the glasses, right?'

Ed Begley Jr
Playboy, February 1987

2   I was never the good girl or the bad girl. I was always the ugly girl.

Sonia Braga
Cannes, 13 May 1985

3   When I first got to Hollywood, I made $40 a week and they named a hairstyle after me and made me into a kind of male Yvonne De Carlo, fooling around in Arabian Nights rubbish.

Tony Curtis
Photoplay, May 1969

4   *The Incredible Two-Headed Transplant*? I ate a baby in that movie. Ate a *baby*!

Bruce Dern
Rolling Stone, 14 December 1978

5   I played all kinds, father rapers, murderers, kidnappers, various psychopaths. I also played dinks. Dinks wear owl glasses and ask Sally Field to go to the prom. And she turns them down.

Richard Dreyfuss
Rolling Stone, 31 July 1975

6   I used to play a lot of lab assistants. I'd be the guy running in, yelling 'The place is on fire?' I'd come in, go out and that was it. I never got shot or died – if that had happened, I would've gotten more screen time than average . . . I did a *Francis The Talking Mule* picture once.

Clint Eastwood
Films Illustrated, February 1981

7   Once I played Cher's dog on TV.

Teri Garr
Washington Post, April 1983

8   I once played a young Nazi and for a short period, to many people, I was this guy who'd come over from Munich and I'd be fine once I learned the English language.

Robert Redford
Playboy, December 1974

---

95   EDITING

1   The basic grammar of film. Asking a director if he does his own editing is like asking a writer if he does his own punctuation.

Alan Alda
American Film, April 1981

2   Scriptwriting is like cooking. Shooting, the part I enjoy most, is like eating. Editing, therefore, is – well, the washing up.

Claude Chabrol
Film Yearbook, 1988

3   I've been accused of editing too much. But audiences get bored quickly.

Bob Fosse (1927–87)
Cue, 1 February 1980

4 When the great actor says the line, you can put the scissors precisely at the point A and it's wonderful. When the star says the line, you hold for four frames longer because something else happens.

Sir David Lean (1908–91) to Michael Caine
Deathtrap publicity release, 1982

5 Harry Keramida, who cut *About Last Night*, said shooting film is the director's way of talking to the editor – cutting film is the editor's way of answering. A dialogue among peers.

Director Edward Zwick
American Cinemeditor, summer 1990

96 EGO

1 I'm munificent. I definitely feel kingly. Same kinda Jew as Napoleon.

Mel Brooks
New Yorker, 1978

2 There's nothing more offensive to me than watching an actor act with his ego.

Robert De Niro
Newsweek, 16 May 1977

3 If I didn't have an enormous ego and a monumental pride, how in the hell could I be a performer?

Jackie Gleason (1918–87)
Time, 29 December 1961

4 I'd have been better than Adolf Hitler. I could've delivered his speeches a lot better. That's for certain.

Klaus Kinski
Film Yearbook, 1984

5 I'm beginning to impress even myself – and I don't like that.

George Lucas
Film Yearbook, 1985

6   To have ego means to believe in your own strength. And to also be open to other people's views. It is to be open, not closed. So, yes, my ego is big, but it's also very small in some areas. My ego is responsible for my doing what I do – bad or good.

Barbra Streisand
Playboy, October 1977

7   You're best when you're not in charge. The ego locks the muse.

Robin Williams
Premiere, January 1988

8   I've never felt so brilliant and intelligent as I feel now.

Franco Zeffirelli
Film Yearbook, 1987

97   ENTERTAINMENT

1   The primary object of the artist is to entertain. The great thing about Mort Sahl or Mozart or Ingmar Bergman is that they're entertaining.

Woody Allen
Newsweek, 24 April 1978

2   I don't like to be entertained.

John Cassavetes (1929–86)
Film Yearbook, 1986.

3   Frivolous, mindless entertainment: that's valuable when it doesn't pretend to be anything else. At least, in my country it is.

Sally Field
Films Illustrated, August 1979

4   What does this mean: entertainer? Entertain what? Who?

Klaus Kinski
Playboy, November 1985

5   *Sullivan's Travels* always inspires me, it reminds you that entertainment is a wonderfully important human need – a good thing to do – and it can also be very ennobling.

Phil Alden Robinson, scenarist-director *Field of Dreams*
Ritz, 1989

98 EUROPEAN FILMS

1   I'm a little bored with the art films we produce in Europe.

Jean-Jacques Annaud
Rolling Stone, No. 485, 1986

2   I don't think Europeans make better films – they can't even keep their johns clean.

Peter Fonda
Time, 16 February 1970

3   The more I go to the movies, the more I like French movies.

Claude Lelouch
French TV, 1986

99 EXTRAS

1   I was an extra for a number of my early years in Hollywood – that Anglo-Saxon Type No. 2008 is perfectly true. You thought you had it made if you got that far at Central Casting. It was quite common to be appearing in several films at the same time, even on the same day. We'd dash from one stage to the next and try to remember which costumes we were supposed to be wearing.

David Niven (1909–83)
Films Illustrated, July 1979

2   I was an extra in many films. Oh, many films! The producers always cast me as the same man. The man in the dinner jacket. Like David Niven and his famous Central Casting label, I was: The Black Tie Type.

Fernando Rey
Knave, August 1986

3   I was an extra for four years. I lived in a seedy hotel in Paris. The first floor was occupied by successful tarts, the second by not-so-successful tarts and the third by out-of-work actors. We used to borrow the tarts' shoes whenever we went for important auditions.

Simone Signoret (1921–85)
Sunday Express, 1962

100 EYES

1   I have the eyes of a dead pig.

Marlon Brando
Screen International, 18 January 1991

2   What a camera likes are eyes which have life and tell a story.

Jeremy Irons
Cinéma, Cinémas, Antenne 2 (French TV), 15 January 1991

3   If you haven't cried, your eyes can't be beautiful.

Sophia Loren
Sunday Express, 6 October 1965

4   If I died today, they might write on my tombstone: 'Here lies Paul Newman, died at 43, a failure because his eyes turned brown.'

Paul Newman
Playboy, 1969

5   Nothing is designed to make somebody feel more like a piece of meat than some chick saying: 'Take off your glasses, I want to look at your baby blues.' What would she say if I said: 'Gee, you really have a great set of tits. Would you mind taking something off?'

Paul Newman
Photoplay, March 1983

6   Eyes are the greatest tool in film. Mr Capra taught me that. Sure, it's nice to say very good dialogue, if you can get it. But great movie acting – watch the eyes!

Barbara Stanwyck (1907–90)
Los Angeles Times, 5 April 1987

101 FACES

1   It's important to keep my face up there on the screen. After all, if one of the movies does well, there's a faint chance I can convince some tired executive that I was partly responsible.

Albert Brooks
Los Angeles Times, 1985

2   I guess it looks like a rock quarry that somebody has dynamited.

Charles Bronson
Sun, 6 September 1976
(But for director Walter Hill: 'There's a lot of poetry in his face' *Photoplay*, January 1987)

3   I've been fighting ten years to make people forget I'm just a pretty boy with a beautiful face. It's a hard fight but I'll win it.

Alain Delon
Films & Filming, 1970

4   People like Brigitte Bardot can speak with their bodies. I guess I speak with my face.

Goldie Hawn
Hollywood Reporter, 16 September 1970

5   Producers seem to feel that I have a medieval face.

Charlton Heston
Photoplay, June 1982

6   I did worry about being classed as a period actor – if you have a long face, as I do, that's always the danger.

Jeremy Irons
Film Comment, 1983

7   Meryl Streep has the most astonishing face on film. Expressions drift over it like mist. It's an eternal face. Like a medieval madonna – and that sexy blonde at the next table.

Producer Stanley Jaffe
Life, December 1987

8   My face is variable. Sometimes, I look very good, sometimes I don't. But it gives the characters a certain ambiguity. That's worked to my advantage.

Meryl Streep
Photoplay, November 1985

9   If you lose weight to keep your ass, your face goes. But if the face is good, forget the ass. I'll choose the face.

Kathleen Turner
Premiere, November 1989

10   I've never liked my face. The left side's predatory, the right more friendly.

Raquel Welch
Vogue, May 1973

102 FAILURE

1 The best film I ever did – *Stardust Memories* – was my least popular film. That may automatically mean it was my best film.
Woody Allen
Time Out, 1 November 1989

2 Nobody stays on top for ever. *Nobody!*
Charles Bronson
Photoplay, November 1979

3 I'm very proud of my flops, as much as of my successes.
Francis Coppola
Film 91, BBC TV, 5 March 1991

4 Failures are inevitable. Unfortunately, in film they live for ever and they're 40 ft wide and 20 ft high.
Harrison Ford
Cinema Papers (Australia), May 1985

5 Film is a personal effort and if you fail, you should fail for the right reasons – it's the only way of growing.
Dustin Hoffman
Films Illustrated, May–June 1980

6 When some of my movies flopped, I took it personally. I really believed that the public didn't like me – me, as a person. But you've got to keep striving to change that.
Steve Martin
Bournemouth Evening Echo, 18 September 1989

7 I know a producer in Hollywood who always throws a party when his film is a flop on the theory that people are happy with someone else's failure.
Producer Arnon Milchan
Film Yearbook, 1987

8 Even with the best creative people in the world, the odds against turning out a successful film are 10:1.
Peter O'Toole
Variety, 11 August 1970

9 I'm not afraid to fail, providing I fail honourably.
David Puttnam
Film Yearbook, 1987

10   Failure is inevitable. Success is elusive.
Steven Spielberg
OM, December 1984

103   FAME

See also 52 Celebrity
240 Success

1   It's other people who change, not me. Sometimes I get a bit paranoid about that.
Sandrine Bonnaire
Guardian, 17 May 1990

2   You can't observe as much if you're observed by others.
Chevy Chase
Playboy, September 1981

3   For years I'd been popular in America not because of my talent but because I was famous.
Cher
Los Angeles Times, 5 December 1982

4   All that concentrated adulation is terribly corroding.
Julie Christie
Sunday Express, July 1965

5   I can't go to Fenwick's or Marks' to pick up a pair of panties without people staring at me. So, I bought a blonde wig. No good! I was recognized trying it on.
Joan Collins
London, May 1978

6   When you live in New York and people are looking at you all the time, the first instinct is that you're going to be mugged – or wondering if my flies were undone.
Tom Cruise
You: Mail on Sunday magazine, 29 January 1989

7 I enjoyed the journey to the top but then I found myself disappointed.

Richard Dreyfuss
Film Yearbook, 1983

8 I don't seem to have the gift it takes to enjoy fame the way it should be enjoyed.

Clint Eastwood
Daily Mail, 14 August 1976

9 I had no expectation of the level of adulation that would come my way. I just wanted to make a living with a regular role in a television series.

Harrison Ford
Photoplay, March 1987

10 You can't be bored by it. You can be pretty embarrassed by it, though. People don't seem to be willing to separate the allure of the character and the actor who plays him.

Paul Newman
Rolling Stone, 5 July 1973

11 If you were me for a month, you might change it to two weeks.

Robert Redford
Ladies Home Journal, 1984

12 The last few months have been really crazy. I can't have a simple dinner. I don't even have time to read a book.

Julia Roberts
Los Angeles Times, 23 March 1990

13 You can't get spoiled if you do your own ironing.

Meryl Streep
Film Yearbook, 1985

14 Why am I so famous? What am I doing right? What are the others doing wrong?

Barbra Streisand
Playboy, October 1977

104 FAMILY

1   Yeah, I have three sons working on *Fool For Love* ... That's
what sons are for. Help you run the farm.

Robert Altman
Paris, March 1986

2   I never used to like babies. I'd always thought if a baby were
more like a chimpanzee, I'd have one. [She had a baby instead.]

Candice Bergen
Film Yearbook, 1991

3   Jock Mahoney married my mother when I was about five or six.
So, for a period, I had Tarzan as a father. But 'Jocko' was Tarzan
even before he played Tarzan!

Sally Field
Cannes, 18 May 1979

4   My father went blind just as my films were starting. And my
mother was deaf. They'd go to the cinema together and one would
say: 'What's he look like?' and the other would say: 'What does he
say?' It's sad but it's also very funny, put it in a film and no one
would believe it.

Marcello Mastroianni
Daily Mail, 2 August 1975

5   I delivered my second son, Ramon. I was so stupid I thought the
placenta was his twin.

Martin Sheen
Sunday People magazine, 20 January 1991

6   I had three children and that's a lot like making a movie. There's
a lot of the same worries. Will it have legs? Will it go wide? How will
it do domestically and what if it goes foreign?

Meryl Streep
Vanity Fair, August 1990

105 FAN MAIL

1 Occasionally they [fan letters] were funny, as in the case of a South African lady of uncertain age who having threatened a breach-of-promise action (rape, on a boat this time) in letters to me, my secretary, my parents and the Rank Organization (to name a few) finally wrote that the Queen was getting very concerned and had been overheard saying to Princess Margaret: 'I say, Meg, Shirley *is* looking peaky – something must be done.'

Dirk Bogarde
His *Cracking the Image* publicity article, 1965

2 Mad people seem to like me. Most of the letters I get are obviously from deranged people with a kink – and offering to share it with me.

John Hargreaves
Films Illustrated, November 1981

3 I used to reply. Dreadful mistake. They show up at the house. My wife answers the door: 'They're gone for the summer. I'm the housekeeper.'

Robert Mitchum
Ritz, No. 134, 1989

4 I send fans a little letter: I'm terribly sorry I cannot answer personally and that my secretary is – because if I answer all the letters I'd be the secretary and the secretary would have to do the acting.

Peter O'Toole
Showtime, 1967

5 Canada is where most of the crazy mail comes from; a lot of frustrated ladies in Canada, apparently. Girls sent me Polaroid pictures of themselves in the nude. One girl sent me pubic hair wrapped in wax paper. Their proposals weren't for marriage.

Burt Reynolds
Penthouse, 1972

106 FANS

1 The local police were always having to come and remove girls
from their nesting-places under the bushes. Like an orphan girl who
twice escaped from a home at Birmingham. We only discovered her
because she used the potting shed as a lavatory which seemed to
indicate an alien presence. I think we got her fixed up as a kennel-
maid which gave her dogs to love in place of me.

Dirk Bogarde
Publicity release, 1964

2 Middle-aged ladies from Peoria telling me 'Mr Brando, we love
you as Napoleon' – Napoleon, for Christ's sake! – and asking for my
autograph, while their husbands shove me against a wall to pose
with the little lady.

Marlon Brando
Time, 24 May 1976

3 People want to fuck movie stars and hug television stars.

Ted Danson
Film Yearbook, 1986

4 His fans say things like: 'Hey, I loved your dad. C'mon, tell the
truth – he's still alive, isn't he?'

Brandon Lee, son of Bruce Lee
Playgirl, October 1988

5 All warts, lenses, terminal dandruff – typical Mitchum fans.

Robert Mitchum
Ritz, No. 134, 1989

6 Under 10, they squeal; from 10 to 15, they giggle; from 15 to 20,
they kind of hang back; over 20, they ignore me.

Christopher Reeve
Playboy, 1976

7 I didn't have young, handsome men for admirers. I had unhappy
creatures from loony-bins. Crackpots who whispered they'd pray for
me, who sent me long poems about God, about reincarnation. These
chosen few with the mark on their foreheads have always been
drawn to me and I to them.

Mai Zetterling
Film Yearbook, 1987

107   FASHION

1   People think I was born in top hat and tails.
Fred Astaire (1899–1987)
Evening Standard, 21 May 1976

2   I try not to dress in a way which offends the world.
Cary Grant (1904–86)
Photoplay, February 1983

3   Everybody looks better in a black tie.
George Hamilton
Playboy, July 1980

4   I wear my sort of clothes to save me the trouble of deciding which clothes to wear.
Katharine Hepburn
Evening Standard, 1969

5   Richard Nixon: 'You dress pretty wild, don't you?' Elvis Presley: 'Mr President, you got your show to run, I got mine.'
Elvis Presley (1935–77)
Albert Goodman, *Elvis*, 1981

6   I kept my own Western costume for most of my films. The hat, in particular. I wore it in every Western until one very sad day it completely disintegrated.
James Stewart
London, January 1966

108   FATHERHOOD IN THREE STAGES

1   I don't care about heirs. Everybody should stop reproducing for a while and adopt all the kids that are loose.
Woody Allen
Esquire, April 1987

2   I'll be profoundly wise and generous, liberal, understanding. I'd be surprised if I'd be less than perfect as a father.
Woody Allen
Time, 25 May 1987

3 The baby's fine. Only problem is he looks like Edward G. Robinson.

Woody Allen
Time, January 1988

109 FAVOURITE ROLES

1 It's a wonderful part. I *don't* have to take my clothes off and I *don't* have to look pretty.

Jamie Lee Curtis (on *Grandview USA*)
Film Yearbook, 1985

2 Robert Altman's *The Long Goodbye* was a Raymond Chandler thriller. I don't remember a thing about making it as I was smashed at the time.

Sterling Hayden (1916–81)
Films Illustrated, February 1981

3 It's a relief to have an unprotected character to play. This guy's an open wound. As the curtain rises, he's face down in a urinal. Sensational!

Paul Newman (not being strictly accurate about *The Verdict*)
Los Angeles Times, 21 November 1982

110 FEMINISM

1 I don't think my film can be accused of being anti-feminist just because the woman is relegated to the role of an object.

Marco Ferreri (on *I Love You*)
Cannes, 1986

2 Men are not the enemy. Women must join with men to form a broader alliance.

Jane Fonda
Photoplay, June 1978

3   We shouldn't stop fighting for our rights but sometimes you just
get so tired of attitudes, egos, weaknesses.

Goldie Hawn
Playboy, January 1985

4   It's too simple to say men and women are equal. You can't make
equals of an apple and pear, they're different.

Dustin Hoffman
Sunday Express magazine, 5 June 1988

111   FEMININITY

1   I have a high feminine component. I grew up cutting out paper
dolls and dressing Deanna Durbin cut-outs. Mia is the one who, at
her farm, drives the tractor and knows how to repair the television
set.

Woody Allen
Time Out, 1 November 1989

2   Acting is an entirely feminine profession and there's a feminine
side of me.

Gérard Depardieu
Time, 6 February 1984

3   My soul is female but the role model is very masculine.

Roy Scheider
Film Yearbook, 1988

4   In life, I am more feminine than Catherine Deneuve.

Jean-Louis Trintignant
F magazine (France), December 1980

112   FILM ACTING

1   How odd – to be working for only two minutes at a time.

Karen Black
Screen International, May 1983

2   The kind of acting I used to enjoy no longer exists because your prime consideration is the budget, running time, the cost – and whether they'll understand it in Milwaukee.

Dirk Bogarde
ABC (American TV), July 1979

3   Spencer Tracy was the first actor I've ever seen who could just look down in the dirt amd command a scene. He played a set-up with Robert Ryan that way. He's looking down at the road and then he looks at Ryan at just the precise, right minute. I tell you, Rob could've stood on his head and zipped open his fly and the scene would've still been Mr Tracy's.

Ernest Borgnine
Rolling Stone, 21 December 1972

4   In a film, you're a puppet. On a stage, you're the boss.

Richard Burton (1915–84)
Time, 26 April 1963

5   They need you. Without you, they have an empty screen. So, when you get on there, just do what you think is right and stick with it.

James Cagney (1899–1986)
Time, 16 November 1981

6   In movie acting, it's not three hours a day but nine hours that you have to be actually on your toes. Plus you dream about the role at night and think about it upon waking. And what is particularly tricky is linking the previous day's work with the following day's – remaining consistent.

Gérard Depardieu
Cyrano de Bergerac publicity release, 1989

7   You've got to donate yourself to the character. You can't say: Jeeze, will I look as sharp as I have in some films?

Clint Eastwood
Film Comment, October 1984

8   Even if it's a shot of my little finger, I act from head to toe.

Marty Feldman (1938–82)
Guardian, 15 September 1976

9   You have to make love to 30 million spectators – and be slightly aloof. You're available and you're not.

Jodie Foster
International Herald Tribune, 26 August 1983

10 You don't have to act in front of a camera. You just have to be concerned and *phfft!* – it begins.

Jeanne Moreau
Time, 5 March 1965

11 Once you've been really *bad* in a movie, there's a certain kind of fearlessness you develop.

Jack Nicholson
Time Out, 20 February 1976

12 You get so *sick* of it, the camera crawling about all over you all day long.

Peter O'Toole
Showtime, 1967

13 It's sad but I can't get genuine enjoyment out of my own work – I can't *see* it. I don't like seeing myself on the screen, I don't *feel* anything.

Robert Redford
Playboy, December 1974

14 It's all about narcissim. Terry Malick called it 'sanctioned vanity'. Everything is attended to. Would you like some Perrier? Anything we can do? May we throw ourselves on the ground in front of you? This unbelievable barrage of indulgence.

Sam Shepard
Newsweek, 11 November 1985

15 I've always been skeptical of people who say they loose themselves in a part. Someone once came up to Spencer Tracy and asked: 'Aren't you tired of always playing Tracy?' Tracy replied: 'What am I supposed to do, play Bogart?' You have to develop a style that suits you and pursue it, not just a bag of tricks.

James Stewart
Time, 29 June 1970

16 Talk low, talk slow and don't talk too much.

John Wayne (1907–79) to Michael Caine
Calgary Herald, 14 September 1987

113 FILM BUSINESS

1   It's very hard to find anyone with any decency in the business. They all hide behind the corporate structure. They're like landlords who kick people out of tenement buildings. There's no compassion and there's certainly no interest in the arts.

Robert Altman
Paris, March 1986

2   You have to be a little unreal to be in this business.

Kim Basinger
Film Yearbook, 1987

3   Three things that people always tell you about the movie business: 'You can fix it in the editing room; it doesn't matter what the critics say; and that there's German money.' You can *never* fix it in the editing, it *does* matter what critics say and there's *no* such thing as German money.

Marshall Brickman
Films Illustrated, November 1980

4   I saw enough of my father's household to know how the business can control your life without you even being aware of it – you have to keep something for yourself.

Michael Douglas
Films Illustrated, September 1979

5   The film business is the only business where a negative is a positive.

Menahem Golan
Cannes, May 1986

6   This is a business and I'm a commodity. Barbra Streisand is a commodity. Clint Eastwood is a commodity. And they want that commodity to pay off. They want the three cherries.

Goldie Hawn
Playboy, January 1985

7   Look at all the film buyers and sellers in Cannes any year and you're basically looking at a lot of shoe salesmen working out whether or not it should be sneakers or lace-ups next year.

David Hemmings
Films Illustrated, November 1981

8   The whole thrust has become a way of missiling the audience, of getting their money and giving them the least amount of quality.

Dustin Hoffman
Films Illustrated, May–June 1980

9   Hollywood is a corporate mentality – like Socialist mentality. All the people are paid to say no. Very few to say yes. Because if you say yes and you're wrong – you're fired.

Russian director Andrei Konchalovsky
Knave, October 1986

10   There are many vampires in the world today – you only have to think of the film business.

Christopher Lee
Films Illustrated, August 1971

11   People always want to call it 'the industry'. It's not an industry now. It was.

Otto Preminger (1906–86)
Films Illustrated, January 1980

12   The business has changed, so the work has changed. It's cartoon movies now for whatever reason. I, personally, think it's because of Reagan and what he brought to this country.

Robert Redford
Havana video publicity release, 1991

13   Film business? I enjoy film – but the business is shit.

Oliver Stone
Film Yearbook, 1987

14   The film business is cyclical and it has always had a crisis mentality. It lurches between crazed optimism and total gloom.

Ned Tanen, ex-chief of Universal Pictures
Film Yearbook, 1985

15   The whole industry is shot to hell now. The only thing that's kept it alive is the growth of population and the increase in ticket prices. We used to have the most inexpensive and accessible medium in the world and now they're doing everything in their power to tear it apart.

John Wayne (1907–79)
Guardian, 24 August 1974

16   Being in the film business is rather like being a tennis player. You have to keep your total concentration and mind on the ball. The minute you fall in love with Tatum O'Neal or get flabby, you've had it.

Michael Winner
Film Yearbook, 1987

114   FILM FESTIVALS

1   I first met Jack Nicholson at Pesaro in ... ah, 1965. We met because we were following the same girl. And since she didn't want me or Jack, we became firm friends ... Or, was that at Cannes?
Bernardo Bertolucci
Cannes, 25 May 1981

2   I never look forward to opening nights at festivals. They're like fund-raising rallies and the movies they show ... usually have titles like *How Tasty Was My Little Frenchman*. They're usually movies that almost everyone can like, at least a little bit.
Martin Scorsese
Film Yearbook, 1985

115   FILM-MAKING

1   Tedious, isn't it?
Woody Allen
Sunday Times, 13 April 1980

2   If you're not careful you may find you're making one film and the leading man is making another.
Ann-Margret
Cinema TV Today, 2 September 1972

3   I enjoy the excitement of working on a well-crewed and exciting picture. It's like a microcosm of society that really works. Because nothing works anywhere else.
Sean Connery
International Herald Tribune, 3 December 1983

4   A film set is a never-ending hell.
Tom Conti
Cannes, 15 May 1983

5   I never enjoyed working in a film.
Marlene Dietrich
Sunday Times, 22 September 1964

6   I still get nervous about work. I feel like a virgin, as if it's my first film. It's great at my age still to be able to get scared.

Jane Fonda (at almost 50)
Sunday Express magazine, November 1987

7   I always start too soon and arrive too late and eventually come back in the middle – stuttering.

Jean-Luc Godard
Sight & Sound, 1982

8   One tends to forget the pain of movie-making. I guess it's like pregnancy – something compels you to go through it again.

Gene Hackman
Films Illustrated, September 1978

9   Between takes, I remember one of the younger actors saying 'God, this sitting around is awful.' And Eddie [Edward G. Robinson] said: 'Yeah, that's true. But I always figure that's what they pay me for. The acting I do for free.'

Charlton Heston
Sunday Express, 17 July 1981

10   The struggle will always be the same – you're still trying to make your own film with someone else's money.

Krzysztof Kieslowski
7 Days, 6 May 1990

11   I always fall in love while I'm making a film. It's such an intense thing, being absorbed into the world of a movie. It's like discovering you have a fatal illness – you live and love twice as deeply. Then you drop out of it, like a snakeskin and you're cold and naked.

Nastassja Kinski
Time, 2 May 1983

12   Film-making is like spermatozoa. Only one in a million makes it.

Claude Lelouch
Film Yearbook, 1985

13   It's too technical a medium and unfair to actors. The acting part, which people watch, is given the least attention. I find that infuriating.

John Malkovich
Film Yearbook, 1986

14   I gave up being serious about making pictures years ago, around the time I made a film with Greer Garson and she took 125 takes to say: 'No.'

Robert Mitchum
Paris Passion, June 1990

15   It's like going into combat except you don't get a Purple Heart. First day is the worst: everybody's real nervous and thinks no one else is. You forget the director is just as nervous. Takes a while to learn how to make the nerves work for you. And the last day, even if the movie has been a real pisser, is very difficult, the intensity of feeling closer to someone.

Michelle Pfeiffer
Champs-sur-Marne (France), 4 June 1988

16   A film set, as Orson Welles was first to say, is the most wonderful electric train a boy could ever be given. What he failed to add was that most of the time it doesn't work.

Frank Pierson
New York magazine, 15 November 1976

17   I don't need a final cut. I only cut the thing once. If they're dumb enough to fool around with it, let 'em do it.

Martin Ritt (1920–91)
Film Yearbook, 1988

18   You can think up a shot in five seconds – five minutes to explain it – three hours to execute it.

Paul Schrader
Los Angeles Times, 18 February 1990

19   To make the movies I make in Hollywood, it's like a gift. And sometimes they even pay me for it.

Martin Scorsese
Film Yearbook, 1990

20   Everything makes me nervous – except making films.

Elizabeth Taylor
Variety, 22 February 1977

116 FILMS

1   An extension of childhood, where everybody wants to be freer, everybody wants to be powerful, everybody wants to be so *overwhelmingly* attractive. Or wants to have comradeship and to be understood.

Marlon Brando
Rolling Stone, 20 May 1976

2   The most expensive art form ever invented. Leonardo didn't need a studio chief for the money to draw a lower jaw. All he needed was a nickle for a pencil. Goya could paint you a national tragedy for $1.69.

Mel Brooks
Newsweek, 17 February 1975

3   I don't think [today's films] stack up to mine. I'm very frank in saying that. They have no merit.

Sir Charles Chaplin (1889–1977)
Show, June 1972

4   A film lives, becomes alive, because of its shadows, its spaces.

Michael Cimino
Variety (Kodak advertisement), 23 July 1980

5   *Paint Your Wagon* was not the smoothest-running picture I've ever been on. I saw it in four different versions: the director's, the producer's, and two cut together by some executives. The director's was the best and that wasn't the one they released.

Clint Eastwood
The Man With No Name, BBC TV (documentary), 23 February 1977

6   I don't look very closely when I'm in them.

Albert Finney
Sunday Times, 6 March 1988

7   I see every movie I do. I don't ever see them twice if I can help it.

Jane Fonda
Time, 16 February 1970

8   Film is a battleground: love, hate, action, death. In a word: emotion.

Samuel Fuller
Films Illustrated, August 1980

9   The only thing I liked about films was looking at the back of my head which otherwise I could only see at the tailor's.

Sir John Gielgud
Time, 15 August 1983

10   I don't think you should *feel* about a film. You should feel about a woman, not a movie. You can't kiss a movie.
Jean-Luc Godard
Rolling Stone, 14 June 1969

11   If there's a way of saying 'I love you,' without saying it – that's film.
Buster Keaton (1895–1966)
Quoted by Dustin Hoffman, *Films Illustrated*, May–June 1980

12   Of course, I find most films banal! Especially in this day and age – they're generally films about other films.
John Malkovich
Paris, 14 November 1990

13   Films have given me an opportunity to do things that normally you'd be locked up for, put into prison and executed for. I can act it out, be paid and go home.
Lee Marvin (1924–87)
Deauville, 4 September 1983

14   A film must be alive. When this happens, it smashes, devours, pulverizes any synopsis, plot, story. It speaks, talks and explains itself. It constantly changes itself, its characters weave in and out of the screen. Their performance is different at each screening.
Spanish director Francisco Regueiro
Cannes, May 1985

15   Motion pictures are for amusement.
John Wayne (1907–79)
Game, June 1975

Footnote: Where would we be without the movies?
Nancy Reagan
Variety, 10 November 1981

---

117   FIRST TIME

1   At 18, I was the oldest virgin in Chelsea.
Jane Birkin
Film Yearbook, 1986

2 I was 13. She was older than me and it was good experience. I can't believe we're talking about this on TV.
James Caan
American TV, December 1975

3 I was 15 and she was a volunteer, a lot older than me. It was marvellous. It didn't happen again until two years later, because at that age I didn't have the dialogue to talk myself into a similar situation.
Michael Caine
American TV, December 1975

4 Fourteen. The first boy I ever slept with – oh, the poor boy, I was really in love with him. He kept bothering me . . . So we did it. 'Now you go home and don't ever talk to me again. That's *it*, OK?' So he left. My next boyfriend was 35.
Cher
Playboy, December 1988

5 I was 17 and he was 33. It was just like my mother said: the pits. But I went out with him later on. I wanted to prove that she was wrong.
Joan Collins
Playboy, April 1984

6 When I was 26 and got married – and it was *hell* waiting.
Bette Davis (1908–89)
Sunday People, 9 December 1984

7 I was the last in my class – 17, almost 18.
Carrie Fisher
Playboy, July 1983

8 First couple of times was a prostitute and it was very unsuccessful. Turned me off.
Henry Fonda (1905–82)
Playboy, December 1981

9 I lost my virginity as a career move.
Madonna
Film Yearbook, 1989

10   On the steps of a church, strangely. I was 15 and what I felt was a gross humiliation. I went out with a friend and we found two very experienced ladies – semi-professional, I think. The only advice I'd had was to take the initiative, so I steered the lady's hand in a certain direction. She said: 'Put that on the mantelpiece – I'll smoke it in the morning.'

Peter O'Toole
Playboy, 1965

11   I was 15. She was a wonderful girl about a year older than me. I had another date with her just recently. She's a schoolteacher now and very happy. I'll remember it all my life.

Burt Reynolds
American TV, December 1975

12   I'd lots of affairs before I married, just love affairs, not sex-love affairs. We'd neck and hug and kiss and play with each other. But no sex. Not 'til I got married. Probably one of the reasons I did get married . . . I was 17.

Mae West (1893–1980)
Sunday Times, December 1969

118 FRIENDS

1   When the chips are not exactly down but just scattered about, you discover who your real friends are.

Richard Burton (1925–84)
Sunday Express, 7 February 1965

2   In all honesty, I don't know what good friendship does, what purpose. I don't understand it.

Sally Field
Playboy, March 1986

3   Damn 'em all except six – and they can be pallbearers. If they stumble, damn them, too.

Stewart Granger
Sunday Express, 26 February 1961

4 The few times I've slept with male friends it's really ruined the friendship.

Margot Kidder
Playboy, July 1981

5 You find out who your real friends are when you're involved in a scandal.

Elizabeth Taylor
Sunday Express, 7 February 1965

119 FUTURE

1 I don't believe in an afterlife although I'm bringing a change of underwear.

Woody Allen
Time, 3 July 1972

2 I'm following the advice of an assistant director of *Hurry Sundown* who said to an electrician who asked him what he should do with his ladder: 'Just go out the door and keep on going until your hat floats.' Then, I'll come up for air and buy a new hat.

Michael Caine
Playboy, 1966

3 The next film I make is what they call 'Big Bucks' in the *Oxford Dictionary*. Just look it up. Under the *Oxford Dictionary* definition of Big Bucks it will say: 'see Dreyfuss, Richard'.

Richard Dreyfuss
London, 7 January 1976

4 I'm doing another picture with Redford. I'm playing Minnie Mouse and he's Mickey.

Paul Newman
Film Yearbook, 1988

5 What I don't want to do is end up being an irrelevant 70-year-old egomaniac.

David Puttnam
Film Yearbook, 1987

120 GENIUS

1 I probably have genius. But no talent.

Francis Coppola
Film Yearbook, 1989
(*See also* 243.4)

2 Genius is taking something difficult and making it simple.

George Hamilton
Nice, 1986

3 Someone who sees things in a way that illuminates them and enables you to see things in a different way. One knows men of genius only through their work. I'd say: [Tennessee] Williams; Eugene O'Neill; [sculptors] Manzu, Henry Moore; Henri Cartier-Bresson, the photographer; in a funny way, Robert Capa, the photographer; Ernest Hemingway; William Faulkner; Dashiell Hammett; Marlon Brando. I've seen flashes of it in others: [Ingmar] Bergman, Vittorio De Sica, Akira Kurosawa.

John Huston
Playboy, September 1985

4 It's easier living with a genius than with an idiot.

Guilietta Masina, wife of Federico Fellini
Film Yearbook, 1985

5 Chaplin was a most terrible phoney. He talked very pretentiously in this half-American/half-Cockney accent. But, of course, he couldn't escape from the unlikely fact that he was a genius.

Lord Laurence Olivier (1907–89)
Sunday Times, 25 November 1979

6 Paul Verhoeven is very intense. At any moment he could blow up beyond belief. This is the behaviour of a genius kinda guy.

Arnold Schwarzenegger
Premiere, June 1990

7 A loud kind of Jewish genius – maybe that's as close as you can get to defining him.

Gene Wilder (on Mel Brooks)
New Yorker, 1978

121   GOSSIP

1   A miserable newspaper woman wrote something implying that
Rock [Hudson] and I spent a lot of time together in San Francisco
leather bars. I loved his response: 'How in the hell did she find out so
quick?'
Blake Edwards
Playboy, December 1982

2   I'm a great gossip. Don't pay any attention to what I'm saying.
Sir Alec Guinness
Time, 31 March 1986

122   GOD

1   I don't believe in God. Just try getting a plumber at the weekend.
Woody Allen
Screen International, 6 October 1990

2   I don't think He belongs to any religion.
Michael Caine
Playboy, 1966

3   I believe God helps those who help themselves.
Bette Davis (1908–89)
Playboy, July 1982

4   I'd rather believe in God – or a good spirit – than in evil.
Gérard Depardieu
Sous Le Soleil de Satan publicity release, 1987

5   God assembled her brilliantly.
John Derek (on Bo Derek)
Photoplay, December 1984

6   In America, the buck is God.
Shirley MacLaine
Evening Standard, 1965

7   If only God could create a lawyer who could make deals in 10
minutes.
Marcello Mastroianni
Look, 8 November 1964

123 GUILT

1   I feel guilty sometimes. It may be that innate English nature – the need to think that you must've done something wrong if you're a success. It's sometimes better if you can say: 'Okay, I'm a failure; *now* will you be my friend?'

Emily Lloyd
Sunday Express magazine, 14 January 1990

2   All my life I've been dogged by guilt because I feel there's this difference between the way I look, which I suppose is good, and what I feel inside me. I get these black glooms, it's my Scottish-Irish blood.

Robert Redford
Sunday Times, 9 March 1980

124 HAPPINESS

1   In St Louis, I knew a fellow who ran a whorehouse simply because it made him happy. Well, I do what makes *me* happy.

Cary Grant (1904–86)
Daily Mail, 6 September 1973

2   If I wasn't happy, I'd be an idiot.

Arnold Schwarzenegger
Film Yearbook, 1991

125 HATES

1   I've a burning resentment that when people meet you, they're meeting some asshole movie actor instead of a person concerned with other things. This *idiot* part of life has to go in the forefront as if it's of major importance.

Marlon Brando
Playboy, January 1979

2   I hate two towns. Edmonton and Aswan. I've enjoyed all the rest. Even New Zealand.

John Cleese
Film Yearbook, 1987

3   I hate the word 'hate'.

Peter Cushing
Sunday Times, 1977

4   I hate long movies.

Clint Eastwood
Playboy, February 1974
(*See also* 147.6)

5   Eggs in general. And then I hate sauce in bottles. The most horrible sound in the world is of a hand smacking the bottom of a Ketchup bottle, only because, as result of that smacking, some ugly, dark-red goo oozes from the neck of the bottle and lays itself over some innocent French-fried potatoes.

Sir Alfred Hitchcock (1899–1980)
London, 21 April 1966

126   HEDONISM

1   I'm not what I'd call a hedonist. Just ignore what you read. I do.

Warren Beatty
Photoplay, April 1982

2   I'm a great romancer – not a libertine.

Michael Caine
Playboy, 1966

3   I was never happily hedonistic. There's no hedonism without a downside.

Anjelica Huston
Vanity Fair, July 1990

127 HEIGHT

1   I failed to make the chess team because of my height.

Woody Allen
Time, 3 July 1972

2   Yul Brynner was shorter. I suggested putting a little block under him. 'You think I want to play it standing on a box? I'll show the world what a big horse you are!' I never had complex about my height after that.

Ingrid Bergman (1915–82) (on *Anastasia*)
The Times, 18 January 1971

3   Girls think you're so cute when you're short – always want to put me in their pocket. Great, as long as it's their breast pocket.

Michael J. Fox
News of the World magazine, 10 July 1988

4   I could have been tall but I turned it down.

Sidney Lumet
Rolling Stone, 20 January 1983

5   I was walking into the commissary on the day Kate [Hepburn] and Spencer met for the first time in the corridor. Kate said: 'I'm afraid I'm a little tall for you, Mr Tracy.' I turned to her and said: 'Don't worry, Kate, he'll soon cut you down to size.'

Joseph L. Mankiewicz (birth of the line usually attributed to Tracy)
McCalls, March 1975

6   People came up: 'I thought you were 6 ft tall.' I'm average height – 5 ft 8 ins, skinny blonde. One guy says to me 'So, where's the fox from *Mystic Pizza*?'

Julia Roberts
USA Today, 23 March 1990

7   I hire people *shorter* than me – except for the big, monster villains.

Sylvester Stallone
Prevue, 1987

8   Frank Lloyd Wright designed the house I was living in. From what I understood, he was having an affair with the wife of the man he was designing the house for. That man was very tall. So Wright, short and vain, designed the house in such a way that a tall person couldn't live in it without severe cranial damage. I hit my head *all* the time.

Donald Sutherland
Playboy, October 1981

128 HEROES

1 George S. Kaufman and the Marx Brothers.
Woody Allen
Time, 3 July 1972

2 Kafka and Kierkegaard are remarkable souls. They visited distant planets of the psyche that no other writers dared before – to some people *they* were the heroes, not Elvis Presley.
Marlon Brando
Playboy, January 1979

3 I'm always stunned when I find out that Roosevelt and Tolstoi weren't Jewish. How could I love them so much?
Mel Brooks
Playboy, December 1974

4 I've played a lot of outcasts – people don't believe in heroes.
Clint Eastwood
Films Illustrated, February 1981

5 I am my own hero.
Peter Fonda
Rolling Stone, 6 September 1969

6 Carole Lombard, Judy Holliday, Marilyn Monroe – just incredibly funny, silly and sweet. I just saw myself in them. My knowingness and my innocence.
Madonna
Time, 27 May 1985

7 I don't feel heroic. Nor anti-heroic.
Jack Nicholson
Daily Mirror, 30 August 1989

8 Spencer Tracy was my god. He was the only actor I've ever written to. We used to write to each other all the time. Katie Hepburn said once: 'Why don't you two guys meet? You'd love each other.' I said: 'I don't want to destroy his illusions – or him destroy mine.'
Anthony Quinn
Films & Filming, 1970

9 The flawed hero is the movie I'm living myself.
Robert Redford
Newsweek, 7 December 1970

10   America loves to make heroes – and then destroy them. Make them real low. Limping is not enough. If they're destroyed real bad, they can even become heroes again.

Burt Reynolds
Film Yearbook, 1989

11   Joseph Wambaugh – he has real integrity. John Lennon – that man never did anything he really didn't want to do and that impresses me.

James Woods
Playboy, April 1982

129   HISTORY

1   The Greeks were good. Greeks were smart. They came up with a lot of things. They came up with Athenian democracy. They came up with hemlock, in case Athenian democracy didn't work. They came up with the Greek salad, one of the best things you'll ever eat in your life. And what's the matter with feta cheese? That ain't gonna hurt anybody.

Mel Brooks
Premiere, September 1981

2   When the details of history no longer serve the function of the story – discard them.

Michael Cimino
Cannes, 20 May 1981

3   History and culture are death.

Klaus Kinski
Time Out, 16 July 1982

130 SIR ALFRED HITCHCOCK

1 We'd do limericks together. One day he pulled up his shirt to show me his belly-button – which he didn't have. He'd had an operation and when they sewed him up, they took it away. His belly-button was gone!

Karen Black
Films Illustrated, June 1981

2 The Donald Spoto biography of Hitchcock was absolute nonsense. Hitchcock couldn't have been a nicer fellow. I whistled coming to work on his films.

Cary Grant (1904–86)
Variety, 6 December 1983

3 I always give a little thought to my appearances and come on as early as possible – don't want to hold them in suspense for the wrong reason! I've been in all my films, on and off. Missed a few. Only cancelled one. It got into the press ahead of time . . . I was going to walk along with a girl and talk to her – in deaf-and-dumb language. My hands would be working very fast. And she turns around and slaps my face. We got letters: 'Please don't make fun of deaf-mutes.'

Sir Alfred Hitchcock (1899–1980)
London, 21 April 1966

4 Blondes are the best victims. They're like virgin snow which shows up the bloody footprints.

Sir Alfred Hitchcock
Sunday Times, 1 September 1973

5 *Psycho* gave me very wrinkled skin. I was in that shower for seven days – 70 set-ups. At least, he made sure the water was warm.

Janet Leigh
Film Yearbook, 1988

6 At the end of *Psycho*, I realized I'd worked with the director who'd been more open to the actor's suggestions and ideas than any I'd worked with – with the possible exception of William Wyler. Since this was the reverse of what I'd expected of Hitchcock, it came as a great surprise.

Anthony Perkins
Cinema, 1965

7   On *Psycho*, if things ever got tense, he'd stop production for five minutes and say: 'Please remember – we're supposed to be enjoying ourselves.'

Anthony Perkins
Los Angeles Times, 28 April 1985

8   What did Hitchcock teach me? To be a puppet and not be creative.

Sylvia Sidney
Film Yearbook, 1984

9   I've never seen Hitchcock look through a camera – some directors never stop.

James Stewart
Variety, October 1983

---

131   HOLLYWOOD BY THE HOME TEAM

1   The people are unreal. The flowers are unreal, they don't smell. The fruit is unreal, it doesn't taste of anything. The whole place is a glaring, gaudy, nightmarish set, built up in the desert.

Ethel Barrymore (1879–1959) in 1932
Leslie Halliwell, *The Filmgoer's Book of Quotes*, 1973
('Unreal' has remained the chief adjective in the Hollywood lexicon ever since)

2   Hollywood is a place where you can make an entire career out of baloney.

Warren Beatty
Weekend, 9 September 1964

3   A cultural boneyard.

Marlon Brando
Daily Express, 3 February 1966

4   Only three things you need if you want to make it in Hollywood. Learn how to make your own salad. Learn how to fall in slow motion. And learn how to cry.

Gary Busey
Film Yearbook, 1987

5   If you say what you mean in this town, you're an outlaw.

Kevin Costner
Time, 26 June 1989

6   I call it Hollyweird. A tickle town, without rhyme or reason. By the time you get down the driveway to collect your mail, you're forgotten.

Frederic Forrest
Daily Express, 15 February 1980

7   If you stay in Beverly Hills too long, you become a Mercedes.

Dustin Hoffman
Time, 29 March 1976

8   The only town where you can die of encouragement.

Pauline Kael
Quoted by Barbara Hershey, *Playboy*, May 1987

9   Strip the phony tinsel off Hollywood and you'll find the real tinsel underneath.

Oscar Levant
Leslie Halliwell, *The Filmgoer's Book of Quotes*, 1973

10   It used to be a great town. My mother used to let us off on Hollywood Boulevard to play. Now, you'd never see your child again.

E.T. scenarist Melissa Mathison
Vanity Fair, August 1990

11   It's like any town.

Jack Nicholson
Time Out, 20 February 1976

12   In Hollywood, if you can't sing or dance, you wind up as an after-dinner speaker.

Ronald Reagan
BBC TV documentary, 1989

13   I look upon going to Hollywood as a mission behind enemy lines. You parachute in, set up the explosion, then fly out before it goes off.

Robert Redford
Evening Standard, 27 September 1976

14   When I'm 60, Hollywood will forgive me. I don't know for what, but they'll forgive me.

Steven Spielberg
Premiere, November 1989

15   Hollywood died on me as soon as I got there.

Orson Welles (1915–85)
Playboy, 1967

16   A rotten, gold-plated sewer of a town. Guys who can't tie their own shoelaces are driving around Beverly Hills in $80 000 cars – 'Hey, look at me, I'm great!' They're not great. They're stupid and arrogant – about being stupid . . . Many times they wouldn't even see me for movies. If California fell into the ocean and I was the only actor left, they'd do a talent search in Paraguay.

James Woods
Knave, July 1980

132   HOLLYWOOD BY VISITING PLAYERS

1   If you write about Hollywood, you can only write farce. It's so way over the top, you can't believe it. It's *Sunset Boulevard*, it really is. And it's cut-throat at the same time.

Dirk Bogarde
Ritz, April 1983

2   People who break their word in Japan kill themselves. People who break their word here kill you.

Michael Caine
Rolling Stone, 27 October 1981

3   Hollywood must have been terrific once.

Peter Finch (1916–77)
Evening Standard, September 1972

4   You can't make a good picture for MGM. Or, if the picture is good, then MGM won't distribute it.

Jean-Luc Godard
Rolling Stone, 14 June 1969

5   Hollywood is simply geared to cheat you left, right and bloody centre.

John Hurt
Film Yearbook, 1986

6   Hollywood reminds me of a monster devouring an enormous amount of people. There's a line in front but he's very picky, this monster. First, you have to be swallowed. Then, keep from being digested. Or, [the] monster produces what happens after digestion.

Russian director Andrei Konchalovsky
Knave, October 1986

7 I long for the days of the old Hollywood with the longterm contracts. The actors were sent out to play by the pool and called in from time to time for a bit of filming. Now we seem to spend half our time getting incorporated.

Roger Moore
Screen International, May 1980

8 It's only a village, you know. Village life around the pump.

Anthony Newley
London, August 1966

9 Hollywood is not my cup of tea – nor am I *its* cup of tea.

Peter O'Toole
Photoplay, April 1988

10 There appears to be a feeling around Hollywood that I am an ungrateful limey or rat fink or whatever who has been abusing everything Hollywood behind its back . . . I didn't go to Hollywood to be ill – I went there to work and found regrettably that the creative side in me didn't accept the sort of conditions under which work had to be carried out. This is a personal matter . . . I have no criticism of Hollywood as a place but only as a place to work in. The atmosphere is wrong for me . . . Anyone is at liberty to say that I'm wrong for the atmosphere, and no doubt will.

Open letter to the industry from Peter Sellers (1925–80)
Daily Variety, 1 July 1964

133 . HOLLYWOODIANS

1 They're all so jealous in Hollywood. It's not enough to have a hit. Your best friend should also have a failure.

Peter Bogdanovich
Film Yearbook, 1986

2 In Hollywood, you live your life for the indoor plant man, the outdoor plant man, the jacuzzi man, the pool man.

Allan Carr
Film Yearbook, 1985

3   One evening a 35-year-old woman in tennis shoes and an old sweater rang the doorbell, stuck a foot in the door and said: 'I want to kill you – your son, as well!' The cops arrested her – and told me 'She wasn't dangerous.' I replied: 'That woman had a gun. Next time, I'll phone you after I'm dead.' I later learned she was a frustrated actress.

Marthe Keller
Unifrance news bulletin, 1977
(*See also* 14.7)

4   Hollywood is full of what we call in Dublin 'gobshites', pricks, phonies.

Pat O'Connor
Cannes, May 1987

5   There are two types of animals roaming the Hollywood jungle. Those who do the screwing, those who get screwed. You have to try and ensure you're one of the former.

Bruce Robinson
Film Yearbook, 1990

6   You can't go for an ice cream there without running into three editors, four producers, two writers and six agents – all talking about their 'properties'.

Roy Scheider
Playboy, September 1980

134   HOMOSEXUALITY

1   I can tell you that Christopher Reeve is not homosexual. When we kissed in *Deathtrap*, he didn't close his eyes.

Michael Caine
Hamilton Spectator (Canada), 14 September 1983

2   Gays grow up watching heterosexual movies – *Now Voyager* – and deciding whether they're Bette Davis or Paul Henreid.

Harvey Fierstein, writer-star of *Torch Song Trilogy*
Time, 20 June 1983

3   I've lived my entire life with heterosexual hatred. All my life, I've been the queer down the hall.

Harvey Fierstein
Playboy, August 1988

4   We live in a so-called heterosexual society which is really male homosexual. Power, press, media, industry all stress male achievements. Heterosexuality was a mask. In the commercial cinema, this heterosexuality appears as basically anti-feminine: you see more male faces on the posters than before. The world is showing its true face at last.

Delphine Seyrig (1952–90)
Unifrance news bulletin, August 1975

135   HORROR

1   Fear is a very strong reaction. It makes people realize that they're alive. Their hearts start to beat faster.

James Cameron, *Aliens* director
Film Yearbook, 1988

2   You've got to send a physical sensation through and not let them off the hook. I like to make it faster and faster and faster and pumping and banging and banging until I get . . . into you!

Tobe Hooper
Film Yearbook, 1988

3   Lon Chaney and Boris Karloff didn't like the word 'horror'. They, like I, went for the French description: 'the theatre of the *fantastique*'.

Christopher Lee
Daily Mail, 25 August 1976

4   I've never been in a horror movie – on purpose – and I'm not about to be.

Peter O'Toole
Photoplay, April 1988

5   Norman Bates is the *Hamlet* of horror roles. Not your standard guy.

Anthony Perkins
Photoplay, November 1986

6 Just because I'm showing somebody being disembowelled doesn't mean that I have to get heavy and put a message behind it.

George Romero
Film Yearbook, 1983

136 HUMOUR

1 The difference between English and American humour is $150 a minute.

Eric Idle
Film Yearbook, 1990

2 A sense of humour is a salvation. It's saved me so far. If you can't laugh, you're dead. I'm laughing all the time – you just never catch it.

Robert Mitchum
Ritz, No. 143, 1989

3 Satire is alive and well and living in the White House.

Robin Williams
Rolling Stone, 25 February 1985

137 HYPE

1 To me, it's much bigger than a film – or an event. The world is in need of direction and help. Everyone's looking for the answers. So this can be a great educator. It's a film very much about good and evil, about two great things on this earth: love and fear. The only two emotions there are. You choose which one to be – good or evil. You choose love or fear. Everything else stems from fear – anger, hatred, jealousy, greed, which causes war, devastation, terrorism, everything that's happening in the rain forests, the way the earth is now. And when something like this happens, it's a real symbol that help is there – and that it's in yourself. If you love yourself, and give out that love, then you can get it back. You can change the earth with that.

Kim Basinger (on not *The Ten Commandments* but ... *Batman*)
Deauville, September 1989

2   The picture is called *Class* but the ad. campaign is anything but. They've put my head on to another body and given me enormous bosoms. All the guys are going to be disappointed.

Jacqueline Bisset
Photoplay, November 1983

3   I generally describe *Brazil* as a post-Orwellian view of a pre-Orwellian world. That bores everyone stiff, so they leave me alone.

Terry Gilliam
Film Yearbook, 1985

4   Wait till you see how big *my* Dick is.

Disney chief Jeffrey Katzenberg on *Dick Tracy*
Premiere, June 1990

5   For a while there, it was it was either me or the Ayatollah on the covers of national magazines. Excessive hype.

Meryl Streep
Time, 7 September 1981

6   It's a movie about making a movie within which there is a movie and within that movie, the film-maker makes a movie.

Orson Welles (1915–85) (on his unseen *Other Side of the Wind*)
Film Yearbook, 1985

138   IMAGE

1   This image people have of Warren Beatty bears no reality to me. It's amazing. It's nice. But it's rubbish.

Warren Beatty
Daily Mail, May 1975

2   Because I'm a Swede I always suffer in films . . . drive audiences out into the night sobbing. Look at *The Bells of St Mary's*. I was happy and gay but there had to be something wrong. So, they gave me TB.

Ingrid Bergman (1915–82)
Sunday Express, 8 December 1963

3   I don't go around saying: 'Hello, did you know I'm the new Olivier?'

Kenneth Branagh
Newsweek, 9 October 1989

4   A spoiled genius from the Welsh gutter, a drinker, a womanizer.
It's rather an attractive image.

Richard Burton (1925–84)
Time obituary, 20 August 1984

5   I'm sort of the boy next door – if that boy had a good
scriptwriter.

Michael Caine
Playboy, 1966

6   The compartment that's easy to put me in is: free-thinking, sexy
broad with a dirty mouth, who pretty much does what she wants.
But there's more to me than that.

Joan Collins
Playboy, April 1984

7   My image is a little wearing. I don't always want to be heavy. It
depends on the material.

Robert De Niro
Photoplay, January 1989

8   Okay, I'm not Doris Day but I'm getting there.

Divine (Harris Glenn Milstead, 1945–88)
Photoplay, September 1985

9   Everybody wants to be Cary Grant. *I* want to be Cary Grant.

Cary Grant (1904–86)
Time obituary, 15 December 1986

10   If you need a ceiling painted, a chariot race run, a city besieged
or the Red Sea parted – you think of me.

Charlton Heston
Photoplay, January 1975

11   I could never understand how Joe Louis was the world
champion when Bogart was the toughest guy in the world.

Anthony Hopkins
Knave, November 1980

12   That's not me you're in love with. That's my image. You don't
even know me.

Kelly McGillis
Premiere, March 1988

13   I don't have the bust to be an image.

Peter O'Toole
Sunday Express, 12 April 1964

14   They see me as having the temperament of the Sundance Kid, the charm of *The Candidate*, the sense of humour of *The Sting* and the wardrobe of *The Great Gatsby*.

Robert Redford
Evening Standard, 27 September 1976

15   After *Last Tango In Paris*, people were insulting me in the street. In restaurants, waiters would bring me butter with a funny smile.

Maria Schneider
VSD magazine (France), 12 November 1980

16   I don't know who Peter Sellers is – except he's the one who gets paid.

Peter Sellers (1925–90)
Time, 27 April 1962

139   IMPROVISATION

1   If an actor can't improvise, perhaps the producer's wife cast him in that part.

Marlon Brando
Playboy, January 1979

2   Judges, juries, prison and probation – they sharpen the imagination. You have to improvise at a moment's notice.

Gérard Depardieu
Films Illustrated, May 1978

3   When you know your text, *that's* when you can improvise.

Jodie Foster
Photoplay, October 1984

4   At Christmas Dustin Hoffman would work at Macy's – demonstrating toys on a stand. I brought my son up there, got him to sit real stiff and Dustin did a big spiel about this life-size doll. We did a lot of improvisations at Macy's. Crazy stuff, false fights – just everything to disrupt the store.

Gene Hackman
Deauville, 8 September 1981

5   Spencer Tracy would improvise with you to help a dull scene –
and steal some of your action. Lee Marvin walked on the *Bad Day
At Black Rock* set with a toothpick in his mouth. Tracy said: 'I
wouldn't use that.' 'Why not?' asked Marvin. 'Because I'm going to!'

Don Taylor
Films Illustrated, January 1979

140   INFLUENCES

1   I don't watch funny movies. I watch Ingmar Bergman. He's
concerned with the silence of God and in some small way, so am I.

Woody Allen
Time, 3 July 1972

2   When I write, I keep Tolstoi around. I want great limits, big
thinking.

Mel Brooks
Film Yearbook, 1983

3   I got into the habit of going to an art house in Glasgow and seeing
films by Godard and Malle. I combed my hair like Maurice Ronet.

Bill Forsyth
Film Yearbook, 1986

4   We all steal but if we're smart we steal from great directors. Then,
we can call it *influence*.

Krzysztof Kieslowski
7 Days, 6 May 1990

141   INTERVIEWEES

1   When you give an interview and the feeling of being outrageous is
present, please place this ball in your mouth and then tape your
mouth shut. If you are still able to say 'oral sex' after doing this, then
you are hopeless.

Letter, enclosing tennis ball and adhesive tape, to Kim Basinger from her father
Film Yearbook, 1990

2   It's most interesting to be embarrassed by a question – or rather, that my answer will embarrass you.

Karen Black
Cannes, May 1981

3   You can say something in a certain spirit, with a smile, but when it appears in print, there's no smile.

Marlon Brando
Playboy, January 1979

4   Actors should keep their mouths shut and hope for the best.

Richard Burton (1926–84)
Playboy, 1963

5   I always give interviews. If the *Poultry Farmers' Weekly Gazette* rings me up, I'm delighted to be asked my opinions on things.

Michael Caine
Sunday Express, 13 February 1965

6   The less you use of what I say the better.

Daniel Day Lewis
Arena, autumn 1989

7   I'm not good at editing how I feel.

Robert De Niro
Playboy, January 1989

8   An unreal situation. You're supposed to be nice and talk about the most private things.

Bo Derek
Films Illustrated, March 1980

9   I'm not too thrilled with the idea of talking about myself.

Clint Eastwood
Playboy, February 1974

10   I wind up saying the most embarrassing things.

Mel Gibson
Photoplay, September 1987
(*See also* 217.8)

11   What you don't remember – make up.

Jean-Luc Godard
IT, 6 September 1968

12   Didn't they warn you? I love to invent – avoiding the truth. I need to dramatize. It's also a form of protection.

Sylvia Kristel
Telegraph Sunday magazine, 17 December 1978

13   I'm not going to be asked any conceptualizing questions, right?
It's the thing I hate most. I've always felt trapped and pinned down
and harried by those questions. Truth is too multi-faceted to be
contained in a five-line summary.
Stanley Kubrick
Rolling Stone, 27 August 1986

14   I remember complaining to Bob Rafelson about all the
interviews scheduled for us. He said: 'It's easy. All you have to do is
change your story every time.' And he would. In one, I read he said
he'd been a Jesuit priest!
Jessica Lange
Washington Post, November 1984

15   I expose myself in an interview – and I assume the interviewer is
exposing himself, too.
Jeanne Moreau
Radio Times, 1977

16   I'm an ex-pressman myself, so I try to be as co-operative as
possible.
Peter O'Toole
Showtime, 1967

17   I'm amazed people read this crap about us – about me most
of all.
Jack Palance
Films Illustrated, 1977

18   Most interviews make me look so perfect, so lucky, so one-
dimensional. I can be terrifically irresponsible and selfish.
Robert Redford
Playboy, December 1974

19   Interviews are like therapy. You don't get the same kind of
feedback. But it's cheaper.
Cybill Shepherd
Film Yearbook, 1988

20   My pet peeve is that I come across as So Serious.
Meryl Streep
Photoplay, November 1985

21   I don't have to answer any man's questions.
John Wayne (1907–79)
Photoplay, June 1961

142 INTERVIEWERS

1   This guy did an unbelievably stupid interview. Trying to be cute, he said: 'What's the dumbest question, you've ever been asked?' I thought for a second and said: 'That's it!'

James Caan
Playboy, February 1976

2   In the middle of a big sequence in *Goldfinger*, the publicity man brought on a French magazine lady. First of all, she asked me what the film was called. I told her. Then, what part was I playing. I told her. Then who was starring opposite me. I said a very famous German actor Gert Frobe. 'Well, I've never heard of her.' I just blew up and walked off the set.

Sean Connery
Playboy, 1965

3   There was a woman from a well-known American newspaper who wanted to know how I spent every minute of the day. What time did I wake up? What did I do first thing? So I told her: 'Well, I probably take a shit.'

Timothy Dalton
Premiere, June 1989

4   I like to keep the journalist puzzled, the charm is in the guessing.

Rock Hudson (1925–85)
Ritz, October 1985

143 KISSING

1   When Clark Gable kissed me, they had to *carry* me off the set.

Carroll Baker
Photoplay, June 1979

2   There's absolutely an art to it. You have to think it's as good as what's coming later.

Kim Basinger
Playboy, May 1986

3 .It becomes a bore – love scenes, kissing scenes. I prefer to fight.

Alain Delon
Films & Filming, 1964

4 When I was in pictures, you had a time limit of about two seconds before cutting away to a curtain blowing – and you couldn't open your mouth. If you had a sinus, you'd just die.

John Derek
London, 17 December 1979

5 I'm fond of kissing. It's part of my job. God sent me down to kiss a lot of people.

Carrie Fisher
Playboy, July 1983

6 I've been kissin' Audrey Hepburn all day and my pucker is tuckered.

James Garner
Panorama (USA), June 1981

7 Before we shot that kissing scene in *The Front*, Woody Allen said: 'I'm going to give you only one lip when we kiss. Because if I give you two, you'll never live through it.'

Andrea Marcovicci
Playboy, February 1989

8 I'm the only one of her partners who never kissed Brigitte Bardot. In *Le Mépris*, I kept saying: 'Do you want to make love?' And she replied: 'You disgust me.' Enough to ruin an actor's career.

Michel Piccoli
Unifrance news bulletin, 1971

9 Jean Harlow – my God, she was *beautiful*! She had this low-cut dress on and I had to kiss her. Well . . . I was just . . . that *just* has to be my most memorable screen kiss.

James Stewart
Photoplay, October 1979

10 You think Cairo was upset? You should've seen the letter from my Aunt Rose!

Jewish Barbra Streisand (on kissing Egyptian Omar Sharif in *Funny Girl*)
Sunday Times, 1968

144   STANLEY KUBRICK

1   If Kubrick hadn't been a film director, he'd have been a General Chief of Staff of the US Forces. No matter what it is – even if it's a question of buying a shampoo – it goes through him. He just likes total control.

Malcolm McDowell
Evening Standard, 31 December 1971

2   Kubrick sounds a tough gig. I guess you'd need to be on steroids to work with him.

Bill Murray
The Irish Times, 16 December 1988

3   Just because you're a perfectionist doesn't mean you're perfect ... Kubrick's impulse has been to master every element of the film-making process. Stanley's good on sound. So are a lot of directors but Stanley's good on designing a new harness. Stanley's good on the colour of the mike. Stanley's good about the merchant he bought the mike from. Stanley's good about the merchant's daughter who needs some dental work. Stanley's good.

Jack Nicholson
Newsweek, 16 May 1980

4   Define Kubrick? Umm ... Gives a whole new meaning to the word meticulous.

Jack Nicholson
Paris, 7 March 1984

5   An incredibly, depressingly serious man, with a wild sense of humour. But paranoid. He's a perfectionist.

George C. Scott
Playboy, December 1980

145   LEGENDS

1   The more you deny a legend the healthier it gets.

Jackie Gleason (1916–87)
Playboy, August 1962

2 To think that after *Hud* and *Cool Hand Luke* and all the other parts I've dug into, I come off as the guy women would most like to go to bed with – it's frightening.

Paul Newman
Playboy, 1969

3 It's good for business if people think I'm a womanizer. I've no motivation to deny it. Unless it begins to dominate the reality of my situation.

Jack Nicholson
Rolling Stone, 29 March 1984

146 LIFE

1 At the core, life is a concentration camp.

Woody Allen (he later put the line in *Manhattan* – and cut it, 'although I do believe that')
Newsweek, 24 April 1978

2 In your 20s, you feel like you're indestructible, that nothing can kill you and you laugh at death. You go on and stay up for days and do as many things as you can and then, in your 30s, you think, well, maybe I'll be around here a little longer, so I'm going to maybe take better care of myself. [He overdosed two months later.]

John Belushi (1949–82)
Rolling Stone, 21 January 1982

3 Surely, life is about something other than reading books about yourself.

Marlon Brando
Playboy, January 1979

4 To get anywhere in life you have to be anti-social. Otherwise, you'll end up being devoured.

Sean Connery
Sunday Express, 30 July 1967

5 It's more a case of my life reflecting my movies than my movies reflecting my life.

Francis Coppola
Film Yearbook, 1990

6   Life's better when it's fun. Boy, that's deep, isn't it?

Kevin Costner
Ritz, No. 134, 1989

7   You wanna know the secret of life? The saliva of young girls.

Tony Curtis
(In a pre-AIDS) Cannes, May 1982

8   There's nothing more ironic or strange or contradictory than life itself.

Robert De Niro
Newsweek, 16 May 1977

9   There was a time when certain people wanted to put me in jail. Now they've gone to jail and I'm still working.

Jane Fonda
Films Illustrated, September 1979

10   I started as a dumb blonde whore. I'll end as one.

Marilyn Monroe (1926–62)
Lena Pepitone and William Stadiem, *Marilyn Monroe Confidential*, 1979

11   For me, life has been either a wake or a wedding.

Peter O'Toole
Photoplay, April 1988

12   Life is like that old Spanish saying: 'He who plants the lettuce doesn't always eat the salad.'

Anthony Quinn
Sunday Express, 13 October 1963

147   LOCATIONS

1   We shot a large section [of *Hannah And Her Sisters*] in Mia's apartment – perfect for me because I always go over there, anyhow.

Woody Allen
Film Yearbook, 1984

2   Never shoot a film in Belgrade, Yugoslavia! The whole town is illuminated by a 20-watt night light and there's nothing to do. You can't even go for a drive. Tito is always using the car.

Mel Brooks
Newsweek, 17 February 1975

3   Between films, I book into a hotel and pretend I'm on location.
Nicolas Cage
Photoplay, August 1979

4   We were going to make *The Corsican Brothers* in Salzburg, but I said no. One really doesn't feel funny in Austria.
Tommy Chong
Cap d'Antibes, 8 May 1983

5   Locations are all tough, all miserable. I never left the sound stage for 18 years at Warners. We never went outside the studio, not even for big scenes.
Bette Davis (1908–89)
Films Illustrated, December 1979

6   What I don't like is *long* locations.
Clint Eastwood
Playboy, February 1974
(See also 125.4)

7   While shooting in Mexico, all conversation was dominated by bowels. During filming, if you'll pardon the expression, you're frightened to fart.
Ian Holm
You: Mail on Sunday magazine, 1988

8   Conditions were somewhat primitive shooting in the Sahara, but I'd shot a film in Texas so I was somewhat used to it.
John Malkovich
Paris, 14 November 1990

9   My pictures always seem to be filmed in places that I can't pronounce.
Roger Moore
Screen International, May 1980

10   Some of the guys were bitching about their hotel rooms. When I started in this business, we used to sleep in tents.
John Wayne (1907–79)
London, January 1974

148 LOOKS

1 My right profile is the worst one. They built all the sets at Pinewood to favour my left profile. I was like Loretta Young – nobody ever saw my right side.

Dirk Bogarde
BBC2 TV, April 1967

2 Elizabeth is a pretty girl but she has a double chin and an overdeveloped chest and she's rather short in the leg. So, I can hardly decribe her as the most beautiful creature I've ever seen.

Richard Burton (1925–84) (on Elizabeth Taylor)
Playboy, 1963

3 There's a lot of good-looking, well-built guys in this business and most of them couldn't play a corpse.

James Caan
Playboy, February 1976

4 It's really a joke that my whole life people thought I was unattractive until now – when I'm getting too old to really be attractive.

Cher
Playboy, December 1988

5 Unattractive people are more obsessed with looks.

Rae Dawn Chong
Playboy, April 1987

6 My skull is too flat. My ears stick out. My mouth is too big. My belly is too round. And my buttocks are too heavy.

Béatrice Dalle
Time, 14 November 1986

7 I was never beautiful like Miss Hayworth or Miss Lamarr. I was known as the little brown wren. Who'd want to get me at the end of the picture?

Bette Davis (1908–89)
Films Illustrated, December 1979

8 Laurence Olivier doesn't look like an actor, either.

Gérard Depardieu
Mulhouse (France), 9 September 1976

9 Blonde hair, pink lips, good figure, talent and sex – that's all I have to offer. It's paid off, too.

Diana Dors (1931–84)
Daily Mirror, 21 May 1956

10   I squint because I can't take too much light.

Clint Eastwood
Newsweek, 23 September 1985

11   I'm idiosyncratically made, both mentally and physically – it doesn't show, does it?

Marty Feldman (1938–82)
Daily Mail, 30 December 1977

12   I like to feel close to the bone.

Jane Fonda
Time, 16 February 1970

13   My teeth are crooked, my nose is broken. I've never thought of myself as beautiful.

Jessica Lange
Playboy, February 1983

14   I've been physically dissected more than any frog in a biology class – my eyebrows, my eyes, my teeth. And now it's my stomach.

Jack Nicholson
Rolling Stone, 29 March 1984

15   The eyes droop, the mouth is crooked, the teeth aren't straight, the voice, I've been told, sounds like a Mafioso pallbearer, but somehow it all works. I'd say between 3 pm and 8 pm, I look great. After that, it's all downhill. Don't photograph me in the morning or you're gonna get Walter Brennan.

Sylvester Stallone
Rolling Stone, December 1985

16   All right, I'm young, I'm beautiful – but you don't have to hate me.

Sean Young
Film Yearbook, 1990

149 LOS ANGELES

1   I fucking hate LA! People talk of LA as this Mecca of enlightened thinking. I get out there and it's a filthy hole.

Alec Baldwin
Premiere, April 1990

2 I've never really adapted myself to life here. I've been here 11 years and my watch is still on New York time.

Mel Brooks
Premiere, September 1981

3 To qualify for a Los Angelean, you need three things: (a) a driver's licence; (b) your own tennis court; (c) a preference for snorting cocaine.

Michael Caine
Photoplay, February 1984

4 Los Angeles is at the end of America – the last place, the extreme. It has extreme people, extreme buildings, extreme cars.

Scenarist Kit Carson
Photoplay, August 1983

5 I remember being flown out to Los Angeles to read for a series. I was terrible. And this director said: 'So, how long you gonna be in California?' And I'm thinking he's probably going to want me to come back. I said: 'Well, just a couple of days.' He said: 'Good. Get a tan while you're here.'

Tom Cruise
Film Yearbook, 1988

6 Los Angeles is where you've got to be to be an actor. You have no choice. You go there or New York. I flipped a coin about it. It came up New York. So I flipped it again.

Harrison Ford
Cinema, 1981

150 LOVE

1 One is never too old for romance.

Ingrid Bergman (1915–82)
Sunday Mirror, 5 May 1974

2 Love is the great incentive – not just sex.

Michael Caine
Playboy, 1966

3   To be in love with your director – that way lies madness. You lose your judgment sometimes in a love affair.

Faye Dunaway
Film Yearbook, 1989

4   Love, when I had it, was a passion which left me lonely and bored.

Jane Fonda
Cinema & TV (South Africa), 31 May 1974

5   Love is blind – and your cane is pink.

Serge Gainsbourg (1928–91)
Equateur publicity release, 1983

6   I believe in love at first sight, though I don't really know if it's love.

Barbara Hershey
Playboy, May 1987

7   Love isn't intellectual – it's visceral.

Kelly McGillis
Playboy, 1986

8   The preparation, the flirtation, the use of the eyes – that's more stimulating than any drugs.

Marcello Mastroianni
Sunday Express, 1967

9   Love emboldens.

Hayley Mills
Sunday Mirror, 17 September 1972

10   Love brings you out of your shell.

Lynn Redgrave
You: Mail on Sunday magazine, 12 November 1989

11   Love wears off too quickly.

Mickey Rooney
Sunday Express, 1 October 1978

12   I have a love interest in every one of my films – a gun.

Arnold Schwarzenegger
Playboy, January 1988

13   The only thing I love in love is all the feelings, the imaginations, the orgsams of the woman. For this reason I'm not a good libertine.

Roger Vadim
Game, March 1975

14 I never loved another person the way I loved myself.
Mae West (1893–1980)
Playboy, 1970

151 LOVERS

1 You love somebody once, you love them for ever – only maybe not as much as the next person.
Warren Beatty
Photoplay, November 1979

2 Bogart could never visualize love affairs without a marriage ceremony – Elizabeth Taylor is the same.
Richard Brooks
Sunday Times, 10 March 1968

3 Every tacky starlet in England who's gotten $25 000 for writing *My Night With* ... always mentions the same 'fab five': George Hamilton, Warren Beatty, Ryan O'Neal, Rod Stewart, David Bowie.
Joan Collins
Playboy, April 1984

4 I can probably count the lovers I've had on my fingers and toes. No – just fingers. One hand!
Jamie Lee Curtis
Clothes Show, November 1988

5 I was never very interested in boys – and there were plenty of them – vying with one another to see how many famous women they would get into the hay.
Bette Davis (1908–89)
Playboy, July 1982

6 Most people think – because of Ursula Andress, Linda Evans and Bo Derek – that I must be the most magnificent lover in the world. I'm not. I'm just terribly honest with the people I love. I love women. I love beauty. And I've never cheated on anyone I've loved.
John Derek
London, 17 December 1979

7   I regret three one-night stands – no, make that four.
Angie Dickinson
Photoplay, January 1985

8   I haven't had that many women – only as many as I could lay my hands on.
Dudley Moore
Playboy, January 1983

9   If I had as many affairs as you fellows claim, I'd be speaking to you today from a jar in the Havard Medical School.
Frank Sinatra
Life, 17 May 1965

10   Great lovers are such a bore. And stupid people most of the time. Limited in the mind. I'm not a great lover.
Roger Vadim
Game, March 1975

11   There's a lot of bad lovers around.
Raquel Welch
Playboy, 1970

12   I don't remember how many lovers I've had. I was never interested in the score – only the game. Like my line: it's not the men in my life that counts but the life in my men. I've been on more laps than a napkin.
Mae West (1893–1980)
Playboy, 1970

152   LOVE SCENES

1   Suddenly, you wind up in bed with a guy on top of you that you wouldn't want to share a cab with.
Candice Bergen
Playboy, December 1989

2   You're very much in love with your husband. Good. I'm very much in love with my wife. Now we can fall in love on-screen. We can really be with each other.
Gérard Depardieu to Sigourney Weaver during *One Woman Or Two*
Playboy, August 1986

3 Awkward, technically difficult: you've got to do acrobatics and contortions so the lighting and camera angles are right. Sorry guys, but love scenes are work.

Michael Douglas
Playboy, February 1986

4 Difficult, unnatural. You say things you never thought of, surrounded by people you don't know, to a girl you've only met a few days before. We Italians know that the real language of love is an inarticulate thing. The words are breathy and broken and often senseless. Yet I've been given love scenes to do that read like political speeches.

Marcello Mastroiani
A Very Private Affair publicity release, 1962

5 It's not entirely acting. When you're doing a love scene, you're actually showing that side of your sexuality.

Kathleen Turner
Photoplay, 1984
(*See also* 223.6)

6 I grew up in a different morality from today. When I did *Lolita* with James Mason, I had to be given drugs to calm me when I was doing a scene in bed with him. In *Alfie*, when I was supposed to be on top of Michael Caine, I had little pillows placed all over his body so we wouldn't touch. He was screaming so much with laughter, we almost didn't get the scene done.

Shelley Winters
Screen International, 12 May 1979

153 LOVE STORIES

1 All romances end in tragedy. One of the key people in a romance becomes a monster sooner or later.

David Cronenberg
Rolling Stone, No. 484

2 The best stories are about first love. Everyone has experienced unrequited love.

Gérard Depardieu
Cyrano de Bergerac publicity release, 1990

3   I don't like watching love stories. Same old eternal triangle.
Jean Gabin (1904–76)
Le Chat publicity release, 1971

---

154   MACHO

---

1   I ain't afraid of nothin'.
David Carradine
On Location magazine, May 1981

2   I think of myself as tough. Cockroach tough.
Michael J. Fox
Sunday Express magazine, 28 January 1990

3   Tales of my toughness are exaggerated. I never killed an actor. Nearly lost a few.
John Huston (1906–87)
Panorama (Belgium), June 1990

4   I dislike it more than any other word.
Burt Reynolds
Photoplay, April 1981

5   If I'm androgynous, I'd say I lean towards macho-androgynous.
John Travolta
Rolling Stone, 18 August 1983

---

155   MAKE-UP

---

1   Men become much *more* attractive when they start looking older. But it doesn't do much for women, though we do have an advantage: make-up.
Bette Davis (1908–89)
Playboy, July 1982

2 I don't wear any more make-up than Reagan.

Pee Wee Herman
Time Out, 17 June 1987

3 Why put make-up on when you only have to take it off again?

Glenda Jackson
People, 18 March 1985

4 It used to take them hours and hours in make-up to give me character. Now I've got the character they take it all out.

Roger Moore
Photoplay, March 1981

5 Sticking a beard on instead of growing one changes your appearance but not your character.

Peter O'Toole
Sunday Express, 12 April 1964

6 My face was always so made up, it looked as though it had the decorators in.

Shelley Winters
Sunday Express, 12 January 1975

156 MARRIAGE

1 It's something that happens to you. Like blight.

Woody Allen
London, 17 August 1965

2 When Mel [Brooks] told his Jewish mother he was marrying an Italian girl, she said: 'Bring her over. I'll be in the kitchen – with my head in the oven.'

Anne Bancroft
New Yorker, 1978

3 It's difficult to be married outside the profession. A lawyer might not understand that going to bed with Gabriel Byrne for three days is work for me.

Ellen Barkin (so, she married Byrne instead)
Photoplay, November 1987

4   I have no intention of getting married. To me, marriage essentially is a contract and there are so many loopholes in it that Wilbur Mills and the entire Ways and Means Committee couldn't figure it out.

Warren Beatty
People, 14 April 1975

5   I'm not exactly *scared* of marriage. It's just that, looking around, it never works.

Julie Christie
Madrid, September 1965

6   The assumption being that you should get married and live with someone for 30 years. If I finish being married five times for seven years each time, that for me will probably be more interesting than one for 35 years. I know you're not supposed to say it, but why not?

John Cleese
Independent, 26 September 1988

7   From the start, marriage was instituted for contemptible, practical reasons – an idea of men.

Catherine Deneuve
L'Express, 1976

8   People change after they're married. They die and become so very bourgeois.

Jane Fonda
Cinema & TV (South Africa), 31 May 1974

9   It's bloody impractical: to love, honour and obey. If it weren't, you wouldn't have to sign a contract.

Katharine Hepburn
Newsweek, 10 November 1969

10   I believe in the marriage state so enormously, I don't want to be responsible for another failure. Besides, I like the bed to myself.

Sarah Miles
Photoplay, December 1982

11   We got married in a kitchen because it was the warmest room in the house. Place smelled of cabbage and a wasted preacher. He kept spitting in the sink.

Robert Mitchum (after, it should be added, his most romantic proposal to Dorothy, quoted in *Film Yearbook*, 1985: 'Marry me and you'll be farting through silk.')
Film Yearbook, 1984

12   Our marriage works because we each carry clubs of equal weight and size.

Paul Newman
Photoplay, April 1987

13   The point of our marriage is that Lola and I are not joined at the hip.

Robert Redford
Daily Mail, February 1977

14   Marriage is a great institution.

Elizabeth Taylor
Film Yearbook, 1987

15   I've never been married or had a child but I want that – very badly . . . Do you know anybody?

Dianne Wiest
New York Times, March 1987

16   She was very naughty to put that in the *New York Times*. Very naughty! But . . . yes, it's true. Do *you* know anybody?

Dianne Wiest
Cannes, 17 May 1987

157   MARRIAGES

1   TWO: My first marriage was not happy. I married him because I was impressed that he knew which wines to order and how to leave his visiting card. Ridiculous reasons.

Jean Seberg (1938–79)
Sunday Express, 22 December 1963

2   THREE: All my marriages were good and what follows love, or should do, is deep friendship.

Ingrid Bergman (1915–82)
Daily Mail, 7 May 1974

3   THREE: I've seen the tremendous change that can happen. Usually, to the man. At any rate, in my case.

Joan Collins
The Observer, 6 October 1985

4 THREE: I never understood my husbands' problems. They couldn't deal with the fact that I was a big star and making more money than they were. Men are so sensitive.

Goldie Hawn
Film Yearbook, 1988

5 THREE: It's tough being married to Raquel Welch.

Raquel Welch
Evening Standard, 7 January 1972

6 FOUR: My first marriage doesn't count. I was 16. It lasted one week.

Jill St John
Sunday Mirror, 30 May 1971

7 FIVE: I'm godammed ashamed of it.

Henry Fonda (1905–82).
Film Yearbook obituary, 1983

8 FIVE: Jack Nicholson and my daughter have lived together for 12 years. That's longer than any of my marriages lasted.

John Huston (1906–87)
Cinecitta, 11 December 1985

9 SEVEN: The morality I learned at home required marriage. I just couldn't have an affair. So I got married all those times and now I'm accused of being a scarlet woman

Elizabeth Taylor
Films Illustrated, October 1980

10 EIGHT: When I say, I do, the Justice of the Peace replies, *'I know, I know.'* I'm the only man in the world whose marriage licence reads: 'To Whom It May Concern'. But to have been married eight times is not normal. That's only half-way intelligent.

Mickey Rooney
Pinewood, 29 September 1978

158 MEDIA

1 Some illiterate, unthinkable idiot will come up: 'Would you have a drink, Mr Burton?' Facetiously, I reply that I'd like a martini because you can't get them in Wales. And immediately, an entire column is built on the fact that there are no martinis in Wales.

Richard Burton (1925–84)
Playboy, 1963

2 We all believe what we read. I read how Tom Cruise and I were two big egos holding up shooting. I know that isn't true – but if I wasn't making a movie with him and I just picked up the paper, I'd believe it. That's interesting, isn't it?

Dustin Hoffman
Sunday Express magazine, 19 February 1989

3 I wish I could sue the *New York Post* but it's awfully hard to sue a garbage can.

Paul Newman
Rolling Stone, 20 January 1983

4 All this brouhaha. It does become a pain. It's only the media who create it. They pick on someone to be the person of the hour.

Meryl Streep
Evening Standard, 1 February 1980

5 The news media has gotten more power today than the railroad in 1890. But in 1890 at least they were trying to set up channels of communication.

John Wayne (1907–79)
London, January 1974

159 MEETINGS

1 I must've been about 10. Kirk Douglas volunteered to adopt me and take me back to Hollywood. He met me when he was filming in Israel. My parents objected even though we were poor. I met Kirk again nine years later in Rome. We were making *Two Weeks In Another Town*. He didn't recognize me.

Daliah Lavi
Sunday Express, 13 June 1965

2 How did I meet Chong? I put an ad. in the paper: 'Learn the joys of rubber clothing. Negroes and excessively hairy men need not apply.' And suddenly, he was there. Like a movie. Like *The Texas Chainsaw Massacre*.

Cheech Marin
Cap d'Antibes, May 1983

3 I met Gary Cooper soon after I came to Hollywood. He asked how many pictures I'd made: 'Two.' He'd made 62. He then asked how were my pictures: 'One good, one bad.' 'You're ahead of the game.' He went on to say of all his films, two out of every five were good.

Gregory Peck
Screen International, 25 October 1977

4 I pounded on her door and when it opened I saw this wonderful vision. She looked extraordinary. I said: 'Well, I'm only going to stay 15 minutes but maybe I can stretch it into four hours.'

Sylvester Stallone (on second wife Brigitte Neilsen)
Rolling Stone, December 1985

5 My dog ran off and I ran after it – wet from the shower, stark naked. And suddenly, there was Francine standing in the doorway. She took one look at me and ran away. She was back a minute later – she had run to get her glasses.

Donald Sutherland (on meeting his wife Francine Racette)
Playboy, October 1981

6 I met Tennessee Williams after I'd done *Cat On A Hot Tin Roof*. I was in hospital with pneumonia and he came to see me. Must have been 57. It was after *Cat* . . . No, it wasn't after *Cat* – yes, it was . . . Must have been . . . Now I'm confused. Must have been after *Cat* but it couldn't have been because Mike [Todd] was killed when I was shooting *Cat*. Well, I was in hospital, but I think it was in New York because that's where we lived. Now, I am confused! Mike was killed in 58. It must have been after. After 1957. Must have been . . .

Elizabeth Taylor
Los Angeles Times, 1988

160 MEETINGS – HOLLYWOOD STYLE

1 Whoever invented the meeting must have had Hollywood in mind. I think they should consider giving Oscars for meetings: Best Meeting of the Year, Best Supporting Meeting, Best Meeting Based On Material From Another Meeting.

William Goldman
Film Yearbook, 1984

2 You go to a meeting and there are all these people wearing tennis shoes -- you know, the latest tennis shoes. And you're depressed that humanity has reached this level.

Coppola's art director Dean Tavoularis
Film Yearbook, 1986

161 MEMORABLE ROLES

1 Although I went all over the world promoting it, I'd never got to see more than the credits before being whisked away. Finally, at Cannes, I was to sit the whole thing through. When I appeared for the first time, I fainted from the shock – and woke up in the ladies' room.

Geraldine Chaplin (on *Dr Zhivago*)
Sunday Times, 1976

2 I'm probably quite proud that I'm the only woman on celluloid ever to have said no to Robert Redford.

Glenn Close (on *The Natural*)
Photoplay, February 1988

3 I got the killer part, that's the truth. It does have Patrick Swayze and Demi Moore but, honey, when I'm on the screen – you've got to be paying attention!

Whoopi Goldberg (on her Oscar-winning *Ghost*)
Starburst, December 1990

4 Acting in *Star Wars*, I felt like a raisin in a gigantic fruit salad.

Mark Hamill
Screen International, 17 December 1977

5 I wouldn't be as rash as to say I played Moses and found God, but one learns from it, certainly. You'd be a bloody fool if you couldn't.

Charlton Heston
Screen International, 22 May 1976

6 If I met Dorothy – me as a woman – at a party, I'd turn her down.

Dustin Hoffman (on *Tootsie*)
Time, 20 December 1982

7 I made a video test and I refused it. I thought it was for shampoo and I didn't want to do any more commercials.

Sylvia Kristel (on *Emmanuelle*)
Game, February 1977

8 Every actor looks all his life for a part that will combine his talents with his personality. *The Odd Couple* was mine. The plutonium I needed. It all started happening after that.

Walter Matthau
Time, 24 May 1971

9 I could actually sit through *Becket*. Not *Lawrence of Arabia* -- I kept thinking 'That's where the camel bit my hand' or 'Imagine, I was only 27 then.' And that awful music they put to it.

Peter O'Toole
Sunday Express, 12 April 1964

10 I had the impression we were going to break new territory; certain paranoias and fantasies, certain delicate, subtle things that go on between two people that I wanted to delve into and capture. But that wouldn't sell as many tickets as me humping Kim Basinger on a coffee table.

Mickey Rourke (on *9½ Weeks*)
Knave, March 1990

11 It's compelling watching people act out the worst thing you've done to someone and the worst thing that's been done to you.

Laura San Giacomo (on *sex, lies and videotape*)
Knave, October 1989

12 If I were to tell you that Chauncey Gardiner was the ultimate Peter Sellers, I'd be telling you what my whole life was about. If I don't portray him, he will ultimately portray me.

Peter Sellers (1925–80) to *Being There* author Jerzy Kosinki
Time, 3 March 1980

13   I didn't give Mr [William] Wyler instructions. I did play *Funny Girl* on stage for three years. I know every line, every word, everything. It's part of myself and I had the right to voice an opinion. It's quite true that it was my first motion picture but it was also Mr Wyler's first musical.

Barbra Streisand
Hello Dolly publicity release, 1969

14   I was 12 at the time, very short and the [*National Velvet*] producer told me I was absolutely right for the part other than my height. I said: 'Well, I'll grow.' And he patted me on the head: 'That's very sweet . . . Jut don't set your heart on it.' But I *did* . . . and in three months, I grew three inches. I did everything. I hung from doors, ate steak for breakfast, lunch and dinner, rode four hours day. I guess I was in that period where children just shoot up – but I thought I'd willed myself into it.

Elizabeth Taylor
Films Illustrated, October 1980

15   I'd been friendly with John Ford for 10 years. He came to me with the script of *Stagecoach* and said: 'Who the hell can play the Ringo Kid?' I said there's only one guy: Lloyd Nolan. Ford said: 'Oh Jesus, can't you play it?'

John Wayne (1907–79)
Time, 8 August 1969

162   MEMORABLE SCENES

1   I was the first man to be seen sleeping with another man's wife in an English film.

Albert Finney (on *Saturday Night and Sunday Morning*)
Sunday Times, December 1975

2   You don't know real heat until you've spent several hours inside a giant condom.

Priscilla Presley (on *The Naked Gun*)
Film Yearbook, 1991

3   I wanted to play [NASA astronaut] Gordon Cooper in *The Right Stuff* a year before they even thought about the movie. I mean, *he fell asleep on the launch pad!*

Dennis Quaid
Munich, 12 February 1989

4 Not flinching – that was the hardest part. I had to stand there looking so happy when I knew any minute the bucket [of blood] was going to fall. For blood they used syrup, the consistency of honey. I couldn't sit down – I'd stick to the chair.

Sissy Spacek (on *Carrie*)
Photoplay, May 1977

163 MEN AND WOMEN

1 Strong women only marry weak men.

Bette Davis (1908–89)
Playboy, July 1982

2 Men are good but women are magic.

Catherine Deneuve
Paris Match, 16 July 1982

3 Men don't understand anything about women and women understand nothing about men. And it's better that way.

Vittorio Gassman
Up magazine, 1987

4 I don't mind living in a man's world as long as I can be a woman in it.

Marilyn Monroe (1926–62)
Rolling Stone, 1985

164 MEN BY MEN

1 The one thing that men and women have in common – they both like the company of men.

Michael Douglas
Playboy, November 1980

2   As women become more liberated, men don't know how to act. They're afraid of looking ridiculous, so they look bored. Sometimes they *really* are apathetic. But most of the time, it's a cover-up, because they honestly don't know what the hell has happened to the relationship between the sexes.

Marcello Mastroianni
Look, 8 November 1964

3   A man who is entirely masculine isn't really normal, is he? I'm not saying he has to be as queer as a three-dollar bill. I mean if he hasn't a certain amount of absolutely feminine in him – feminine, mind you, not femininity – I doubt he'd be very interesting.

Lord Laurence Olivier (1907–89)
Daily Mail, 26 March 1979

4   I don't see many men today. I see a lot of guys running around television with small waists, but I don't see many men.

Anthony Quinn
Film Yearbook, 1985

165   MEN BY WOMEN

1   A woman isn't complete without a man. But where do you find a man – a real man – these days?

Lauren Bacall
Daily Mail, 27 November 1972

2   I never wanted to be a man. I feel sorry for them.

Glenn Close
Film Yearbook, 1990

3   I've *always* liked men better than women.

Bette Davis (1908–89)
Playboy, July 1982

4   My mother said it was simple to keep a man: you must be a maid in the living-room, a cook in the kitchen and a whore in the bedroom. I said I'd hire the other two and take care of the bedroom bit.

Jerry Hall
Film Yearbook, 1987

5   Only when a woman decides not to have children, can a woman live like a man. That's what I've done.

Katharine Hepburn
Daily Mail, 21 July 1979
(*See also* 256.3)

6   Men can be a great deal of work for very little reward.

Glenda Jackson
People, 18 May 1985

7   Young men seem so nervous of me.

Sylvia Kristel
Game, February 1977

8   Men like to see women as objects ... That image of totally contrived sexuality, with bleached hair, pushed-up tits and make-up an inch thick, still works. A dolly is safe. You don't have to invest your emotions or real feelings of life and commitment. You can just get your dick up, stick it in and then say: 'So long, sweetie.'

Theresa Russell
American Film, April 1989

9   I called up this guy, who was quite attractive, connected, well educated and nice, and I said: 'About our evening tomorrow, let me tell you, if you think we're going to end up in bed, we're *just* not . . .' And he said: 'Oh, no, no, no.' And without fail, midnight, and I'm pushing him out the door. Men don't believe what you say.

Kathleen Turner
Film Yearbook, 1991

10   Men looked upon me as a challenge to their manhood and thought they had to have a shot.

Raquel Welch
Daily Mail, 20 February 1979

166   THE METHOD

1   The Method is Judeo-Christian: if you go through pain, you can't miss. Rubbish. I'm more interested in the box itself than what's in it. How *v.* why.

Isabelle Adjani
The Driver publicity release, 1977

2   Stanislavsky helps the weak. The idea of a Stanislavskian self-indulgence is anathema to me. I hate this public display of a personal rat biting a personal stomach.

Richard Burton (1925–84)
Playboy, 1963

3   The Method is a lot of nonsense.

Sir Charles Chaplin (1889–1977)
Radio Times, 1972

4   All Stanislavsky ever said was: 'Avoid generalities.'

Anthony Hopkins
Films Illustrated, December 1980

5   The Method was all built up by the media into something it's not. I started the Actors Studio. That was *my* idea. I got Lee Strasberg in – a born teacher. Lee formulated The Method. But all really good actors live by their spiritual content. It's about when the emotion is real and not simulated. Brando – that's the *real* thing. He wouldn't say he worked with The Method.

Elia Kazan
Photoplay, August 1983

6   Method actors give you a photograph. Real actors give you an oil painting.

Charles Laughton (1899–1962)
Quoted by Jackie Gleason (1916–87), *Playboy*, 1962

7   If it works, *that's* The Method.

Jack Nicholson
Evening Standard, 29 September 1976

8   Duke [John Wayne] used to say to me: 'To hell with all that Method stuff. You don't hafta act. Just react.'

Slim Pickens (1919–83)
Honeysuckle Rose publicity release, 1980
(*See also* 253.10)

9   We exponents of horror do much better than those Method actors. We make the unbelievable believable. More often than not, they make the believable unbelievable.

Vincent Price
Sunday Express, 1964

10   A lot of claptrap is talked about The Method as though the British actor didn't have one. It's just that we tend to be *quieter* about it.

John Schlesinger
Film Yearbook, 1988

11   There's no such thing as The Method. The term method-acting is so much nonsense. There are many methods, many techniques. My father merely used a method of teaching based on the ideas originally propounded by Stanislavsky – self-discipline, how to think out a role and use imagination. That's all.

Susan Strasberg, actress-daughter of Lee Strasberg
Scream of Fear publicity release, 1961

12   I have no method. I've a smattering of things learned from different teachers. Nothing I can put in a valise, open up and say: 'Now which one would you like?'

Meryl Streep
Life, December 1987

167   MONEY

1   What, after all, is money? Can you eat it, drink it – make love with it?

Warren Beatty
Evening Standard, 23 April 1969

2   I could've made more money if I'd sold torn T-shirts with my name on them. The Brando T-Shirt would've sold a million.

Marlon Brando
Daily Express, 3 February 1966

3   I had a dream. A vision. Of money in the bank. And I said: If I make a big picture that everybody laughs at they'll give me *money* . . . and when when I'm an old man, I'll go visit my money in the bank.

Mel Brooks
Films Illustrated, January 1982

4   I've done the most unutterable rubbish, all because of money –
when the lure of the zeros was simply too much.

Richard Burton (1925–84)
Time, 20 August 1984

5   Where I come from, if there's a buck to be made, you don't ask
questions, you go ahead and make it.

James Cagney (1899–1986)
Newsweek, 14 May 1973

6   Anyone who says that money can't buy happiness is putting out
propaganda for the rich. I've had 35 years of not having any money
and I'd now like, in all justice, fairness and decency, to have 35 years
of absolute luxury – and if I can get it, I will. But if I can't, I won't
shoot myself. I'll shoot somebody else.

Michael Caine
Playboy, 1963

7   I never ask anybody what they earn and don't tell anybody what
I earn. I want all I can get. I'm entitled to it. I don't believe all this
stuff about starving in a garret or being satisfied with artistic
appreciation only.

Sean Connery
Playboy, 1965

8   I'm personally not interested in money.

Attributed to Disney chief Michael Eisner, reputedly Hollywood's highest-paid
executive: $65 753 per day, $24 million a year

9   I'm very rich. That's what you wanted to hear, isn't it? People
would like to know exactly how rich. But it's none of their goddam
business.

Harrison Ford
Time, 25 February 1985

10   If you make an American film with a beginning, middle and end,
with a budget of less than $5 million, you must be an idiot to lose
money.

Menahem Golan
Cannes Daily, 8 May 1986

11   I've always lived above my income. When I was earning $100 a
week, I spent $200 . . . always borrowing against my future earnings.
That's why I'm not the only one who wants me to be a success.

Laurence Harvey (1928–73)
Sunday Express, 10 February 1963

12   I've always had a good head for deals – not for handling money. Until he died, my father used to send me my allowance, which was how I preferred it.
Katharine Hepburn
Film Yearbook, 1987

13   They said I was worth $500 million. If I was worth that much, I wouldn't have visited Vietnam, I'd have sent for it.
Attributed to Bob Hope

14   If all the system can offer its talent is the crap it does, then producers should pay through the eyes, ears, nose, mouth – any orifice you can think of.
Glenda Jackson
People, 18 March 1985

15   I make movies for money. Exclusively for money! So I sell myself at the highest price. Exactly like a prostitute.
Klaus Kinski
Playboy, November 1985

16   I'll do anything for money – even associate with my agent.
Vincent Price
TV Times, 1969

17   My boyfriend keeps telling me I've got to own things. So, first I bought this car. And then he told me I oughta get a house. 'Why a house?' 'Well, you gotta have a place to park the car.'
Julia Roberts
Los Angeles Times, 23 March 1990

18   I'm so naive about finances. Once when my mother mentioned an amount and realized I didn't understand, she had to explain: 'That's like three Mercedes.'
Brooke Shields
Film Yearbook, 1987

168   MARILYN MONROE

1   Kissing Marilyn was like kissing Hitler – sure, I said that. It wasn't *that* bad. But you can see through that line: there was this woman, beautifully endowed, treating all men like shit. Why did I have to take that?

Tony Curtis
Game, September 1975

2   She's something different to each man, blending somehow the thing she seems to require most.

Clark Gable (1901–60)
Playboy, 1986

3   This lady would come to our pizza parlour every Sunday – only place in town where we kids could hang out. Wasn't much room, so she asked to join our table. She chatted about schools, hobbies, ambitions. Never mentioned movies. We didn't know what to call her. 'I'm Marilyn,' she said. And she became our friend. None of us knew who she was. We didn't have a cinema. I was always going on about wanting to act – and got my drama scholarship to the American Academy of Dramatic Art – all through Marilyn.

Jackelyn Giroux
Cannes, May 1987

4   Next to her, Lucrezia Borgia was a pussycat.

Assistant director David Hall
Sunday Times, 9 September 1973

5   Oh, it was a tragic thing to witness. particularly since there was something ever so appealing about her. What interests me now is the fact that interest in her endures. They're asking the same questions – you are – that they were 15 years ago. Simple – she's still alive.

John Huston
Rolling Stone, 19 February 1981

6   During *We're Not Married*, she came running towards me and asked breathlessly: 'Where's the men's room?' I pointed and off she raced. I've never understood that.

Nunnally Johnson
American Film, October 1981

7   Marilyn was blowing take after take, either fluffing or forgetting a line completely. Every man and woman on the set was loathing her. I said: 'Don't worry, darling, that last one looked very good.' She looked at me, puzzled, and said: 'Worry about what?' I swore then that I'd never attribute human feelings to her again.

Nunnally Johnson
American Film, October 1981

8   I could watch her movies for ever. Whether you were a dog or a cat or a woman or a guy, you just *loved* her.

Nastassja Kinski
Playboy, May 1983

9   Young lady, I think you're a case of arrested development. With your development, somebody's bound to get arrested.

Groucho Marx (on the *Love Happy* set 1949)
Playboy, May 1979

10   When Pearl Harbour was attacked, I was working at the Lockheed airplane factory in the sheet metal department running a shaper and a drop hammer. My partner was a guy named Jim Dougherty, married to a girl named Norma Jean Baker. So I knew her since 16. She was not a very sexy girl. She had no sex appeal whatsover. She had a lot of serious physical problems. Yes, really. And very shy.

Robert Mitchum (they co-starred in *River Of No Return* in 1954, directed by No. 12 below)
Ritz, No. 134, 1989

11   She was the victim of ballyhoo and sensation – exploited beyond anyone's means.

Lord Laurence Olivier (19078–89)
The Observer, 3 May 1987

12   Directing her was like directing Lassie. You need 14 takes to get each one of them right.

Otto Preminger (1906–86)
Photoplay, September 1982

13   The facts, as we've found them, do not support a finding of foul play – to the contrary. Permit me to express the faint hope that Marilyn Monroe be permitted to rest in peace. She's entitled to that.

Los Angeles DA, John Van der Kamp
Variety, 4 January 1983

14 Marilyn doesn't need script approval. If she doesn't like something, she just doesn't show up.

Producer Henry T. Weinstein
Sunday Times, 9 September 1973

15 I've never met anyone as utterly mean as Marilyn Monroe. Nor as utterly fabulous on the screen. And that includes Garbo.

Billy Wilder
Photoplay, September 1982

Footnote: Remembering Munroe [*sic*], the actress.

Headline in the *Independent*, 31 July 1987

169 MORALITY

1 To me, it's much more moral to live with the man you love without signing a piece of paper than to live legally in an atmosphere of boredom which can eventually turn to hate.

Ursula Andress
Sunday Mirror, 1971

2 I don't have a moral plan. I'm a Canadian.

David Cronenberg
Film Yearbook, 1985

3 I haven't seen a woman take a moral stand in a film for about 20 years.

Glenda Jackson
Daily Mail, 8 December 1976

4 I was born in a revolution, lived through 2½ world wars. I grew up watching people avoid issues. I want to stand for something more.

Anthony Quinn
A Star For Two publicity release, 1990

170 MOVIES

1 Everyone wants to get into movies for some reason, but there aren't any movies left.

Dirk Bogarde
Ritz, April 1983

2 Movies are in major trouble. They're aiming most of the movies at children – the most mindless, uninformative and vulgar bunch of projects.

Robert De Niro
Photoplay, November 1984

3 Movies are fun. But they're not a cure for cancer.

Clint Eastwood
Film Yearbook, 1986

4 Movies are bourgeois.

Richard Gere
Photoplay, November 1983

5 Pictures are not wine. We don't believe in laying them down to gather dust.

Menahem Golan
Cannes, May 1985

6 Movies are 70 years old – an infant art form.

Dustin Hoffman
Films Illustrated, May–June 1980

7 I thought that you played around with Lauren Bacall for a little while, then you met Doris Day and settled down. Boy, was I wrong! That's the lie movies gave to me.

Henry Jaglom
Film Yearbook, 1985

8 Making movies is better than cleaning toilets.

Klaus Kinski
Playboy, 1985

9 How many movies do you see that you really like?

Amy Madigan
Washington Post, May 1985

10   You go to the movies for four reasons. To laugh, cry, get scared, get a hard-on. If you can do all four – hey it's the ultimate pizza combo, man!

Cheech Marin
Playboy, 1982

171   MYTHS

1   Movies are the repository of myth. Therein lies their power. An alternative history, that of the human psyche, is contained and unfolded in the old stories and tales. Film carries on this tradition.

John Boorman
Money Into Light, 1985

2   There's a tendency for people to mythologize everybody evil or good. Elvis Presley – bloated, over the hill, adolescent entertainer suddenly drawing people to Las Vegas – has nothing to do with excellence, just myth.

Marlon Brando
Playboy, January 1979

3   I am not a myth.

Marlene Dietrich
Sunday Times, 22 September 1964

4   Myths are a waste of time. They prevent progression.

Barbra Streisand
Playboy, October 1977

172   NAMES

1   Yeah, my real name is Coppola. I changed it because they'd think I was some nepotism-oriented kid.

Nicolas Cage
Photoplay, August 1987

2   Bo – it's cute. Sure, I know what the initials mean.

Bo Derek
Films Illustrated, March 1980

3   If we'd known he was going to be an actor, we'd have given him a fancier name.

Mrs Alice Finney, Albert's mother
Telegraph weekend magazine, November 1990.

4   The studio guys thought my name was too pretentious for a young man. As an alternative, I suggested the dumbest I could think of: Kurt Affair.

Harrison Ford
Playboy, March 1988

5   My mother was such a movie fan, she named me for her idol Dustin Farnum and my brother, Dr Ronald Hoffman, for her other favourite Ronald Coleman.

Dustin Hoffman
Stage & Cinema (South Africa), 28 June 1968

6   It's better than Crash and Brick which were the other two suggestions. It might have been worse – Flip or Fluke!

Rock Hudson (1925–85), born Roy Scherer
Sunday Express, 25 November 1962

7   Change it to what – Tiffany? It's been an advantage. It's unforgettable. I'm the only one.

Swoosie Kurtz
Champs-sur-Marne (France), 3 June 1988

8   If I ever [change it], it will be something smoother, more phonetic like Marilyn.

Jo Anne Pflug
M*A*S*H publicity release, 17 May 1969

9   My cousin, Rip Torn, persuaded me not to change my name: You shouldn't change what you are in the search for success.

Sissy Spacek
Photoplay, April 1977
(See also 172.13)

10   It's of Dutch origin. It just means a line – something they'd put down when they couldn't write.

Meryl Streep
Photoplay, December 1986

11 One thing's for sure. No child of mine will have a name like Kiefer.

Kiefer Sutherland
Young Miss, January–February 1988

12 People who know me well, call me Elizabeth. I dislike Liz.

Elizabeth Taylor
Look, 15 August 1961

13 I like my crazy name. Even during the time I didn't work people remembered it because it was always cropping up – in crossword puzzles, stuff like that.

Rip Torn. (He married actress Geraldine Page and their New York bell-push read: 'Torn-Page')
Los Angeles Times, May 1987

173 NICKNAMES

1 It's been misspelt a lot. He decided on it. It's not Bog-*ey*. He signed with an *ie*. And that's good enough for me.

Lauren Bacall (on Humphrey Bogart)
Paris, April 1990

2 As a child, I was called Lady Jane by relatives. My middle name is Seymour.

Jane Fonda
Photoplay, October 1983

3 People in the street still call me Popeye – and *The French Connection* was 15 years ago. I wish I'd another hit – and a new nickname.

Gene Hackman
Film Yearbook, 1987

4 Wal, I guess everybody knows the story by now. Used to have this [pause] dawg called Duke. He'd follow me to school, ya know. Used to stay at the fire [pause] station and wait for me. Firemen knew his name but [pause] not mine. So, he as Big Duke and I was Little [pause] Duke.

John Wayne (1907–79) telling the tale for the (pause) 50 000th time
Game, June 1975

174 NUDITY BY MEN

1 I like to be naked in movies, I've a reputation to uphold.

Alec Baldwin
Premiere, April 1990

2 Stripping naked is not entertainment. It's for voyeurs and I'm damned sure I'm not going to feed their imaginations and let them get their licks from seeing me totally nude.

Charles Bronson
The Mechanic publicity release, 1972

3 That's what I object to about modern movies. Any pantry sweetheart can take their clothes off and she's interesting to the average audience.

Sir Charles Chaplin (1889–1977)
Show, June 1972

4 It was Jamie's idea to have me naked in one scene. When I first thought it up, both of us were nude. Jamie [Lee Curtis] said: 'That's not right. It's so much funnier if he's naked – because Wanda's always in control.'

John Cleese (on *A Fish Called Wanda*)
Deauville, September 1989

5 It's my body. That's what I work with.

Gérard Depardieu
Paris Metro magazine, 25 May 1977

6 Audiences want to see Bo nude. They'll tell us when they're bored.

John Derek
Photoplay, December 1984

7 Nobody's gonna come and ask me to take my clothes off. What am I saying? I did – didn't I? In *The Rounders*. Went bare-assed. But it was a funny scene.

Henry Fonda (1905–82)
Hollywood Reporter, 1970

8 All the fuss about her [Sarah Miles] appearing nude in this film amused me. Her parents were shocked. Their servants were surprised to see their young mistress in the nude. I should've thought it a splendid way of keeping one's domestic staff happy.

Laurence Harvey (1928–73) (on directing *The Ceremony*)
Sunday Express, 10 February 1965

9   We have two girls today and they're both stark naked. They're embarrassed. They shouldn't be. Everybody on the set has seen it a thousand times before. Nobody gives a monkey's uncle, unless you've got three tits.

David Hemmings, shooting *Blow Up*
London, 29 June 1966

10   Never in my films! It's too easy – a complete cliché these days.

Sir Alfred Hitchcock (1899–1980) (when he relented in *Frenzy*, the nude was, of course, a corpse)
London, 21 April 1966

11   I won't show my wanker. There's got to be some mystery left.

Dennis Quaid
Premiere, October 1987

12   There was a bit of male nudity in *Lassiter* and that was handled well. It did not stick out.

Tom Selleck
Ritz, 1985

13   When I see a film and somebody takes their clothes off, I'm out of the movie. I've immediately forgotten her character and I'm thinking: Oh, that's Greta Scacchi and she's taken her shirt off.

Steven Soderbergh
Knave, October 1989

---

175   NUDITY BY WOMEN

1   I've nothing against it. We're born this way.

Ursula Andress
Dublin Castle, October 1965

2   I would not, could not, be naked for the cameras.

Candice Bergen
Premiere (UK), 1970

3   We've all seen it. We go home – we *are* it.

Rae Dawn Chong
Playboy, April 1987

4   Had I not done the work that involved nudity, I don't think I'd be working right now. It has given me a career and let me hold on to my self-esteem.

Jamie Lee Curtis
Playboy, 1985

5   I don't walk around naked like that even at home. I don't like nudity. It's not my style.

Béatrice Dalle
Journal du dimanche (France), 6 April 1986

6   I don't mind being naked because I like the sensuality of a nice body. Trouble is food is fun and exercise is boring.

Bo Derek
Film Yearbook, 1983

7   I'm not prudish about exposing my body. I'm much more uptight about exposing my mind to the wrong people.

Lauren Hutton
Daily Mail, 17 November 1977

8   Nudity in the flesh doesn't bother me. But having my mind uncovered – that scares the hell out of me.

Margot Kidder
Playboy, July 1981

9   I can't bear being seen nearly naked. I'm not exactly a tiny woman. When Sophia Loren is naked, this is a lot of nakedness.

Sophia Loren
Sunday Mirror, 30 August 1964

10   *Moi*, in the altogether? Honey, *no* studio has that much money.

Bette Midler
Photoplay, May 1986

11   Breasts and bottoms look boringly alike.

Lee Remick
Loot publicity release, 1970

12   Nudity is easier if there are two of you.

Greta Scacchi
The Times, 7 December 1984

13   I promised myself never to be photographed nude. Why should I show all my cards at the beginning of the game – what could I do for an encore?
Raquel Welch
Playboy, 1970
(*See also* 178.10)

14   Nowadays, they just throw in a naked body to help the plot, 'cos all the great plots have been done and it's monotonous.
Mae West (1893–1980)
Playboy, 1970

15   I think it's disgusting! Shameful! And damaging to all things American. But if I were 22 with a great body, it would be artistic, tasteful, patriotic and a progressive, religious experience.
Shelley Winters
Cinema X, 1970

176   OLD MOVIES

1   I never watch my old films, never have. I have a blanket I carry around to cover the television set in hotel rooms.
Sterling Hayden (1916–86)
Films Illustrated, February 1981

2   Our old mistakes do come back to haunt us. Especially with video.
Peter O'Toole
Photoplay, April 1988

3   Looking at *Mrs Miniver* on videotape and looking at *Mrs Miniver* on 35 mm good black and white film is the difference between observation and inspiration.
Steven Spielberg
Los Angeles Times, 3 December 1989

177   OSCAR NIGHT

1   This is the morning of the day of the night of the Oscars.
American TV, 8 April 1975

2   There's a car blocking the entrance. Does anybody here have a Mercedes?

Johnny Carson
9 April 1983

3   It's just a meat parade in front of an international television audience – degrading to have actors in competition with each other.

George C. Scott
Evening Standard, 9 February 1971

4   I came to Hollywood in 1928 – the same time as the Oscar – and we plan to be around for a long time to come.

John Wayne (1907–79) presenting Best Film, 9 April 1979
(He died two months later)

178   OSCARS

1   Nothing would disgust me more morally than winning an Oscar.

Luis Buñuel (1900–83)
Variety, 1971

2   Well, the rear of it looked like my first husband Ham Nelson's bare behind. And Ham's middle name was Oscar. But whether or not I named it officially isn't going to make a bit of difference in my life.

Bette Davis (1908–89)
Playboy, July 1982

3   I will *not* be there and put up with that shit.

Henry Fonda (1905–82) (three months before he finally won)
Playboy, December 1981

4   Anyone who's semi-conscious knows not to take the Academy Awards seriously. They're a game show.

Kevin Kline
Deauville, 14 September 1985

5   It's not about deserving to win – because no one deserves to *lose*. I thought I might win for *The Apartment* until Elizabeth Taylor had her tracheotomy.

Shirley MacLaine
Playboy, September 1984

6   I was a little high. I had to pee – bad. I kept popping Valium like candy. I was praying: Please don't let it be me.

Al Pacino (his prayer was heard)
Playboy, December 1979

7   I grew up in Los Angeles and the Academy Awards seemed like California politics. Weird. An awful lot of extravagance for nothing. The awards always went to people who had done better work before or later.

Robert Redford
Playboy, December 1974

8   Jack Nicholson knows how to play the game. If Jack shit bricks, they'd give him an Oscar.

Mickey Rourke
Playboy, January 1985

9   I really wanted it [for *Anatomy of a Murder*]. I became anxious and I didn't like that in myself. I said: 'I'm never going to allow myself to be put in that position again, of wanting something just for what it is.' Once I got the nomination [for *Patton*] I made it perfectly clear should I win, I would not accept it. I didn't do what Marlon did. I didn't wait until I won the fucking thing and tell them to jam it up their ass – which I think is rude.

George C. Scott
Playboy, December 1980

10   I told Howard Koch if I'm ever *nominated*, I'll be there to collect – in the nude.

Raquel Welch
Playboy, December 1979
(*See also* 175.13)

11   I don't care what they say to the press, I've never met an actor in my life who doesn't have an acceptance speech going through his head every day.

James Woods
Films Illustrated, April 1980

179 OSCAR WINNERS

1 I don't believe my wife has ever made love to an Academy Award winner before.

F. Murray Abraham
Best Supporting Actor, 15 March 1985

2 They reside with my father – who polishes them. Well, I'm certainly not going to put Oscars in my house.

Woody Allen
Time Out, 1 November 1989

3 If New York is the Big Apple, then Hollywood must be the Big Nipple.

Bernardo Bertolucci as *The Last Emperor* scored nine
April 1988

4 You're all sweet, wonderful people.

Sir Charles Chaplin (1889–1977) receiving his honorary Oscar, 10 April 1972.
('I hated all of them,' he admitted to *Sunday Times*, 22 January 1978)

5 The first time I hardly felt it because it was all so new . . . But now I feel it . . . You like me! You *like* me!

Sally Field, collecting her second
25 March 1985

6 When I won my first one, I was so contained – numb. All I could think of was: Don't fall down. I didn't have any underwear on.

Sally Field
Playboy, March 1986

7 My mother polishes them to an inch of their lives until the metal shows. That sums up the Academy Awards – all glitter on the outside and base metal coming through. Nice presents for a day. But they don't make you any better.

Glenda Jackson
People, 18 March 1985

8 I deserve this.

Shirley MacLaine, Best Supporting Actress, 9 April 1984.
(Later: 'I don't know what I said. Was it all right?')

9 A long time ago winning was pretty important but it's like chasing a beautiful woman. You hang in there for years, then she finally relents and you say: 'I'm too tired.'

Paul Newman
Photoplay, April 1989

10   I'd like to win more Oscars than Walt Disney and I'd like to win
them in every category.

Jack Nicholson (so far, he has won two Oscars in two categories)
Rolling Stone, March 1984

11   You have refused to be intimidated by the threats of a small
band of Zionist hoodlums whose behaviour is an insult to Jews all
over the world and their great and heroic record of struggle against
fascism and oppression.

Vanessa Redgrave
Best Supporting Actress, 29 March 1978

12   All I've won since is three days on *Bright Lights, Big City* as
Michael J. Fox's mother. That's what an Oscar does for you.

Dianne Wiest
Cannes, May 1987

180   PERSONALITY

1   People often confuse personality with talent.

Alain Delon
Films & Filming, 1964

2   I'm just me. That's all. I don't want to be a personality.

Richard Gere
Photoplay, November 1983

3   He is personality functioning.

Katharine Hepburn (on Cary Grant)
The Times, 8 January 1984

4   Personality is everything that's false in a human, everything
that's been added on to him and contrived.

Sam Shepard
New York Times, January 1984

5   You may say all my parts are the same. That's just what I want
you to think. You get lost on the screen if your personality doesn't
show through.

John Wayne (1907–79)
Guardian, 24 August 1974

6 It's not merely talent that brings them your way in Hollywood, but being noticed and talked about. I discussed it with my press agent and quite cold-bloodedly we invented this personality – a dumb blonde with a body and a set of sharp sayings.

Shelley Winters
Sunday Times, 2 May 1972

181 PHILOSOPHY

1 Every end is a beginning – or every beginning is an end.

Sonia Braga
Cannes, 13 May 1985

2 Whatever doesn't kill you, makes you stronger.

Marlon Brando (following Nietzsche)
International Herald Tribune, 28 September 1990

3 My Uncle Joe was a philosopher, very deep, very serious. Never eat chocolate after chick'n, he'd tell us, wagging his finger. Don't buy a cardboard belt.

Mel Brooks
Playboy, December 1974

4 You have to have something to get you out of bed. I can't do anything in bed anyway.

George Burns
Playboy, June 1978

5 Be like a duck, my mother used to tell me. Remain calm on the surface and paddle like hell underneath.

Michael Caine
Deathtrap publicity release, 1982

6 Never do anything you wouldn't want to be be caught dead doing.

John Carradine (1906–88) to son David
Film Yearbook, 1985

7 People try to change the world – instead of themselves.

John Cleese
The Times, 12 December 1987

8   We've no control over our conception, only over our creation.
Tony Curtis
Cannes, May 1982

9   If something doesn't come up the way you want, you have to
forge ahead. If you think it's going to rain, it will.
Clint Eastwood
Newsweek, 23 September 1985

10   My only enemy is me.
Elliott Gould
Photoplay, April 1979

11   You learn as much from the hand that you lead across the street
as it learns from you. Do you know what I mean?
William Hurt
Film Yearbook, 1985

12   Anything you have to acquire a taste for was not meant to be
eaten.
Eddie Murphy
Film Yearbook, 1986

13   There are two Newman's Laws. First, it's useless to put on your
brakes when you're upside down. Second, just when things look
darkest, they go black.
Paul Newman
Playboy, April 1983

14   I'm not a philosopher. Guilty bystander, that's my role.
Peter O'Toole
Sunday Times, 20 May 1990

15   You are your brother's keeper – and if you don't feel you are,
then you're not very philosophic.
Shelley Winters
That Lucky Touch publicity release, 1975

182 PLASTIC SURGERY

1   It's my body and if I want to do it like Michael Jackson, I will. My nose bothered me for a long time. Now it's smaller and I'm happy. If I wanna put my tits on my back, they're *mine*!

Cher
Playboy, December 1988

2   There's something horrid about a face-lift.

Joan Collins
Playboy, April 1984

3   You see women in America who've had face-lifts – faces as smooth as melons. It makes my stomach turn to think about voluntarily putting myself under a surgeon's knife.

Glenda Jackson
Daily Mail, 24 November 1978

4   When the time comes, I'm gonna have a face-lift, jaw-lift, eye-lift. Everything that's falling *will* be lifted. And the things that can't be lifted *will* be *moved*.

Little Richard
Film Yearbook, 1989

5   Plastic surgeons are always making mountains out of molehills.

Dolly Parton
Playboy, October 1978

6   I've considered having my nose fixed. But I didn't trust anyone enough. If I could do it myself with a mirror . . .

Barbra Streisand
Playboy, October 1977

183 POLITICAL OFFICE

1   If you ever hear that I'm running for office, you'll know that I've become a much more unselfish person than I am now.

Warren Beatty
People magazine, 14 April 1975

2 I'd love to enter politics. I will one day. I'd adore to be Prime Minister. And yes, I believe very strongly in Fascism.

David Bowie
Playboy, September 1976

3 Being Mayor of Carmel was a little bit time consuming. But there were some things that needed doing.

Clint Eastwood
Film Monthly, April 1989

4 Jane for president? Why not? Why not? She'd be good at anything she tried.

Henry Fonda (1905–82)
Playboy, December 1981

5 May I say, as long as actors are going into politics, I wish for Christ's sake that Sean Connery would become King of Scotland.

John Huston (1906–87)
Rolling Stone, 27 October 1981

6 Politics? Ah, the real entertainment . . . Some Californian people with a lot of money came to me and said they'd support me if I ran. I said if I could play six weeks in Vegas and do two pictures a year, I'd do it.

Shirley MacLaine
Playboy, September 1984

7 We stayed with one of my friends who had a book in which people were asked to write down their secret ambitions. Ronald Reagan wrote he'd like to be president. All those years ago!

Patricia Neal (on Reagan in 1949)
Photoplay, October 1986

8 I've been approached. But I won't run. Because I can barely, just barely, handle the aspect of my life that's public right now.

Paul Newman
Playboy, April 1983

9 People told me I could be Governor of California or the Senator, if I wanted to go that way. It wouldn't be the life for me. *They* live in a goldfish bowl.

Gregory Peck
Films Illustrated, October 1980

184 POLITICIANS

1 We should really call all politicians actors.

Marlon Brando
Newsweek, 13 March 1972

2 If presidents don't do it to their wives, they'll do it to the country.

Mel Brooks
Playboy, December 1974

3 I hate all politicians. They're the biggest bunch of bums you can find.

Michael Caine
Look, 30 May 1967

4 I listen to Reagan speak and I want to throw up.

Henry Fonda (1905–82)
Playboy, December 1981

5 We vote for a person: 'Seems like he's got integrity.' An actor is trained a long time to fake integrity.

Dustin Hoffman
Premiere (UK), 1970

6 I spent about 15 minutes with Jimmy Carter in the White House. God, I was uncomfortable. But that's my problem, not his.

Paul Newman
Rolling Stone, 20 January 1983

7 Nothing to see in their eyes. They all talk as though they're addressing a room filled with 40 000 people.

Robert Redford
Playboy, December 1974

185 POLITICS

1 I'm a Communist at heart.

Richard Burton (1925–84)
Variety, 31 July 1973

2 I've never voted in my life. I've no interest in secular politics or religion. I was probably a Communist at 16, a Socialist at 22 and now I'm quite definitely a capitalist.

Michael Caine
Independent, 25 May 1987

3 A rich man's sport or a prostitute's sport.

Richard Dreyfuss
Game, August 1976

4 I've always considered myself too individualistic to be either right-wing or left-wing.

Clint Eastwood
Newsweek, 23 September 1985

5 British people have a Socialist mind and a Conservative heart.

Albert Finney
Evening Standard, 12 November 1970

6 I'm a capitalist. I'm a producer.

Jean-Luc Godard
Variety, 8 October 1980

7 For me, *E.T.* is the greatest political film of all time. I think that Spielberg should be given the Nobel Peace Prize for that film.

Claude Lelouch
Film Yearbook, 1984

8 Like the movie business, politics are not what they were. Not the way it should be.

Robert Redford
Esquire, 1988

9 I don't go near politics.

Lynn Redgrave
TV Times, 1981

10 I'm as left-wing as it's possible to be.

Vanessa Redgrave
Sunday Mirror, 1969

11 If I'd been a Communist, I'd tell you to mind your own business. As I, and my husband, have never been Communist, I will tell you that.

Simone Signoret (1921–85)
Face To Face, BBC TV, 1962

12   I'm a Democrat with Republician underpinnings. I'm liberal about a lot of things but I'm bullish about America.
Steven Spielberg
Film Yearbook, 1987

186   PORNOGRAPHY

1   I don't know anything about French movies – I don't go to pornographic films.
Anonymous Roman Catholic anti-Godard's *Hail Mary* protester
New York, August 1985

2   Women especially are nice to me. I'm not a threat to them like Marilyn Monroe must have been. People sensed that she was naughty – but you never knew how naughty. Me, you know *exactly* how naughty I am.
Marilyn Chambers
Film Yearbook, 1986

3   I fell asleep during *Deep Throat*.
Joan Collins
Photoplay, 1978

4   The old stag films with the guys in masks, black socks and garters were more fun. So bad they were good. These new ones aren't any better. They're just in colour.
Clint Eastwood
Playboy, February 1974

5   Close to 17 000 stores are selling and renting video cassettes in the United States. The X-rated biz has become a home and hearth industry. We finally took sex out of the theatres and put it back in the bedroom where it belongs.
David F. Friedman, chairman, Adult Film Association of America
Film Yearbook, 1986

6   *Deep Throat* – I thought it was about giraffe.
Bob Hope
Playboy, December 1973

7   I can't say I was desperate and needed the money. I'd be a hypocrite if I did. *Deep Throat* was something I believed in and a fantastic opportunity for me to act. I loved every minute of it. We all have to start somewhere. Marilyn Monroe did it with that calendar, Lana Turner with a sweater. I had to go a little bit better.

Linda Lovelace
New Musical Express, 15 June 1974

8   I was naive, sure. Linda Lovelace was a robot who did what she had to do in order to survive and be alive today. I'd like to see pornography totally wiped out ... and everybody that's in it in a mental institution.

Linda Marchiano (ex-Lovelace)
London, 7 April 1981

187   POWER

1   They say he's obsessed with women. But he isn't. He's obsessed with power. He likes to dominate men as well as women.

Gabriel Byrne (on Warren Beatty)
Film Yearbook, 1988

2   Very powerful [people] have had what I call conscious deaths. Their egos have died a couple of times. Once you've had that, no one can hurt you anymore. No one can take anything away from you. You just gain. That kind of understanding is *really* power.

Rae Dawn Chong
Playboy, April 1987

3   No question – the more powerful men are, the more sexy they are.

Angie Dickinson
Photoplay, January 1985

4   The only power an actor has is the ability to say: 'No.'

Lou Diamond Phillips
Drama Logue, 4 February 1988

5   I've opened my mouth on a lot of subjects. And I thought the more prestige you get, I'd have the power to do what I like. It's not true.

Vanessa Redgrave
Evening Standard, 28 February 1969

6   Power corrupts but lack of power corrupts absolutely.
Orson Welles (1915–85)
Screen International, 6 October 1990

188   PRESS

1   I know that movie stars are over-rewarded in our society and that
the press has to cut people like me down to size. So, they make me
into an insane eccentric with an incredible fear of losing my youth,
who lives in a bomb shelter, who contemplates or is going through
plastic surgery, who has devastating relationships with women. It
goes through cycles. First, they say that women like me too much;
then, that women don't like me at all; then, that they like me too
much again. Somewhere along the way they say I secretly like men –
but then that men don't like me! I'm old, I'm young, I'm intelligent,
I'm stupid. My tides flow in and out.
Warren Beatty
Time, 3 July 1978

2   The American press is the most decadent, most unethical, most
lying profession I've ever come across. And I know of what I speak.
There was never a truthful thing written about *Apocalypse Now* in
four years. About the budget. About what we were doing. About the
film.
Francis Coppola
Films Illustrated, October 1979

3   Tabloid journalism in Britain is a great training ground for
Hollywood. If you can survive there, Hollywood is not the great nest
of sharks you think it's going to be.
Twins co-scenarist William Davis
Film Yearbook, 1990

4   I'll know my career's going bad when they start quoting me
correctly.
Lee Marvin (1924–87)
Quoted by Clint Eastwood, *Film Monthly*, April 1989

5   I'm not worried about the press. All those guys want to write screenplays for Robert Redford.

Hollywood's top agent Mike Ovitz
Premiere, January 1990

6   My aunt in Knoxville would bring newspapers up, which we used for toilet paper. Before we used it, we'd look at the pictures.

Dolly Parton
Playboy, October 1978

7   When they've treated me unfairly, I struck back. I've turned the other cheek. Hell, I've turned all four cheeks and I still get the short end.

Frank Sinatra
TV Guide, 1977

8   I don't care what you say about me. Just be sure to spell my name wrong.

Barbra Streisand
Time, 10 April 1964

9   I'm tired of malicious articles slandering me.

Barbra Streisand
Playboy, October 1977

189   PRIVACY

1   I still have the privacy that all celebrities crave, except for those celebrities who feel that privacy reflects some kind of failure on their part.

Albert Brooks
Playboy, July 1983

2   I didn't become an actress so that my life could be exposed. It's really the only thing that makes me contemplate quitting.

Michelle Pfeiffer
Vanity Fair, February 1989

3   I wish I was the same girl making *One Million Years* BC – all open, optimistic and confident. Now I realize why all the stars yell and scream about their privacy – you don't really have any.

Raquel Welch
Man, 1967

190 PRODUCERS

1   Once I became interested in stories and getting stories told, I realized I had to be a producer to get them told the right way.

Warren Beatty
Photoplay, July 1975

2   I'm not interested in directing. Now, producing! I noticed when it starts to rain, the only person who goes back to the hotel is the producer.

Michael Caine
The Ottawa Citizen, 17 September 1982

3   I was always a director and I just produce for myself as it gets rid of the producer who's usually an unpleasant person.

Michael Winner
Film Yearbook, 1987

4   Producers are assholes. How's that for a quote? They're schmucks, they're deal-makers. They know all the tricks of the trade but they don't know the trade, itself. Producers know how to steal money, how to put together packages. They're liars and thieves. They have no value in life. They don't believe in anything.

James Woods
Playboy, April 1982

191 PRODUCERS BY STARS

1   What's extraordinary is that I've never worked with this man [David Puttnam]. As far as I know, I've met him only three times. And yet he goes around saying these horrible things about me.

Dustin Hoffman
Los Angeles Times, 3 April 1983
(*See also* 192.4)

2   George Harrison is a sweet sort of hapless character who doesn't have a mean bone in his body.

Madonna
Rolling Stone, 5 June 1986

3 Everybody's worked with a jerk in their lives and I'd work with David Puttnam tomorrow – if he's got a script.

Bill Murray
The Irish Times, 16 December 1988

4 Extraordinary man. I've never known a greater vulgarian – not even Kruschev. He calls my wife [Joanne Woodward] Joan.

Paul Newman (on Jack Warner)
Playboy, 1969

5 Collaboration – that's the word producers use. That means, don't forget to kiss ass from beginning to end.

Sam Shepard
Newsweek, 11 November 1985

192 PRODUCERS ON STARS

1 To me she [Kim Basinger] is Marilyn Monroe, Brigitte Bardot and Judy Holliday in one girl – with the talent of Julie Christie. She's the most talented girl I've seen in my life. Just looking at her makes me want to screw her.

Menahem Golan
GQ, December 1985

2 He's a strange, difficult boy, but the most wonderful actor of his generation. He reminds me of Brando and James Dean. He's only at half-speed now. If he could concentrate for eight out of 12 hours, instead of three, he could be the greatest actor. He may never realize his full potential. That may be his tragedy.

Alan Marshall (on Mickey Rourke)
Arena, July 1989

3 Howard Hughes said one time: 'My God, Mitch, you're just like a pay toilet – you don't give a shit for nothin'.'

Robert Mitchum
Ritz, No. 143, 1989

4 My experience with him [Dustin Hoffman] was an unhappy one. There seemed to be a malevolence in him, a determination to make other human beings unhappy.

David Puttnam
Film Yearbook, 1984
(*See also* 191.1)

193 PRODUCING

1 If Delon is to be sold, why shouldn't he be sold by Delon.
Alain Delon
Films & Filming, 1964

2 The reason I started Malpaso was I saw a lot of inefficiencies and thought I can screw up as good as the next person. I'd rather be the cause of my own demise.
Clint Eastwood
Film Comment, October 1984

3 Producing life is better than producing films.
Cary Grant (1904–86) (on fatherhood at 62)
Daily Mail, June 11 1976

4 I do it simply because someone has to. It's a thankless task more akin to hotel management.
David Hemmings
Screen International, 11 May 1978

5 Keep Films is a company formed by Jules Buck and myself for the purposes of getting rich. We'll make films with anyone who interests us – even United Dairies.
Peter O'Toole
Scene, 12 December 1962

6 I'd rather direct. Any day. And twice on Sundays.
Steven Spielberg
Rolling Stone, 24 October 1985

194 PSYCHOANALYSIS

1 I was in analysis for years because of a traumatic childhood. I was breast-fed through falsies.
Woody Allen
Newsweek, 24 April 1978

2 There's streak of madness in the family. I've a horrible fear it's genetic. One of the reasons I've never been in analysis is I've always been afraid of what I might find out.
David Bowie
Photoplay, September 1983

3   I'd rather go mad than see a psychiatrist.

Michael Caine
Playboy, 1966

4   I first went into analysis because the group I went around with –
Paul Newman, Natalie Wood, James Dean, Marlon Brando, Joanne
Woodward – were in analysis. It was the done thing.

Joan Collins
The Observer, 6 October 1985

5   The British have always been so anti-analysis – in every sense of
the word.

Sean Connery
Evening Standard, 24 March 1972

6   Almost went three times – almost. Then I decided what was
peculiar about me was probably what made me successful. I've seen
some very talented actors go into analysis and really lose it.

Bette Davis (1908–89)
Playboy, July 1982

7   My life has been off balance. So I went into analysis as one would
go to a dentist for a toothache. To cure it.

Gérard Depardieu
Time, 6 February 1984

8   I know too many people who use it as a crutch. Give us this day
our daily analysts.

Dustin Hoffman
Time, 7 February 1969

9   I once went – my mother insisted. She came with me. I decided to
lie about everything. I told him my mother was terrible to me, I'd
had an unhappy childhood, my parents fought all the time. Finally,
my mother got so mad, she hit me. The doctor advised we should
both be put away as crazy and dangerous.

Melina Mercouri
Sunday Express, 15 August 1965

10   It helped me to have a more realistic appraisal of myself, to get
in touch with my emotions. Some of it was effective. Some of it was
helpful. A lot of it was irrelevant.

Paul Newman
Playboy, April 1983

11   My therapy was all Reichian, which is all sexual.

Jack Nicholson
Rolling Stone, 29 March 1984

12 I don't go for this auto-cannibalism. Very damaging.
Peter O'Toole
Daily Mail, 1 October 1973

13 Some people have analysis. I have Utah.
Robert Redford
Daily Mail, February 1977

14 Four visits. I kept laughing. I couldn't get serious. If it helps you, it helps you. If standing on your head on roof helps you, it helps you – if you think so.
George C. Scott
Playboy, December 1980

15 I solve my problems with the movies I make. Where there's a character in conflict in a movie, some part of that character is part of me that needs to be straightened out.
Steven Spielberg
Film Yearbook, 1987

16 Couches are for one thing only.
John Wayne (1907–79)
Time, 8 August 1969

195 PUBLIC

1 I love people too much to be just the object of their taste, their fashion. I want the public to love me, sure. But not to adore me.
Gérard Depardieu
Films Illustrated, May 1978

2 You can't live up to what people expect. Nobody can. But I guess that's my problem not theirs.
Mel Gibson
Rolling Stone, 29 August 1988

3 The public are people like me who don't know what to do. So, they go to the movies.
Marcello Mastroianni
Il Corriere Della Sera, 3 August 1985

4 The second you step out of the confines of the personality the public has set for you, they get incensed. Public reaction tends to keep actors as personalities instead of allowing them to act. It's a very corrupting influence.

Paul Newman
Photoplay, 1977

5 I'm afraid the public knows me too well. They know every shade of voice, every trick, every goddammed movement I can make.

Lord Laurence Olivier (1907–89)
Newsweek, 1979

196 PUBLIC RECOGNITION

1 In New York, people aren't impressed – unless you're an athlete. You can be the Pope and they'll say: 'Hey Pope, howya doin'?' Al Pacino walking down the street and it's: 'Hey, Al – the movie *Author, Author!* – it sucked!' But if you're Mike Tyson: 'Mike, I love ya!'

Alec Baldwin
Premiere, April 1990

2 On the train, people say: 'Aren't you the girl in *The Golden Child*?' I say: 'Yes.' And they say: 'Wot you doin' on a train then?'

Charlotte Lewis
Ritz, No. 118, March 1987

3 I was in the ladies room with her when I was about 14 and this drunk lady came in and started saying: 'Oh, Judy, whatever happens, never forget the rainbow.' And Mama said, exiting grandly: 'Madame, how *could* I forget the rainbow, I've got rainbows up my ass.' Oh yes, she could be a terror.

Liza Minnelli
Rolling Stone, 10 May 1973

4 People come up: 'God, I know you, I *know* you!' And I say: 'Yeah, we went to high school together.' And for a few seconds, they'll actually believe it.

Dennis Quaid
Premiere, October 1987

5   People walk up to me: '*Taxi Driver*, right?' People get actors confused. A guy pays his $4, sees a face, goes home; he doesn't remember.

Roy Scheider
Cue, 1 February 1980

6   My biggest nightmare is I'm driving home and get sick and go to hospital. I say: 'Please help me.' And the people say: 'Hey, you look like . . .' And I'm dying while they're wondering whether I'm Barbra Streisand.

Barbra Streisand
Playboy, October 1977

197   PUBLICITY

1   First time I went to America to promote *The Family Way*, the man from Warner Brothers called: 'Please spend some more money, godammit!' A couple of years later, I went back to promote *Twisted Nerve* and they were demanding to know what I wanted: drugs, chicks, booze, anything? It got so ridiculous, I actually had to ask the film company not to send any more women around.

Hywel Bennett
Daily Mail, 19 April 1975

2   I'm not going to place myself at the feet of the American public and invite them into my soul. My soul is a private place.

Marlon Brando
Playboy, January 1979

3   I don't think it's ever been the actor's job to sell a film. I find it demoralizing. If he can't stand to go to premieres and get groped by middle-aged ladies, there's no reason for him to have to.

Paul Newman
Cinema TV Today, 6 January 1973

4   They held up *The Outlaw* for five years. And Howard Hughes had me doing publicity for it every day, five days a week for five years.

Jane Russell
Cinéma, Cinémas, Antenne 2 (French TV), 1985

5   I'm not some bosomy starlet. I don't need to fall in with the demands of the ritual publicity machine.

Frank Sinatra
Sunday Express, 7 August 1966

6   A picture is worth a thousand words – 10 000! If you want publicity, you can't sit around waiting for it. You've got to throw it in their faces.

Edy Williams
California magazine, January 1984

198   QUALITY

1   It's up to us to produce better-quality movies.

Lloyd Kaufman, producer of *Stuff Stephanie In The Incinerator*
Cannes, May 1989

199   Q & A

1   *Why make so many films and not return to the stage?* Because I couldn't bear not to have somewhere to go in the mornings.

Richard Burton (1925–84) to Gabriel Byrne
Film Yearbook, 1989

2   Joan Rivers: *You've had a lot of lovers. Who was your best lover?*
Joan Collins: Your husband.

American TV, 1984

3   *How many husbands have you had?* You mean apart from my own?

Zsa Zsa Gabor
American TV, 1985

4   *How would you answer the people calling you a naive actor?* Fuck 'em!

Bob Hoskins (interviewing himself)
Lunettes Noires pour les Nuits Blanches, Antenne 2 (French TV), 1988

5 *You've just made* The 5th Monkey *and Kim Novak's comeback,*
The Children. *Which is the most difficult to act with: monkeys or
children?* Kim Novak.
Ben Kingsley
Cannes, May 1990

6 *You've probably been in more movies with Dean Martin than Jerry
Lewis?* I've probably been in more movies with Dean Martin than
even Dean Martin has.
Shirley MacLaine
Playboy, September 1984

7 *When are you going to direct again?* When they let me.
Jack Nicholson
Cannes, 16 May 1981

200 RACE

1 I had to change my name from Segal to Benson because of
anti-semitism. When I was 10 or 11, I went up for an audition and
they said: 'That ugly little Jewish kid.' So I wasn't getting any work.
I changed my name and started doing okay.
Robby Benson
Playgirl, August 1979

2 Our relationship with the [American] Indians is unprecendented
in history. No group of people has ever so consciously and cruelly
suppressed another group as Americans have the Indians.
Marlon Brando
Playboy, January 1979

3 My comedy comes from the feeling that, as a Jew, and as a
person, you don't fit into the mainstream of American society. It
comes from the realization that even though you're better and
smarter, you'll never belong.
Mel Brooks
Newsweek, 17 February 1975

4   Actors have no colour. That is the art form. They ask me all the time: 'Well, what would you really like to do, Whoopi?' I say: 'I wanna do *A Lion In Winter*.' They say: 'But-but-but-but – Eleanor of Aquitaine was . . . y'know . . .!' I say: 'Thin? Old?' They say: 'But you are . . . y'know . . .' And I say: 'Thin? Old?' 'No, Whoopi, you are . . . *black*!' I say: '*No!*' As if I didn't know.

Whoopi Goldberg
Deauville, September 1990

5   It was a hot day in 1957, when I was 11. I walked over to the public water fountains. One was marked WHITE, the other COLOURED. Who wants coloured water, I thought, as I headed to the WHITE fountain. I want the white, clear water. Instantly, about eight guys from the show grabbed me. Nothing was said. But at that moment, I understood something new: coloured meant me.

Gregory Hines
Playboy, September 1986

6   The biggest lie is that if you're American it doesn't matter what race, creed, nationality you are – the colour of your skin doesn't matter, it's the person that you are and if you do a good job, you can succeed. Bullshit! Race has everything to do with everything.

Spike Lee
Paris Passion, December 1989

7   I use racial slurs but I don't hate anybody.

Eddie Murphy
Rolling Stone, 12 April 1984

8   I hate to think my avenues of artistic expression were circumscribed by my colour.

Sidney Poitier
Showtime, 1967

9   A lot of Italians have played Indians. Well, someday, I'd like to play an Italian.

Creek Indian actor Will Sampson (1934–87)
Photoplay, 1976

10   One lady told me that before she saw *Sounder*, she didn't believe black people could love each other, have deep relationships in the same way as white people.

Cicely Tyson
Daily Mail, 23 February 1973

201 *RAMBO*

1 I wouldn't have made the picture – is it *Rainbow? Rambo?* – whatever its name is – I wouldn't have made it even if I'd known it was going to make so many millions of dollars.

John Huston (1906–1987)
Cinecitta, 11 December 1985

2 It's true – I was thinking of Rimbaud. I began the novel in 1969 while studying for my PhD in American Lit. at Penn. State University. I had my BA in English Lit., so I was broadening out. I was reading Rimbaud when my wife came from the supermarket she had some apples. Rambo apples! Of such accidents . . .

Rambo creator David Morrell
Knave, June 1986

3 I love *Rambo* but I think it's potentially a very dangerous movie. It changes history in a frightening way.

Steven Spielberg
Rolling Stone, 24 October 1985

4 Rocky gets his power from the people around him – his family. Rambo has nothing. Rambo is an experiment gone wrong.

Sylvester Stallone
Rolling Stone, December 1985

5 When President Reagan stood up and said: 'Having seen *Rambo* I know what to do with Libya,' it was the kiss of death. He made Rambo a Republican.

Sylvester Stallone
Sunday Express magazine, 17 July 1988

6 *Rambo IV* is the last one. It's concerned with environmental issues. Rambo will be working for, like, Greenpeace.

Sylvester Stallone
Cap d'Antibes, 13 May 1990

202 RELIGION

1 My real obsessions are religious – to do with the meaning of life and the futility of obtaining immortality through art.

Woody Allen
Time, 30 April 1979

2   I don't believe in organizations telling people what to do in the obedience sense.

Susan Anspach
Cannes, 24 May 1981

3   The weak rely on Christ, the strong do not.

Richard Burton (1925–84)
Playboy, 1963

4   I'm a Zen-Buddhist student first, actor second. If I can't reconcile the two lives, I'll stop acting. I spend more time off-screen than on.

Peter Coyote
Cannes, 8 May 1987

5   I believe in reincarnation, divorce and abortion.

Laura Dern
Rolling Stone, February 1986

6   My idea of a religious experience would be standing on Half Dome looking down into Yosemite Valley.

Clint Eastwood
Newsweek, 23 September 1985

7   I only believe in the SEBF Association. Screw Everybody But Fields.

W.C. Fields (1879–1946)
Quoted by Bob Hope, *Playboy*, December 1973

8   I'm an agnostic – means I don't know the answers.

Henry Fonda (1905–82)
Playboy, December 1981

9   I'm a retired Christian with a capital C. I was brought up Catholic and educated by nuns whose hands had never felt a man. All I believe in that a No. 11 bus goes along the Strand to Hammersmith but I know it isn't being driven by Santa Claus.

Peter O'Toole
Daily Mail, 16 June 1972

10   Basically, I'm for anything that gets you through the night – be it prayer, tranquilizers or a bottle of Jack Daniels.

Frank Sinatra
Playboy, 1962

203 REPUTATIONS

1   Because I first appeared in *Behind The Green Door* when I was 19, everyone thinks I'm stuffed away in some geriatric ward now.

Marilyn Chambers at 35
Film Yearbook, 1986

2   People thought I was sleeping with the entire Mormon Tabernacle Choir. They believe what they want to believe.

Cher
Rolling Stone, 29 March 1984

3   To some people I *am* rude and aggressive – they provoke about 50% of it by their attitude to me. I can't go around with a welcome mat around my neck.

Sean Connery
Playboy, 1965

4   I suppose many people don't even know if I'm still alive – well, perhaps I'm not.

Douglas Fairbanks Jr
Film Yearbook, 1990

5   I've met those who I thought were – perhaps – connected with the Mafia and they weren't all that dreadful.

John Huston (1906–87)
Cinecitta, 11 December 1985

6   People found out I came from this upper-class background, a wealthy industrial family, very traditional. I had this reputation of being a playboy, making films for the sake of something to do. That really got on my nerves, because I was working very hard at what I was doing. If I'd been more gifted, it would have been easier.

Louis Malle
Today, 28 January 1990

7   My reputation as a wild man, you gotta understand was always a little . . . well, hmm, exaggerated. Christ, my *mother's* had stranger things happen to her.

Lee Marvin (1924–87)
Rolling Stone, 21 December 1972

8   You wanna be bad, don't be bad in a Hollywood restaurant, with a bunch of wimpy photographers. Punching a photographer – what's that? Try going to jail. Plenty of guys there who'll kick your ass for a nickel.

Mickey Rourke (on Sean Penn)
Film Yearbook, 1988

9   People don't credit me with much of a brain. So why should I disillusion them.

Sylvester Stallone
Film Yearbook, 1984

10   There's all this hodge-podge that (a) I'm a stupid girl who just happens to be attractive; (b) a film star without being seen in a film; and (c) that I connived my way to fame and fortune.

Raquel Welch
Showtime, 1967

204   RETIREMENT

1   I'm a retired film-maker.

Ingmar Bergman
Film Yearbook, 1985

2   I couldn't retire.

Sean Connery
Film Yearbook, 1985

3   I will not retire while I've still got my legs and my make-up box.

Bette Davis (1908–89) (and she didn't)
TV Times, 1972

4   I never retired. I just did something else.

Doris Day
Time, 29 July 1985

5   When you're not interested in trying new things that's when you should start hitting golf balls.

Clint Eastwood
Films Illustrated, February 1981

6   Quitters don't win and winners don't quit.

Elliott Gould
Photoplay, 1977

7   It wasn't so much a question of me finishing with movies. Movies finished with me.

Stewart Granger
Radio Times, 5 October 1972

8   No press conference announcing a last film. I'd just steal away. Best way because, if by chance after two or three years something interesting comes up, I would not – like Sinatra – have to say: 'Well, I've thought it over and decided to come back.'

Sophia Loren
Paris, 23 February 1974

9   I think about it. Every morning! But some years ago I lost a lot of money. The cupboard was bare.

Robert Mitchum
Ritz, No. 143, 1989

10   Actors never retire. They're just offered fewer parts.

David Niven (1909–83)
Evening Standard, 29 October 1976

11   My days as an actor are numbered.

Robert Redford
Photoplay, January 1977

12   I wish to announce, effective immediately, my retirement from the entertainment world and public life.

Frank Sinatra
Evening Standard, 24 March 1971
(Two years later, Ole Blue Eyes is back and: 'I'll do what I'm doing for another five or six years, then get the hell out before becoming a bore.' *TV Guide*, April 1977)

205   REVIEWS

See also 68 Criticism
69 Critics

1   When Rex Reed wrote that I had a face like an open sandwich, that was the best moment so far. It's just a thing of mine – I've always wanted to be compared to deli food.

Albert Brooks
Playboy, July 1983

2 I'd get *really* worried if we got all good reviews. You mean we fooled them *all*?

Tommy Chong
Playboy, September 1982

3 You can't believe reviews, good or bad.

Joan Collins
Screen International, 19 May 1979

4 My agent, a great man called Lew Wasserman, took me to the public library to borrow a book on acting by Stanislavsky. Then, we went to the *New York Times* and he had them pull out the reviews of Grant, Gable and Cagney in the 30s. 'If you still feel depressed after reading those notices,' he said, 'you can start on the book.' I couldn't believe it. Their notices were diabolical. They'd all been slaughtered in their early days.

Tony Curtis
Sunday Express, 10 October 1965

5 His Kraft is Ebing.

Washington critic Margot Kernan (on Woody Allen)
Film Yearbook, 1984

6 She runs the gamut of emotions from A to B.

Dorothy Parker (1893–1967) (on Katharine Hepburn in *Spitfire* 1934)
('Extremely accurate and funny,' Hepburn told *The Times*, 28 April 1969)

7 If I kept all my bad notices, I'd need two houses.

Roger Moore
Time, 1 November 1982

8 Whenever I got a good review, I'd think the studio paid for it. Or, perhaps, I'd met the critic and they'd liked me. I just didn't believe that something good was being written about me for no reason. It's taken me a long time to be convinced.

Michelle Pfeiffer
Los Angeles Times, 3 March 1985

9 I wish I could be like Shaw who once read a bad review of one of his plays, called the critic and said: 'I have your review in front of me and soon it will be behind me.'

Barbra Streisand
Playboy, October 1977

206 ROCK 'N' ROLL

1 I'd like to see John Lennon play Trotsky.

Jean-Luc Godard
Rolling Stone, 14 June 1969

2 I saw what happened to Elvis Presley which is why I never wanted to be a star in the first place.

Goldie Hawn
Playboy, January 1985

3 I cast actors from rock because they're sensitive to what people want. They're performers. Their antennas are screwed on right. They don't mind getting right in there and having a go at the truth.

Nagisa Oshima
Photoplay, September 1983

4 I don't think of them as singers. They're performers, prepared to get up and perform. They're free of a pattern of acting I'm not happy with.

Nicolas Roeg
Game, August 1976

207 ROLES BY ACTORS

1 I'd never [play] a pimp or a drug-runner. I wouldn't do anything I wouldn't want my guru to see.

Saxophonist-turned-actor Clarence Clemons
Film Yearbook, 1986

2 I can't fix my car though I play characters who can.

Kevin Costner
Time, 26 June 1989

3 I tend to be drawn to characters who are totally outside my own experience, whose motivations I don't understand. Anyone who isn't like me. God, yes, as unlike me as possible!

Daniel Day Lewis
Arena, autumn 1989

4 I prefer to be like a gambler: if you don't throw, you'll never know.

Robert De Niro
Screen International, May 1976

5 I don't play rabbits! I couldn't do what Robert Redford does.

Gérard Depardieu
Mulhouse (France), 9 September 1976

6 I do the kinds of roles I'd like to see if I were still digging swimming pools and wanted to escape my problems.

Clint Eastwood
Time, 9 January 1978

7 Film people find it difficult to *place* me. The number of films that deal with crowned heads of Europe is rather limited.

Sir John Gielgud
Radio Times, 4 November 1971

8 I think I gave my best performance, perhaps, during the war – pretending to be an officer and gentleman.

Sir Alec Guinness
Film Yearbook, 1984

9 I've played three presidents, three saints and two geniuses – and that's probably enough for any man.

Charlton Heston
Evening Standard, 1969

10 The hardest role for me would be something I had no interest in – in the worst script ever written. Now, *that* would be a challenge.

Dustin Hoffman
Cinéma, Cinémas, Antenne 2 (French TV), 1989

11 I've played everything except midgets and women.

Robert Mitchum
Ritz, No. 143, 1989

12 I've a feeling that the film character enters my body as *if I were a medium*. I get so damned deep into it, I become another living person.

Peter Sellers (1925–80)
Sunday Dispatch, 25 September 1960

13 I've played the kinda man I'd like to have been.

John Wayne (1907–79)
Daily Mail, 18 January 1974

208 ROLES BY ACTRESSES

1 I wish sometimes I could play roles I don't believe in. It might give me a wider range.
Ingrid Bergman (1915–82)
Sunday Express, 8 December 1963

2 I'm either offered window-dressing parts in large movies – or little art films no one ever sees. People think the movies I end up doing are my real choices. I do the best things I'm offered.
Jacqueline Bisset
People, 5 May 1980

3 At my age, you don't get much variety – usually some old nut who's off her track.
Katharine Hepburn
The Times, 28 April 1969

4 Women's roles – forget it. You're either the prostitute. Or this rash of this contemporary women – like, the city DA, who's divorced, who has these two fabulous kids and can take care of them and also has a great sex life. That superwoman kind of thing.
Amy Madigan
Washington Post, May 1985

5 I choose my roles carefully so that when my career is finished, I'll have covered all our current history of oppression.
Vanessa Redgrave
Film Yearbook, 1984

6 In my movie, I play a 17-year-old girl because I was 17 at the time of making it.
Brooke Shields
Photoplay, February 1984

7 I've played bad women, wicked women – and they don't pay. If you play them too well, people hate you.
Simone Signoret (1921–85)
Face To Face, BBC TV, 1962

8 I'm always offered straightforward women with integrity. Even in *Half Moon Street*, I'm a hooker with integrity.
Sigourney Weaver
Playboy, August 1986

209 ROOTS

1 Part of him is Swiss. Therefore, he is partly a banker.
John Boorman (on Jean-Luc Godard)
Money Into Light, 1985

2 Cockneys are poor, but they are never defeated and they always smile. I'll be a Cockney until I die.
Michael Caine
Playboy, 1966

3 Like most Celts, I'm moody.
Sean Connery
Sunday Express, 1967

4 We Welshmen like to think of ourselves as heroes.
Timothy Dalton
Photoplay, November 1986

5 I'm Czech, German and Irish – so I'm all mixed up.
Jim Jarmusch
Cannes, May 1986

6 Show a Welshman 1001 exits, one of which is marked 'Self-Destruction' and he'll go right through that one.
Joseph L. Mankiewicz
Time, 26 April 1963

7 I was born Greek. I will die Greek.
Melina Mercouri when the Colonels cancelled her passport. (Elected to the Greek parliament in 1977, she became Culture Minister in 1981)
Look, 8 May 1976

8 I come from a very good family, descendants from Alfred the Great.
Mae West (1893–1980)
Playboy, 1970

210 RUMOURS

1 I don't know why people think I'm running around with everybody. A friend told me: 'I hear you went out with Daryl Hannah.' I said: 'I did? How was I?'
Tom Cruise
Film Yearbook, 1988

2   According to the doctors, I'm only suffering from a light form of premature baldness.

Federico Fellini (after four headlined days in a Rome clinic)
Variety, 1986

3   Most memorable rumour about me? That I wanted to eat my son's placenta! How do you defend yourself against something like that?

Barbara Hershey
Playboy, May 1987

4   Best thing I ever heard was that I married Sean Penn. And I'd never even met him.

Kelly McGillis
Playboy, 1987

5   Rumours? They're all true. Booze, broads. Make up some more if you want to.

Robert Mitchum
Paris Passion, June 1990

6   There were even stories going around about how I was . . . well, getting my secretary to peel grapes.

Sylvester Stallone
Film Yearbook, 1983

---

211   SALARIES

---

1   If you're Dustin Hoffman and you get $5 million with your share of the percentage, you're not in a hurry to make another film. I make a lot less. But I have the same standard of living as Dustin, so I have to make a lot of movies.

Michael Caine
Film Yearbook, 1985

2   I ask for the money I want, they pay it. It's that simple.

Harrison Ford
Film Yearbook, 1984

3   You get to a certain point with the money when it doesn't really matter. Uncle Sambo's going to get most of it, anyway.

Gene Hackman
Hollywood Reporter, April 1972

4 It's true. I get $50 000 a year from the profits from *The Bridge on the River Kwai*. Sounds like something. Until you break it down: 10% goes to the agent, 20% is withheld for taxes, 50% of what's left goes to my ex-wife. Add up other things I hadn't thought of – and I end up seeing about $5800 a year from my 10% of the gross profits.

William Holden (1918–81)
Photoplay, September 1978

5 Nobody is worth what they pay me.

Burt Reynolds
Penthouse, 1972

6 Eleven million dollars is what Jack Nicholson got for *Batman*. Eleven million! He was in *Ironweed*, if you recall. OK. All right. He was in *Heartburn*, if you remember. OK. I was in *Out of* fucking *Africa*, remember? *Kramer vs. Kramer*! *Deer Hunter*! I'm saying it's a guy's game. If I asked for $11 million they would laugh. In my face.

Meryl Streep
Premiere, December 1989

212 SCHOOLDAYS

1 I was always the creative kid who was a nerd. I listened to Vivaldi, wrote poetry and actually did my homework.

Laura Dern
Rolling Stone, February 1986

2 I was a wise-ass at school. Pretty much equal parts – wise and ass.

Cheech Marin
Rolling Stone, 14 December 1978

3 I hated school. Even to this day, when I see a school bus it's just depressing to me. The poor little kids.

Dolly Parton
Playboy, October 1978

4   I was an ugly little kid with a big mouth, an obnoxious show-off.
Nobody liked me. I was bossy, prim and determined. I looked
middle-aged and the other kids thought I was one of the teachers.
Meryl Streep
New York Times magazine, 4 February 1980

213   SCIENCE FICTION

1   I don't know what my part is about. Take my name: Obi Wan
Kenobi. I haven't a clue what it's meant to mean.
Sir Alec Guinness (on *Star Wars*)
Daily Mail, 17 December 1977

2   I'm not crazy about science fiction and I'd never read *Dune*. When
Dino's [De Laurentiis] office called me, I thought they said: *June*.
David Lynch
Film Yearbook, 1986

214   SCRIPTS

1   I really don't like reading scripts. It's a real effort for me, which is
not very good. I might throw something good out – like a *Platoon*.
Nicolas Cage
Cannes, 9 May 1987

2   Every asshole has a script in his back pocket.
Director Larry Cohen
Film Yearbook, 1986

3   I hate reading scripts. They're not interesting. No photos!
Béatrice Dalle
French TV, 1987

4   About 40 a week come into my business manager's office. My car
mechanic gets a stack, too!
Harrison Ford
Deauville, September 1982

5   There are no great scripts – just great films.

Malcolm McDowell
Photoplay, March 1977

6   They literally spring out of the parking lots at you with scripts –
nobody can read a thousand scripts a year and still work.

Jack Nicholson
Time Out, 20 February 1976

7   In my naivety, I handed in a screenplay for *Sparkle* that was over
300 pages long. When I asked: 'Howda like the story?' – the answer
was: 'Which one?'

Joel Schumacher
Film Yearbook, 1987

8   With Francis [Coppola], a script is like a newspaper. You get a
new one every day.

Art director Dean Tavoularis
Film Yearbook, 1991

9   The text is never important. One has to say it, play it, of course.
What is vital is what's in-between the words – behind them.

Jean-Louis Trintignant
Films Illustrated, July 1979

10   L.B. Mayer tried to get me to write stories for the blonde one
[Jean Harlow]. 'Give her a sophisticated story,' he says. And I says:
'If I got good ideas, L.B., I gotta keep 'em for myself.'

Mae West (1893–1980)
Playboy, 1970

215   SECOND GENERATION

1   Emilio Estevez and Charlie Sheen both look like their dad – but
they don't look like each other.

Director Chris Cain
Deauville, 7 September 1986

2   On my 17th birthday, my mother gave me a set of luggage.
'What's that for?' She said: 'Guess.' And I moved out right away.

Nick Cassavetes (on mother Gena Rowlands)
Playgirl, October 1988

3   I thought it'd be easy to get into movies as Charlie Chaplin's daughter. And I suppose it was. Except I wasn't much good as an actress – really terrible at the beginning.

Geraldine Chaplin
Sunday Times, 1976

4   I decided to be an actress at nine and my mom [actress Diane Ladd] was against it. So, when I was 11, I got my own agent.

Laura Dern
Rolling Stone, February 1986

5   If I'd known what a big shot Michael was going to be, I would've been nicer to him as a kid.

Kirk Douglas
Playboy, February 1986

6   There's a certain bit taken away from you because you physically look like your father and may sound like him. People will remind you about it all the time which is debilitating. Now [my brothers] have their oldest brother to worry about as well. I feel for them. I know I had a certain amount to overcome with *Spartacus* as a father image.

Michael Douglas
Films Illustrated, September 1979

7   I wish I had their guts.

Henry Fonda (1905–82) (on Jane and Peter)
People, 7 April 1975

8   When I did *The Happy Hooker Goes To Hollywood*, my father told me: 'That's one of the worst pieces of shit I've ever seen and you stunk.' Quote. Unquote.

Chris Lemmon
Playgirl, October 1988

---

216   SELF-PORTRAITS (FEMALE)

---

1   I'm a wreck. I get hurt very easily. I don't have a tough shell. I'm so insecure – it's pretty stupid for me for me in this business, isn't it?

Rosanna Arquette
Rolling Stone, 9 May 1985

2   I don't smoke. I don't drink to speak off. I don't take drugs at all.
I take care of my two children. I've been married twice, once for 11
years and once for three. I don't go out with more than one man at a
time. But you know what it is: I dress strange.

Cher
New York Times, January 1984

3   I have a good mind but I don't like to bore anyone with it.

Rae Dawn Chong
Film Yearbook, 1988

4   I'm independent, strong, determined. I live off my nerves. I'm a
sensualist. I enjoy pain and happiness and all the emotions.

Julie Christie
Daily Mail, September 1965

5   I'm a giraffe. I even walk like a giraffe with a long neck and
legs. It's a pretty dumb animal, mind you.

Sophia Loren
Sunday Times, 1 April 1979

6   I'm certain I was a prostitute in some other life. I just have
empathy for them.

Shirley MacLaine
Playboy, September 1984

7   I'm working my way toward divinity.

Bette Midler
Rolling Stone, 9 December 1982

8   A large part of me is pure nebbish – plain, dull, uninteresting.
There's a more flamboyant part, too. Obviously.

Barbra Streisand
Rolling Stone, 24 June 1971

9   I'm Mother Courage, baby. I've been through it all.

Elizabeth Taylor
Photoplay, 1981

217   SELF-PORTRAITS (MALE)

1   I'm not as normal as I appear.

Woody Allen
Time, 14 April 1976

2   I am Richard, son of Richard – for I am both my father and my son. Devious, difficult and perverse. A mess of contradictions.

Richard Burton (1925–84)
Playboy, 1963

3   I have the worst possible character and am constantly hurting people, especially those who love me most. I learned very young that no one's going to tolerate me. I either charm people or they detest me.

Alain Delon
Stage & TV (South Africa), 1973

4   Describe myself? That's a tough one.

Robert De Niro
Deauville, 4 September 1988

5   I'm not worldly, a bit of a savage really. I love the trees, the isolation, the soul. I've a mystic temperament, an independence that prevents me from constantly looking into myself. I'm not suicidal but alive, excessive, bloody-minded, above all a traveller without need for medicaments to assist my journey.

Gérard Depardieu
The Observer magazine, 3 April 1990

6   I'm a sonuvabitch. Plain and simple. Why try to act the nice guy?

Kirk Douglas
Daily Express, February 1964

7   I'm an ordinary, 42-year-old creaky set of bones and I have to work out to get in shape for a film.

Harrison Ford
Time, 25 February 1985

8   I'm a guy that dances on tables, puts lampshades on his head, sticks his dick out in crowds. But I'm married now, got kids. I figure: Stay healthy, live longer.

Mel Gibson
Rolling Stone, 29 August 1985
(*See also* 141.10)

9   I'm like the man I play so often – indolent.

Marcello Mastroianni
Look, 8 November 1964

10   I'm very 50s-Zen – all tributes are false, all is vanity.

Jack Nicholson
Rolling Stone, March 1984

11   I'm nuts, I'm weird but I'm great.

Al Pacino
Cinema & TV (South Africa), 4 October 1974

12   There is no me. I do not exist. There used to be a me but I had it surgically removed.

Peter Sellers (1925–80) (four months before his death)
Time, 3 March 1980

---

218   SEQUELS

1   Bruce Willis was offered something like $7.5 million for *Die Hard II*. But they offered me less than for the first one. *Less!* What do they think actors want to do sequels for, anyway. It's for the money!

Bonnie Bedelia
Film Yearbook, 1991

2   Cardinal rule – *always* get yourself killed off in a picture that looks like it's gonna be a success, sweetheart.

Lee Marvin (1924–87)
Rolling Stone, 21 December 1972

3   I sure tried like hell to get out of *Jaws II*. I pleaded insanity. I went crazy in the Beverly Hills Hotel. My act was so convincing that Barry Diller, head of Paramount where I was making *Sorcerer*, actually called to see if I was stable enough to do *his* picture. But nothing got me out of *Jaws II*.

Roy Scheider
Playboy, September 1981

4   A sequel is the last thing the world needs right now.

Yahoo Serious, refusing any *Young Einstein II*
Film Yearbook, 1991

219 SEX APPEAL

1 Sex appeal is in your heart and head. I'll be sexy no matter how old or how my body changs.

Sonia Braga
Movieline, December 1990

2 If anyone thinks I look sexy stripped in *The Music Lovers*, they must think Minnie Mouse is sexy.

Glenda Jackson
Reveille, 20 February 1971

3 Nuns are sexy.

Madonna
Time, 27 May 1985

4 Where do you think I'd be if I hadn't got whistles?

Marilyn Monroe (1926–62) in 1952
American Film, October 1981

5 If a woman thinks she's sexy, she is.

Burt Reynolds
Penthouse, 1972

6 Oh, I'm never dirty, dear. I'm interestin' without bein' vulgar. I have – taste. I *kid* sex. I was born with sophistication and sex appeal but I'm never vulgar. Maybe it's breedin'.

Mae West (1893–1980)
Playboy, 1970

220 SEX BY MEN

1 Sex is the most fun I ever had without laughing.

Woody Allen
Today, 23 July 1989

2 Of course, Ginger was able to accomplish sex through dance. We told more through our movements instead of the big clinch. We did it all in the dance.

Fred Astaire (1899–1987)
Time, 16 November 1981

3   Even the promiscuous feel pain.

Warren Beatty
People, 14 April 1975

4   I'm a bisexual. So, I've had all these girls try to get me over to the
other side again. 'C'mon David, it isn't all that bad. I'll show you.'
Or, better yet: 'We'll show you.' I always play dumb.

David Bowie
Playboy, September 1976

5   Four kids by three different women – I had a real Ford assembly
line going throughout much of my life. If you're rich and famous,
getting laid a lot isn't difficult. I knew what I was doing but I didn't
know why. I still don't have all the answers.

Marlon Brando
Time, 24 May 1976

6   Sex has to be behind locked doors. If what you're doing can be
done out in the open, you may as well be pitching horseshoes.

George Burns
Film Yearbook, 1984

7   It's not all that important to me. It would be important if I wasn't
getting any.

Michael Caine
Playboy, 1966

8   I don't say anything during sex. I've been told not to. Told during
sex, in fact.

Chevy Chase
Playboy, September 1981

9   When you have AIDS, you're judged on how much sex you've
had and what kind. But *there's nothing wrong with having had a lot of
sex*, with putting your arms around someone, holding them, feeling
great.

Harvey Fierstein
Playboy, August 1988

10   Sex for a fat man is much a do about puffing.

Jackie Gleason (1916–87)
Playboy, August 1986

11   Masturbation is always very safe. You not only control the
person you're with but you can leave when you want to.

Dudley Moore
Playboy, January 1983

12   I'm preoccupied with sex – an area of human behaviour that's underexplored, in general. And I like virgin territory.

Jack Nicholson
Sunday Express magazine, 30 July 1989

13   It's best, natural.

Robert Redford
Photoplay, August 1976

14   I don't care about sex anymore. It's been years since I made love. Nowadays I so much prefer motorcycles.

Mickey Rourke
Film Yearbook, 1989

15   I don't believe most women are as quickly or as indiscriminately aroused as most men are. It's a peculiar male problem to want to copulate with almost anything that moves.

Roy Scheider
Playboy, September 1980

221   SEX BY WOMEN

1   I mean if I were out in the desert and I'd no one to do it with, I still wouldn't do it with girls.

Karen Black
Film Yearbook, 1985

2   Sex is not a fad like the hula-hoop – it's here to stay.

Marilyn Chambers
Cannes, 11 May 1983

3   Having sex with someone you're not crazy about – I don't think I'm grown up enough.

Cher
Playboy, December 1980

4   I really don't find it a terrible turn-on when somebody says: 'I've made love to every one of my leading ladies – don't break my record.' A good trick – a man can't stand to be laughed at.

Joan Collins
Playboy, April 1984

5   God's biggest joke on human beings.

Bette Davis (1908–89)
Playboy, July 1982

6   My father, a surgeon and urologist, studied sex professionally all
his life. Before he died at 82, he told me he hadn't come to any
conclusions about it at all.

Katharine Hepburn
Daily Express, 1969

7   The world revolves around sex. If it were worked out to the
satisfaction of all parties, the world would have no problems. It
affects most things: murder, war, making money. They have to do
with power and power has to do with sex.

Lauren Hutton
Playboy, March 1981

8   Sex is like washing your face – just something you do because you
have to. Sex without love is absolutely ridiculous. Sex follows love, it
never precedes it.

Sophia Loren
Daily Mail, 27 March 1979

9   I used to think sex was like having dinner. I don't think that now.
Sex is a serious undertaking. My view is more spiritual. It's the most
intimate exchange of human energy. You live with the interaction of
those sparks for a long time afterwards.

Shirley MacLaine
Playboy, September 1984

10   Pussy rules the world.

Madonnna
Omnibus documentary, BBC TV, 1 December 1990

11   Sometimes I look at my skin and say: Oh, my God, it doesn't
look so good – I have to have more sex!

Paulina Porizkova
Film Yearbook, 1990

12   Being good in bed means I'm propped up with pillows and my
Mom brings me soup.

Brooke Shields
Film Yearbook, 1990

13   I don't know anyone who laughs *during* orgasm. Sex is serious.
On the other hand, I'm not saying *foreplay* is.

Raquel Welch
Playboy, December 1979

14   An orgasm a day keeps the doctor away.

Mae West (1893–1980)
George Eells and Stanley Musgrove, *Mae West*, 1982

222   SEX FILMS

1   We held an end-of-picture party at the ladies' health club location. We actors were at the bar, very elegantly dressed. But the whole crew – grips, sparks, secretaries – all stripped off and were romping around in the pool as we'd done in the shooting two days before. All these naked camera-crew men with their big beer-bellies were cavorting all over the place! That's when I started to think the film would appeal to a lot of people.

Joan Collins (on *The Stud*)
London, May 1978

2   Jesus Christ, you'd think there had never *been* any sex until recent years.

John Huston (1906–87)
Films Illustrated, March 1980

3   Tits and sand – that's what we used to call sex and violence in Hollywood.

Burt Lancaster
Photoplay, April 1983

4   Americans don't like sexual movies – they like sexy movies.

Jack Nicholson
Rolling Stone, March 1984

5   There is too much sex on the screen. I've balled and brawled my away around and I'm no prude, but sex is something to be enjoyed not sniggered over or gaped at.

Peter O'Toole
Daily Mail, 16 June 1972

223   SEX SCENES

1   I may not be a great actress but I've become the greatest at screen orgasms – 10 seconds' heavy breathing, roll your head from side to side, simulate a slight asthma attack and die a little.

Candice Bergen
Daily Mirror, 1971

2   Darling, if I get excited during this scene, please forgive me. And if I *don't* get excited, please forgive me.

Tom Berenger to a co-star in a bed scene (often attributed to George C. Scott)
Playboy, 1982

3   Too many actresses are afraid to be emotionally naked and have to fake the passion – unreal and not sexy.

Sonia Braga
Movieline, December 1990

4   Many of my peers are fornicating on the screen for money. It's so hilarious when they start rolling around in bed. The sex they portray looks pretty pathetic to me. Doesn't look like any sex I've ever had.

Katharine Hepburn
Daily Mail, 21 July 1929

5   I've only once come to blows with a director – Antonioni – when we were making *Blow Up*. We had this scene in which David Hemmings came into a room while I was making love to another man. I thought it important to know if the gentleman lying on top of me was my husband or my lover. So I asked Antonioni. 'It doesn't matter,' he said.

Sarah Miles
Sunday Times, 11 July 1976

6   One can act sexuality to a certain extent. But there's a grey area there. Nobody can be petted, touched and kissed without feeling something. 'Cut!' is a very good cold shower!

Kathleen Turner
Playboy, May 1986
(*See also* 152.5)

7   It's not that difficult to lie around naked on top of Debbie Harry all day, you know what I mean? Certain instincts take over after a while and make the scene really play.

James Woods
Deauville, 9 September 1983

224   SEX SYMBOLS

1   Me – sex symbol? I tell ya, there are 10 million women out there that *don't know who I am!*

Nicolas Cage
Cannes, 9 May 1987

2   American's sexiest actor? I suppose Richard Gere, really. I think he's too busy flashing his balls. On the screen, I mean.

Joan Collins
Playboy, April 1984

3   I don't think you can take it too serious. Oh, it's very flattering – but The Sexiest Man Alive . . .? There are few sexy dead ones.

Sean Connery
Sunday Express magazine, 8 April 1990

4   Perhaps one can be a sex symbol when one is 20. There's insolence, youth, a certain lack of confidence. But at 40 – it would be a remarkable sadness.

Gérard Depardieu
The Observer magazine, 3 April 1990

5   I was the first home-grown sex-symbol, rather like Britain's naughty seaside postcards. When Marilyn Monroe's first film was shown here, *The Asphalt Jungle*, a columnist actually wrote: 'How much like our Diana Dors she is.'

Diana Dors (1931–84)
Daily Mail, 11 February 1978

6   *Emmanuelle* is . . . Well, she's nothing, really.

Sylvia Kristel
Game, February 1977

7   You have to be born a sex symbol. You don't become one. If you're born with it, you'll have it even when you're 100 years old.

Sophia Loren
Radio Times, October 1979

8   I'm too mature, mentally and soon physically, to continue being any kind of sex-symbol.

Robert Redford
Photoplay, January 1981

9 · In real terms, that means someone most men would like to go to bed with. It's better than being labelled a washerwoman. But the disadvantages outweigh the advantages – eclipses everything else about you. A sex goddess isn't a real living thing. She's a plastic lady. She's Superwoman. No intellect, no emotions, no anything. Just a man-eater, the dominant woman. I don't happen to be any of these things.

Raquel Welch
Playboy, 1970

10   They never had sex-symbols in films until I came. Or, they called it something else, 'cos nobody used the word sex till I used it in my play.

Mae West (1893–1980)
Sunday Times magazine, December 1969

225   SEXUALITY

1   Sidney Poitier, as a black artist and a man, is also up against the infantile, furtive sexuality of this country. Both he and Harry Belafonte are sex symbols, though no one dares admit that, still less use them as any of the Hollywood he-men are used.

James Baldwin (1924–87)
Look, 23 July 1968

2   The sins of the flesh have always been very attractive to me – all of them.

Michael Caine
Playboy, 1966

3   You can't be a movie star without it – and it's a big burden.

Jane Fonda
Cannes, May 1989

4   I don't want to imply racism, but black sexuality makes people uncomfortable.

Spike Lee
Knave, March 1987

5   The ability to enjoy your sex life is central. I don't give a shit about anything else. My obsession is total.
Dudley Moore
Playboy, January 1983

6   Most people are afraid of their feelings in this area. Reich says we form our personalities, our families and our government around this neurotic armour.
Jack Nicholson
Sunday Express magazine, 30 July 1989

7   When I wanted something, I'd use my sexuality on men and not necessarily by fucking them. I wouldn't have to fuck them, just be around them, going out and having fun and making them feel real smart.
Theresa Russell
American Film, April 1989

8   Richard is a very sexy man. He's got that sort of jungle essence that one can sense.
Elizabeth Taylor (on Richard Burton)
John Cottrell and Fergus Cashin, *Richard Burton: Very Close Up*, 1973

226   SHAKESPEARE

1   I don't like Shakespeare's comedies. I like his serious plays better. I prefer things that are sad and serious.
Woody Allen
Today, 13 July 1989

2   I've never been that keen on Shakespeare.
Joan Collins
Evening Standard, 31 August 1979

3   If I played Hamlet, they'd call it a horror film.
Peter Cushing (he was Osric in Olivier's 1948 version)
Film Yearbook, 1986

4   Shakespeare is great. But I'd rather have the same problems in a contemporary situation where people can relate to it more directly.
Robert De Niro
Rolling Stone, 25 August 1988

5   A lot of actors who play *Henry V* can't play my characters.
They'd be ludicrous.

Clint Eastwood
Playboy, February 1974

6   I'm playing Shakespeare – and I may not win.

Mel Gibson (on his *Hamlet* film)
Film Monthly, January 1991

7   Norman Mailer will play *King Lear*. He's a natural! He has five
daughters and a crazy life.

Menahem Golan on plans for Jean-Luc Godard's film. (Mailer didn't play *Lear*)
Cannes, May 1986

8   When you've played Montano in *Othello* a couple of times, let me
tell you, you never want to do it again. I mean, five months being the
guy who runs out at the start of the second act and says: 'What, from
the cape, can you discern at seas?' – it begins to grate.

Tom Hanks
The Times, 17 October 1988

9   Bob [Mitchum] is one of the very great actors – his resources have
never been fully tapped. He could play *King Lear*.

John Huston (1907–87)
Radio Times, 6 December 1962
(*See also* 226.11)

10   An actor can do *Hamlet* right through to *Lear*, men of every age
and every step of spiritual development. Where's the equivalent for
women? I don't fancy hanging around to play Nurse in *Romeo and
Juliet*. Life's too short.

Glenda Jackson
Daily Mail, 24 November 1978

11   All the tough talk is a blind. He's a literate, gracious, kind man
and he speaks beautifully – when he wants to. Bob would make the
best *Macbeth* of any actor living.

Charles Laughton (1899–1962) (on Robert Mitchum)
Paris Passion, June 1990
(*See also* 226.9)

12   I'd make a wonderful Lady Macbeth. I'll wear a pair of
platform shoes or something.

Bette Midler
Time, 2 March 1987

13   Hard to understand, hard to do. I always try to reassure the audience initially that they're not going to see some grotesque, out-sized dimension of something they can't understand or sympathize with – then there's no end to where you can lead them ... Young actors shouldn't have to wait until they're film stars, like dear Marlon, before they play it [Shakespeare]. It's not right that you should risk your neck in the stuff when you've achieved such a height of fame.

Lord Laurence Olivier (1907–89)
Life, 1965

14   My old, true love! After the kings and the princes get through talking about their greatness, the gravedigger comes out to tell what's really going on.

Roy Scheider
Playboy, 1980

15   *Othello* is a part I've dreamed of playing. It's me, the Moor. It hasn't been played by a Moor before.

Omar Sharif
Film Yearbook, 1985

16   You could spend a lifetime on *Hamlet*, the most complex, most ambiguous, richest character in all literature. You can't make a *Hamlet* without breaking eggs!

Jean-Louis Trintignant
Paris, 14 December 1978

17   Lady Macbeth, with her ruthless single-mindedness, is just like Mrs Thatcher. No room for weakness or compassion.

Julie Walters
The Times, 21 October 1985

227   SMILES

1   You're never fully dressed without a smile.

Bud Cort
Film Yearbook, 1986

2   I was in the right place at the right time and said the right thing. And had a charming smile.

Eddie Murphy
Time, 11 July 1983

3 My best feature's my smile. And smiles – praise heaven – don't get fat.

Jack Nicholson
Photoplay, September 1986

228 SOBRIETY

1 Sobriety's a real turn on for me. You can see what you're doing.

Peter O'Toole
Film Yearbook, 1984

2 I'm thrilled, happy – and sober.

Maureen Stapleton, collecting supporting actress Oscar
29 March 1982

229 SONG AND DANCE

1 Singing has never been particularly easy for me.

Julie Andrews
Time, 23 December 1966

2 I had some ballet training but I didn't like it. It was like a game to me.

Fred Astaire (1899–1987)
Benny Green, *Fred Astaire*, 1979

3 Once a song-and-dance man, always a song-and-dance man. Those few words tell as much about me professionally as there is to tell.

James Cagney (1899–1986)
Time obituary, 1 April 1986

4 I'm not a ballerina. I'm a hoofer.

Leslie Caron
Radio Times, December 1971

5   I'm the worst singer in Western Europe. I mean, horrendous. I was in *Half A Sixpence* on Broadway in 1965 on condition that I mime.

John Cleese
Playboy, November 1987

6   Fred Astaire danced himself so thin I could almost spit through him.

Bing Crosby (1904–77)
Daily Mail, February 1971

7   Dirty dancing can be very satisfying. It's a form of safe sex.

Jennifer Grey
Film Yearbook, 1989

8   I don't care what crown a guy wears, I don't care if he's president, the one person I was ever speechless around was Fred Astaire – the greatest dancer who ever lived. He's almost perfection.

Goldie Hawn
Playboy, January 1985

9   I never wanted to be a dancer. It's true! I wanted to be a short-stop for the Pittsburg Pirates.

Gene Kelly
Variety, 12 November 1985

10   I can sing as well as Fred Astaire can act.

Burt Reynolds
Photoplay, April 1976

11   I hated singing. I wanted to be an actress. But I don't think I'd have made it any other way.

Barbra Streisand
Playboy, October 1977

12   I *started* as a singer – in the Deanna Durbin days.

Elizabeth Taylor
Look, 15 August 1961

230 SPECIAL EFFECTS

1 It's verging on insanity. I spend all my time talking to characters who are not there, fighting weasels and being thrown out of clubs by gorillas.

Bob Hoskins (on shooting *Who Framed Roger Rabbit*)
Premiere, November 1989

2 I started work in January but *King Kong* didn't actually show up until August. Most of the time I was playing to a spot on the ceiling.

Jessica Lange
Photoplay, May 1977

3 A few years from now, if you can still portray a human being, you'll be quite a valuable commodity.

Jack Nicholson
Film Comment, 1983

4 I don't do effects for anybody anymore. I don't even want to do effects for myself.

Hollywood's top special-effects technician Douglas Trumbull
Film Yearbook, 1985

231 STARDOM

1 This is all very funny. Today I am a star -- and tomorrow?
Isabelle Adjani
The Driver publicity release, 1977

2 I didn't set out to be a star. If you do, you engage in manipulation. You do stuff to be liked. I didn't want to be endorsed: I wanted to be listened to. I had ideas about things.
Kevin Costner
Time, 26 June 1989

3 This star stuff eats you.
Tom Cruise
You: Mail On Sunday magazine, 29 January 1989

4   To become a star is the beginning of the end. I really don't want
to be saddled with a screen persona.

Beverly D'Angelo
Photoplay, December 1983

5   Today everyone is a star – they're all billed as 'starring' or 'also
starring'. In my day, we earned that recognition.

Bette Davis (1908–89)
Films Illustrated, December 1979

6   A Hollywood star is death as far as acting is concerned. I don't
want people to recognize me in the streets. I don't want to do what
real stars have to do – repeat themselves in film after film after film,
always being themselves.

Robert De Niro
Screen International, May 1976

7   If I start to become a star, I'll lose contact with the normal guys I
play best.

Gene Hackman
American Film, March 1983

8   Stardom equals freedom. It's the only equation that matters.

Dustin Hoffman
Radio Times, March 1977

9   Stardom? I never touch the stuff.

John Lithgow
Photoplay, September 1986

10   All you need is one incredible vehicle – a financial, artistic and
cinematic success – for your launching pad. The hardest thing is to
get your rocket launched.

Yvette Mimieux
Newsweek, 4 March 1968

11   There are no more stars – stardom being defined, I suppose, as a
guarantee that the picture will make money.

Paul Newman
Rolling Stone, 5 July 1973

12   There are two ways up the ladder, hand over hand or scratching
and clawing. It's sure been tough on my nails.

Jack Nicholson
Time, 12 August 1974

13 I'm just waiting for somebody to say I'm a fag – that's when you're really a big star!
Burt Reynolds
Penthouse, 1972

14 You can't last if you don't *love* it.
John Wayne (1907–79)
Photoplay, June 1968

232 STARS

1 Stars, they don't exist anymore.
Isabelle Adjani
Unifrance bulletin, 1974
(*See also* 241.1)

2 Of course, you start with dreams of being a star. You want recognition, public recognition. And why not? You're doing public work.
Alan Bates
Sunday Times, 3 October 1971

3 In your heart of hearts, you know perfectly well that movie stars aren't artists. Shakespeare said: 'There's no art to find the mind's construction in the face.'
Marlon Brando
Playboy, January 1979

4 Most movie stars – I hate that term – are not very bright. Same goes for television stars.
Joan Collins
Playboy, April 1984

5 A star is just an actor who sells tickets.
Charles Dance
Woman's Hour, BBC Radio 4, April 1989

6 A star remains pinned on a wall in the public imagination.
Catherine Deneuve
L'Express, 1976

7   What makes a star? Hmm. Everything! Charisma – what I used to call in drama school, the shine. Internal, emotional, physical energy – it goes beyond the body and you can't control it.

Faye Dunaway
Film Yearbook, 1989

8   I have one question. By 'Star Of Tomorrow', do you mean Friday? Because if it's just tomorrow, Friday's not a good day for me. I have all these appointments. Could we change it to Saturday?

Christine Lahti, receiving a film industry award
Film Yearbook, 1987

9   It's someone you don't mind spending two hours in a cinema with – even if the film is bad.

Claude Lelouch
French TV, 1988

10   I turned down dinner with Mickey Rourke. Because he's a star. To me, a star is inaccessible, mysterious, an impossible dream – and should stay that way. Adjani's a star. Deneuve's a star. Not me.

Miou-Miou
Cinéma, Cinémas, Antenne 2 (French TV), 1989

11   You're not a star until they can spell your name in Karachi.

Roger Moore
Film Yearbook, 1987

12   If I could only be a star rather than an actor, I'd probably stop acting.

Jack Nicholson
Newsweek, 7 December 1970

13   I can cope. After all, I'm a fucking movie star.

Peter O'Toole
Playboy, August 1982

14   I've become the No. 1 box-office star in the world not because of my movies – but *in spite* of them.

Burt Reynolds
Playboy, October 1979

15   I knew that with a mouth like mine, I just hadda be a star or something.

Barbra Streisand
Daily Mirror, 26 June 1964

16   Stars don't cry.

Mae West (1893–1980)
Playboy, 1970

233   STARS BY DIRECTORS

1   Depardieu is absolutely somebody of today. He's a *mec*. Really, a *mec*. A guy! He could be a factory worker – which never happened with a French star before; maybe Gabin, but only in a *folklorique* way. Gérard's full of blood and sensitivity. He's ugly. He's real. You want to make friends with him. Have you ever dreamt of making Liz Taylor a friend – *non*!

José Benazeraf
Game, March 1977

2   I like Bob. I just don't know if he likes himself.

Francis Coppola (on Robert De Niro)
Playboy, January 1989

3   I was too shaken to make the announcement. No one else could do it, either. Audrey [Hepburn] said simply: 'I'll do it.' Taking a hand microphone, she said: 'The President of the United States is dead. Shall we have two minutes' silence to pray or to do whatever you think is appropriate?' When the chips are down, Audrey is there.

George Cukor (1899–1983)
Daily Mail, 1964

4   John Wayne – a splendid actor who's had very little chance to act.

John Ford (1895–1973)
Time, 8 August 1969

5   She's the one they all watch. Her gift is emotion and exceptional lucidity of thought. Vanessa [Redgrave] has an access to her feelings without parallel. She's the least flustered, most completely focused actress – she barely needs to study a part.

David Hare
Time, 6 February 1989

6   Very professional – but infuriating.

Gene Kelly (on Barbra Streisand)
Photoplay, July 1982

7   Robert Redford is the centre of America – blond, blue-eyed, tall and thin.

Barry Levinson
Film Yearbook, 1986

8   She has her father's unseductibility.

Josh Logan (1908–88) (on Jane Fonda)
Time, 15 February 1970

9   Most people think of him as a legendary star. I don't but only because we go to the toilet together.

Sidney Lumet (on Sean Connery)
Sunday Times magazine, 5 November 1989

10   Tom Hanks is in what I'd call the Hat Pack. You know, a bunch of guys who occasionally wear hats and that's about as wild as they get.

Garry Marshall
Rolling Stone, October 1986

11   Jack Nicholson always tells the truth – in acting and in life. He has something that Brando also has – complete comfort with and in his body.

Mike Nichols
Newsweek, 7 December 1970

12   There are three things I never saw Elizabeth Taylor do. Be on time. Tell a lie. Be unkind to anyone.

Mike Nichols
Variety, May 1986

13   Warren Beatty is always on the up. He travels light and takes one small suitcase from coast to coast. I guess you'd call him a very rich migrant worker.

Arthur Penn
Time, 3 July 1975

14   She looks like a professional virgin – not Marilyn Monroe or Lolita, but the niece of a man who'd make her sit in his lap.

Roman Polanski (on Catherine Deneuve)
Look, 30 April 1968

15   You can't get him to do something that's false. He marches to his own Walkman.

Phil Alden Robinson (on Kevin Costner)
Time, 26 June 1989

16   I'd let my wife, children and animals starve before I'd subject myself to something like that again.

Don Siegel (on working with Bette Midler on the aptly-titled *Jinxed*)
Premiere, November 1989

17   With the exception of Lassie, Sean Connery is the only person I know who's never been spoiled by success.

Terence Young
Rolling Stone, 27 October 1983

234   STARS ON DIRECTORS

1   Because he was a special kind of actor, [Elia] Kazan is the best actor's director, he understands things that other directors do not. Chaplin reminded me of what Churchill said about the Germans: either at your feet or at your throat. A remarkable talent but a monster of a man. Gillio Pontecorvo started carrying a gun – was going to use it if I didn't do what he said. Hysterically superstitious, he had two pocketfuls of lucky charms. On Thursdays, you couldn't ask him questions. If there was anything purple on the set, he'd get rid of it – including the wine at lunch.

Marlon Brando
Playboy, January 1979

2   You told me he was young but you didn't tell me he was *that* young. I have ties older than him.

George Burns (on Martin Brest)
Knave, May 1985

3   He's in my family and there's not many directors of whom you can say that.

Julie Christie (on John Schlesinger)
Film Yearbook, 1989

4   I call Oliver Stone the Van Gogh film-maker. His films are intense, vibrant, explosive, unrelenting – just like he is. Watching him in action is like seeing Bruce Springsteen live for the first time.

Tom Cruise
Los Angeles Times, 17 December 1989

5   There'll never be another John Ford. He had, instinctively, a beautiful eye of the camera. He was so egomaniacal. He never would rehearse, didn't want to talk about a part. If an actor started to ask a question, he'd either take those pages and tear them out of the script or insult him in an awful way.

Henry Fonda (1905–82)
Playboy, December 1981

6   Do it – try it – fight – write – act – direct – indulge – survive. John Huston can do it all. And he rubbed my back when I was sick. He sets his work on fire . . . David Lean knows more about films than a banker knows about money.

Katharine Hepburn
Panorama (USA), March 1981

7   I'd like to spend the rest of my life doing nothing but Billy Wilder films.

Jack Lemmon
Films & Filming, November 1969

8   Billy Wilder's very dominating. He knows what he wants and he's absolutely certain. Willy Wyler will try maybe four different ways. Billy is almost always right – Willy is, too.

Shirley MacLaine
Films & Filming, February 1962

9   Fellini's my favourite – between us, I don't know who's more of a child.

Marcello Mastroianni
Gente, 23 August 1985

10   Howard Hawks called me up about *El Dorado*. 'What about doing a Western with Duke Wayne?' Sounds good – where? 'Let's shoot it down in Old Tuscon, Arizona.' Wonderful, great location, nice town – what's the story, Howard? 'No story, Bob. Just characters. Stories bore people.'

Robert Mitchum
Knave, June 1990

11   He's the only guy who could double-park in front of a whore-house. He's that fast.

Paul Newman (on Sidney Lumet)
Rolling Stone, 20 January 1983

12   Roman Polanski has no time to listen to actors but Milos Forman insists on talking about every scene.

Jack Nicholson
Screen International, 14 February 1976
(*See also* 82.6)

13   Alan Parker wears those glasses to look like an Oxford don. But he's really a street kid and that's what makes him a great director.

Mickey Rourke
Arena, July 1989

14   I've worked with the biggest tyrants: Preminger, Welles, Visconti. Despots – they have contempt for most actors. When they meet someone who stands up to them, everything's great.

Romy Schneider (1938–82)
Sunday Express, 23 May 1965

15   Claude Lelouch is both detestable and adorable. He likes to lie. Lying is his poetry.

Louis Trintignant
Michel Boujut, *Un Homme à sa fenêtre*, 1977

16   Bergman taught me how little you can do, rather than how much.

Liv Ullmann
Time, 4 December 1972

17   No one remembers the names of directors anymore[!].

John Wayne (1907–79)
Photoplay, June 1968

---

235   STARS ON FEMALE STARS

---

1   She is one of a selected few who aren't actors by our standards but if you put them on a screen they emanate something – something I frankly don't understand. Brando has it, Monty Clift used to have it and, of course, Garbo had it.

Richard Burton (1925–84) (on Elizabeth Taylor)
Playboy, 1963

2   She was a fresh-faced, wholesome, well-scrubbed kid. To go from that to an overt sex-symbol with Vadim and totally to turn around and become not only a committed women's liberationist and political figure but a brilliant actress in amazing films that have tremendous commercial and entertainment value as well as being works of art, and work with her husband in politics, put all her salary into his political movement *and* do her own washing at the laundrette *and* help her father – she's too much for me!

Joan Collins (on Jane Fonda)
Films Illustrated, August 1978

3   Working with Bette Davis was my greatest challenge and I mean that kindly. She liked to scream and yell. I just sit and knit. During *Whatever Happened To Baby Jane?*, I knitted a scarf from Hollywood to Malibu.

Joan Crawford (1904–77)
Variety, April 1973

4   Catherine Deneuve is the man I've always wanted to be.

Gérard Depardieu
F magazine (France), December 1980

5   I don't have a fond memory of Mae West. She did her own thing to the detriment of everyone around her.

Cary Grant (1904–86)
Variety, 17 July 1984

6   Too bad she's not queen of some country.

Goldie Hawn (on Ingrid Bergman)
Time, 6 October 1980

7   I taught her to cuss, she taught me to dress.

Shirley MacLaine (on Audrey Hepburn)
Evening Standard, 1965

8   I'd love to work with Barbra Streisand again. In something appropriate. Perhaps, *Macbeth*.

Walter Matthau
Photoplay, April 1982

9   She's got the Oscar. She's got Yves [Montand]. She's smart. They respect her. She's got everything. What have I got?

Marilyn Monroe (1926–62) (on Simone Signoret)
Lena Pepitone and William Stadiem, *Marilyn Monroe Confidential*, 1979

10   Karen Black is the most lucid actress I've worked with. You tell her where it's at and she grabs it.

Jack Nicholson
Time, 9 June 1975

11   Doris Day is one of the most difficult actresses I've met. She spent so much time crying.

David Niven (1909–83)
Showtime, 1964

12   I was very impressed by Doris Day, actually. She was terribly professional and used to get up to the studio early to have her legs made up *under* her nylons.

Natasha Parry
International Herald Tribune, April 1983

13   Bette Davis is my bloody idol. I admire her more than any film star.

George C. Scott
Playboy, December 1980

14   The kind of girl you know Mother would love, the kind they built musicals around.

Frank Sinatra (on Audrey Hepburn)
Photoplay, August 1982

15   Garbo, on screen, is flawless.

Meryl Streep
Photoplay, November 1985

16   Streisand [in *Hello, Dolly!*] has the unmitigated gall to imitate me. Garbo does more thinkin' than talkin'. Theda Bara had a nice mean quality and Clara Bow had cute sex. Lana [Turner] did very well, too. But there's nobody in my class.

Mae West (1893–1980)
Playboy, 1970

236   STARS ON MALE STARS

1   He's the kind of guy that when he dies, he gives God a bad time for making him bald.

Marlon Brando (on Frank Sinatra)
Daily Mail, 30 March 1977

2 One day, God said 'Let there be prey,' and he created pigeons, rabbits, lambs and Gene Wilder.
Mel Brooks
Newsweek, 17 February 1975

3 Clint Eastwood appears to do nothing and does everything, reducing everything and everybody – like Mitchum and Tracy.
Richard Burton (1925–84)
Films Illustrated, February 1981

4 Warren Beatty doesn't drink, he doesn't smoke, he plays the piano beautifully, he's extremely intelligent, learned, knowledgeable. You look for something to get him on and you can't.
Gabriel Byrne
Film Yearbook, 1989

5 Sean Connery is utterly wonderful both as an actor and in what he does: 'So I'm bald and 10 pounds overweight, so what?' He's still the most attractive man on the screen.
Joan Collins
Playboy, April 1984

6 He can really throw you. That's one of the great joys of working with Mickey Rourke. He's like me. He likes to see what could happen – not to play so specifically. I like that, it's alive . . . actually happening. You have to respond to him, with that same kind of spontaneity, so it keeps you on your toes.
Faye Dunaway
Barfly publicity release, 1987

7 Secretly, I think Bob [Redford] is afraid of women. He likes to tell them what to do. He likes them to be subservient. He treated me as if I were an extra or something.
Jane Fonda
Evening Standard, 27 September 1976

8 The actor who's in everything is Gérard Depardieu. I've never seen a French film he wasn't in except *La Cage aux Folles* and he might be in the chorus of that for all I know.
Gene Hackman
Film Yearbook, 1989

9 Spencer [Tracy] was a typical American product. He never gussied it up. He just did it, let it ride along on its enormous simplicity.
Katharine Hepburn
The Times, 28 April 1969

10 Charlton Heston wears a hairpiece. His character in *A Man For All Seasons* [on stage] was bald. Instead of doing without his hairpiece, he put a bald pate *over* it.

Dustin Hoffman
Premiere, January 1989

11 I'm here to speak about his wit, his charm, his warmth, his talent . . . At last, a real acting job!

Burt Lancaster (at a Kirk Douglas tribute)
Variety, 15 April 1987

12 Past lives leaking through and confusing him in this life.

Shirley MacLaine (on Peter Sellers)
Playboy, September 1984

13 Duke [John Wayne] was born Marion Morrison. He was working on *The Alamo* in Texas. Laurence Harvey was walking along a parapet. Duke just shouted up to him: 'Jesus Christ, can't you at least walk like a man.' And Larry leaned over and said: 'Speaking to me, Marion?'

Robert Mitchum
Ritz, No. 143, 1989

14 He's the actor of the new generation. I don't mean one of – he is *the* one.

Yves Montand (on Gérard Depardieu)
Time, 6 February 1984

15 Bob Redford is a star in the shower. No water spray would dare him a hassle. The water would never be too hot or too cold and the eggs at breakfast would always come out of the pan perfect.

Paul Newman
Daily Mail, February 1977

16 We had dinner with him. We're driving home and I'm thinking: God, here's old Paul [Newman] – what is he, 60, 61? He looks great, feels great, has a lot of money, gives to great causes, he's in love with his wife, he races his cars when he wants to, makes a movie when he wants to, he's incredibly happy and still has the face that looks the way it did when he was 20. God, by the time we got home, I wanted to shoot myself.

Robert Redford
Esquire, 1988

17 Richard Burton is one of the finest actors of this generation.

Elizabeth Taylor (Burton replied: '*One* of . . . ?')
Time, 4 October 1982

237 MERYL STREEP

1 Like De Niro, Meryl Streep has no limits.
Robert Benton
Time, 7 September 1981

2 Meryl Streep is an acting machine in the same sense that a shark is a killing machine.
Cher
Film Yearbook, 1989

3 She's going to be the Eleanor Roosevelt of acting.
Dustin Hoffman
Newsweek, 7 January 1980

4 The danger in talking about Meryl Streep is she tends to sound boring – she's so perfect.
Sydney Pollack
Film Yearbook, 1983

5 Meryl Streep is the greatest living actor that America has, man or woman.
Bruce Willis
Playboy, November 1988

6 I can't say anything bad about Meryl Streep – and I love to say bad things about people.
James Woods
Newsweek, 7 January 1980

238 STUDIOS

1 Ten years ago, the studio heads thought the audience were sheep. Now, they think they're snails with Down's Syndrome.
Albert Brooks
Playboy, July 1983

2 Sometimes they give you so much rope you forget it's around your neck. But it always is. You feel it when they yank it.
James L. Brooks
Film Yearbook, 1985

3 Studios underestimate audiences, feeling they won't be interested in anything reflecting a different background. Some of my most successful films were the ones I was advised not to make.

Jane Fonda
Photoplay, October 1983

4 They're simple people. They understand the needs of a real artist. You only have to make $40 million with a film for them to appreciate the value of what you want to do next!

Terry Gilliam
Film Yearbook, 1985

5 You have to reconcile what you think is good with what you think is profitable.

Tom Pollock, president of Universal Pictures
Los Angeles Times, 17 December 1989

6 They try to break you. They tie you up in deals, keep you off the market, keep you waiting.

Franc Roddam
Film Yearbook, 1985
(*See also* 247.2)

7 I haven't been able to find anybody running a studio that even knows that movies are 35 mm and run at 24 frames per second.

Douglas Trumbull
Film Yearbook, 1985

8 Most studio moguls would be selling cars if it weren't for the nepotism in Hollywood – used cars that don't run.

Joseph Wambaugh
Films Illustrated, April 1980

9 The banks and stock promoters have taken over. The moguls may not have been moral but they worked a 50-week schedule. They *built*.

John Wayne (1907–79)
Game, June 1975

239 STUDIO SYSTEM

1 They gave me away as a prize once – a Win Tony Curtis For A Weekend competition. The woman who won was disappointed. She'd hoped for second prize – a new stove.

Tony Curtis
Sunday Express, 10 October 1965

2 Universal signed me as a contract player – which is a little lower than working in the mail room.

Clint Eastwood
Playboy, February 1974

3 The guy who was vice-president of Columbia at the time – 'Kid,' he says. (They always called me 'Kid', probably because they didn't know who the hell I was.) 'Kid, siddown. Lemme tellya story. First time Tony Curtis ever appeared in a movie, he delivered a bag of groceries. *A bag of groceries!* You took one look at that person and you knew that was a star. Kid – you ain't got it.'

Harrison Ford
Films Illustrated, April 1978

4 The system is geared towards overworking the stars. There aren't too many stars around to haul the freight.

Jack Nicholson
Time, 12 August 1974

5 The head of publicity of the Hollywood studio where I was first under contract told me: 'You're a piece of meat, that's all.' It wasn't very nice but I had to take it. When I made my first screentest, the director explained to everyone: 'Don't listen to her, just look.'

Kim Novak
Daily Mail, 12 June 1980

240 SUCCESS

See also 52 Celebrity
103 Fame

1 I notice that the width of a Hollywood smile in my direction is commensurate with how much my last picture grossed.

Marlon Brando
Time, 24 May 1976

2   Success helps you ease up.

Mel Brooks
Newsweek, 17 February 1975

3   When you reach the top, that's when the climb begins.

Michael Caine
Playboy, 1966

4   Success has no nationality. There's some good actors from New York not known in Los Angeles.

Gérard Depardieu
Films Illustrated, May 1978

5   Before I'd met Julie [Andrews], some people were conjecturing about her success. I said: 'I can tell you what that is. She has lilacs for pubic hair.'

Blake Edwards (on his wife)
Playboy, December 1982

6   Success is a very tough mistress. For years, while you're struggling, she wants nothing to do with you. Then, one day you find yourself in the room with her and even though the key is on the inside, you can't leave. 'You've made your choice,' she says, 'I don't care how exhausted you are – you're going to stay here for the rest of your life making love to me.'

Peter Finch (1916–77)
Sunday Express, 15 November 1964

7   Sex and money are the two most desirable things in the world. I've worked really hard to get to a position where I haven't got time to enjoy either as much as I'd like.

Michael J. Fox
Photoplay, July 1987

8   In Britain, any degree of success is met with envy and resentment.

Christopher Lee
Films Illustrated, 1978

9   Sometimes I get the feeling that if I have any more success it's going to be obscene. I'm embarrassed by it.

George Lucas
Film Yearbook, 1985

10   The more success you have, the less you use the things that got you there in the first place. You end up doing what I call Retirement Acting – merely exhibiting your former skills.

Walter Matthau
Sunday Express, 15 April 1979

11   Success or failure in films are exactly the same. They're both imposters.

Paul Newman
Daily Mail, February 1977

12   It's like an American tradition. A person gets successful and then he's supposed to change for the worse. It's silly.

Barbra Streisand
Playboy, October 1977

13   Success? Ah yes, the first three-piece suit, first lawsuit . . .

Robin Williams
Playboy, 1979

241   SUPERSTARS

1   Superstars don't exist anymore.

Isabelle Adjani
Rolling Stone, 26 August 1976
(*See also* 232.1)

2   You look at Harrison Ford and you *listen*. He looks like he's carrying a gun, even if he isn't.

Carrie Fisher
Vanity Fair, August 1990

3   Sylvester Stallone is frustrated with his myth. Yet he finds it difficult to try not to live up to it – bodyguards, girls, all that is there. He wants out but is afraid to get out of it. He's like Gina Lollobrigida. She's still as she was 35 years ago, doesn't change anything – not even her dresses.

Russian director Andrei Konchalovsky
Deauville, September 1989

4   We always knew it would be Elizabeth Taylor for *Sweet Bird of Youth*. After all, *her life* is a Tennessee Williams play.

TV producer Peter Locke
Los Angeles Times, 1988

5   Bob Redford is the superstar – and I'm not.

Paul Newman
Daily Mail, February 1977

6   Warren Beatty can say 'No' simply and I can't, while I can say 'Yes' simply and he can't.

Jack Nicholson
Rolling Stone, March 1984

7   I don't like the word 'superstar'. It has ridiculous implications. These words – star, stupor, star, superstar, stupid star – they're misleading. It's a myth.

Barbra Streisand
Playboy, October 1977

8   World cinema for me means Meryl Streep, Robert De Niro, Jack Nicholson. They're so natural, I don't know if they're acting a script or improvising.

Russian actress Elena Yakovleva
Cannes, May 1990

242   SWEARING

1   They tend to overdo the vulgarity. I'm not embarrassed by the language itself. But it's embarrassing to be listening to it, sitting next to perfect strangers.

Fred Astaire (1899–1987)
Newsweek, 31 May 1976

2   I especially love swearing in Italian.

Nastassja Kinski
Playboy, May 1983

3   Carole Lombard was a wonderful girl. Swore like a man. Other women try, but she really did.

Fred MacMurray
Film Yearbook, 1988

4 I've got a filthy mouth but it's my only sin.
Eddie Murphy
Film Yearbook, 1990

5 Ever since *Slapshot*, I've been swearing more. You get a hangover from a character like that . . . I knew I had a problem when I turned to my daughter one day and said: 'Please pass the fuckin' salt.'
Paul Newman
Rolling Stone, 20 January 1983

243 TALENT

1 Talent lies in your choice of drama coach.
Stella Adler (Marlon Brando's choice)
Quoted by Robert De Niro, *American Film*, March 1981

2 Great talent is an accident of birth.
Woody Allen
Newsweek, 24 April 1978

3 I'm a skilled, professional actor. Whether or not I've any talent is beside the point.
Michael Caine
Film Yearbook, 1985

4 You know when I knew I had some talent? I'll tell you the day I knew because I remember it. It was right dab smack in the middle of *Apocalypse Now* in the middle of the Philippines and one day, I knew I had talent.
Francis Coppola
Film Yearbook, 1983
(*See also* 120.1)

5 If I have some success, it might be because I have some talent.
Gérard Depardieu
Films Illustrated, May 1978

6 I'm working with a handicap. I have no talent.
Audie Murphy (1924–71), America's most decorated World War II soldier turned movie star
Time obituary, 14 June 1971

7 Having talent is like having blue eyes. You don't admire a man
for the colour of his eyes. I admire a man for what he does with his
talent.

Anthony Quinn
Sunday Express, 1960

8 There's never any talent without a little strain of madness.

Jean-Louis Trintignant
Films Illustrated, July 1979

244 TELEVISION

1 I adore TV – like everyone else. But I watch very little. There's so
very little worth watching.

Bernardo Bertolucci
Film Yearbook, 1989

2 TV? Never! I don't want my audience going for a piss or making
tea while I'm hard at work.

Dirk Bogarde (he relented)
Sunday Times, 15 October 1978

3 Too much emphasis on celebrity bullshit these days. Every time
you turn around, there's another goddam TV talk show – what
Connie Francis had for breakfast today. And people eat it up. That's
kinda scary – like they don't have anything better to do than *that*.

John Goodman
Premiere, February 1990

4 TV has changed the world by changing people's attitudes. When
they are born with a TV set in their room – well, you can't fool them
anymore.

Roman Polanski
Time, 8 December 1967

5 Such an ugly piece of furniture.

John Waters
Cannes, May 1990

245 TRUTH

1   Death is the only, inevitable truth.

James Dean (1931–55)
Photoplay, September 1985

2   We Swedish believe in telling the truth. We feel love and truth go together. Then you know love is not dependent on illusions.

Britt Ekland
Cinema and TV (South Africa), 22 March 1974

3   Film is truth, 24 times a second.

Jean-Luc Godard
Sunday Times, 1966

4   I once asked Barbara Stanwyck the secret of acting. She said: 'Just be truthful – and if you can fake that, you've got it made.'

Fred MacMurray
Variety, 15 April 1987

5   Last thing people want is truth.

Sylvester Stallone
Antenne 2 (French TV), 1989

6   All good actors work the same way. They just stand there on their own two feet and tell the truth.

James Woods
Deauville, 9 September 1983

246 TYPECASTING

1   You keep getting offered the same role you got the Oscar for. Every time you complain, they don't change the script, they just offer you more money.

F. Murray Abraham
Quoted by Geraldine Page (1924–87), *Time Out*, June 1986

2   After all those years of playing Mr Clean, I was afraid to comb my hair for fear of scratching my halo.

Troy Donahue
Grandview USA publicity release, 1984

3   After *The China Syndrome*, I was getting sent every morose, sicko, wacko diseased script – cancer, poison, you name it – to come down the tubes. If it's off-the-wall, send it to Mikey!

Michael Douglas
Photoplay, October 1984

4   Typecast? I certainly hope so. I spent seven years without working. I got two kids to bring up.

Andy Garcia
Premiere, September 1989

5   I'm typecast anyway – as *me*.

Roger Moore
Daily Mail, 11 June 1979

247   UNEMPLOYMENT

1   It seems much easier for these people to rent my films, look at them and make notes – than to give me a job.

Underground legend Kenneth Anger
Independent, 18 January 1990

2   I was off the screen for 18 months. It's hard for me to not to work but I refused to be broken.

Franc Roddam
Film Yearbook, 1985
(*See also* 238.6)

3   In Hollywood, you're a veteran if you've had a job of more than six weeks' tenure with one company.

Jack Valenti, president of Motion Picture Association of America
Variety, 1985

248   VILLAINS

1   Because I'm the only actor who ever killed John Wayne in a picture, producers have pegged me for a villain.

Bruce Dern
Photoplay, April 1976

2   Virtue is not photogenic and bad guys are more interesting to play.

Kirk Douglas
Photoplay, July 1987

3   If you're going to be bad, be real bad. In film-making, once the spaghetti is going through the machine at 11 cents a foot or whatever, the thing is to use it and I did. I leaned on people, real hard.

Lee Marvin (1924–87)
Sunday Express, 27 March 1966

4   If it were not for villains, there'd be no heroes.

Sir Peter Ustinov
Screen International, 9 October 1976

5   The heavies in my day were kid stuff compared to today. Our villains had no redeeming qualities. But there's a new morality today. A villain is a guy with a fraility. Heroes are villains.

Richard Widmark
Variety, 16 November 1976

249   VIOLENCE

1   Violence is extremely beautiful.

Brian De Palma
Film Yearbook, 1985
(*See also* 255.5)

2   When *Play Misty For Me* came out, I was criticized for knocking the leading lady through a window. But it was a simple question of survival. She was trying to put a knife in my forehead.

Clint Eastwood
Newsweek, 25 September 1985

3   There's always been violence in cinema, theatre and literature. But it is society's tolerance of violence in society that's probably responsible for violent behaviour more than any motion picture or television show. The attitude, at least in America, seems to be: this isn't bothering me so why should I be bothered about it?

Clint Eastwood
Film Monthly, April 1989

4 My films won't send people out into the streets with axes or anything. The Shirley Temple movies are more likely to do that. After listening to *The Good Ship Lollipop*, you just gotta go out and beat up somebody. Stands to reason.

Lee Marvin (1924–87)
Sunday Express, 27 March 1966

5 *Bonnie and Clyde* didn't kill Martin Luther King, man.

Michael J. Pollard
Films & Filming, 1969

250 WAR

1 I was put in the combat engineers. We would throw up bridges in advance of the infantry but mainly we would just throw up.

Mel Brooks
Newsweek, 17 February 1975

2 I found out why war is hell – army authority is absolute. You are defended and judged by the same kind of people who accuse and prosecute you.

Michael Caine
Playboy, 1966

3 In many movies, including *Platoon*, war looks like fun. In reality, a dead body is a very ugly thing and it's hard to carry. Life isn't cheap and I wanted to rub that in the audience's face.

Patrick Duncan, director of *84 Charlie Mopic*
Film Yearbook, 1990

4 When I got back from the war in 1945, I refused to make war pictures.

James Stewart
Time, 29 June 1970

251 WEIGHT

1 Thing I look forward to the most about retiring is *not* having to worry about my weight.

Charles Bronson
Photoplay, January 1987

2 It's very important that you're slim in Hollywood. You just remember the camera adds a little.

Sybil Danning
Starburst, 1982

3 I'm answering this question for the 6000th time. It was very easy. I just had to get up at 6.30 am and eat breakfast at 7 am in order to digest my food to eat lunch at 1 pm in order to digest my food to eat a nice dinner at 7 pm. So, it was three square meals a day – pancakes, beer, milk.

Robert De Niro (on gaining 60 lbs for *Raging Bull*)
American Film, March 1981

4 I try to stay in shape. There's no roles for fat leading men.

Kirk Douglas
Photoplay, August 1969

5 I'm very much bigger than I was, so what? It's not really fatness, it's development.

Anita Ekberg
Daily Mail, 2 September 1972

6 I've been overweight since I was four. I don't want to overinflate my role and my job, but isn't there more to me than what I weigh?

Jack Nicholson
Rolling Stone, 29 March 1984

7 I find it really disappointing that a lot of American actors will go to great lengths to gain weight or lose weight or dye their hair [for roles] – and use the same voice.

Kathleen Turner
Film Yearbook, 1986

8 A lot of vices are secret but not gluttony – it shows. It certainly shows on me.

Orson Welles (1915–85)
Playboy, 1967

252 ORSON WELLES

1 I know little about Orson's childhood and seriously doubt if he ever was a child.

Joseph Cotton
Film Yearbook, 1989

2 When I talk to him, I feel like a plant that's been watered.

Marlene Dietrich
Sunday Times, 22 September 1964

3 He was the most talented man I've ever worked with – indeed, ever seen.

Charlton Heston
Variety, 5 November 1985

4 Orson is not a man who could bow down to idiots. And Hollywood is full of them. Orson has a big ego – but he's completely logical. He's a joy! An amateur – I mean that in the very best sense of the word. He loves pictures and plays and all things theatrical.

John Huston (1906–87)
Rolling Stone, 19 February 1981

5 Impossible! But I loved him. He was so misused, abused. Big tragedy! He had the metabolism of a falcon. He burnt ideas so quickly. We'd talk about a sequence over breakfast. He'd start walking up and down, smoking his cigar and, in a minute, he'd be changing it into another idea and then another – in the end he was telling a different story and possible film. That was Orson. A genius!

Fernando Rey
Knave, August 1986

6 Not true there was a cabal preventing Orson making more films. He simply never fulfilled himself after that magnificent start. His own fault – lack of self-discipline.

Director Robert Wise (editor of *Citizen Kane*)
Paris Passion, December 1989

253 WESTERNS

1 Those Italians were jerks, they even called their films by titles like ours – *A Dollar in the Teeth*, can you believe it? And there was this Italian actor who called himself Clint Westwood. *Westwood!*

Clint Eastwood
Sunday Times magazine, 1969

2 Everybody knows nobody ever stood in the street and let the heavy draw first. That's where I disagree with the [John] Wayne concept. I do all the stuff Wayne would never do. I play bigger-than-life characters but I'll shoot a guy in the back. I go by the expediency of the moment.

Clint Eastwood
Variety, 14 September 1976

3 I'd sure hate to see the genre disappear.

Clint Eastwood
Cannes, 12 May 1985

4 Fifteen out of nearly 80 films isn't that many. Trouble is I hate horses and I hate riding.

Henry Fonda (1905–82)
Photoplay, October 1976

5 You can tell any story in a Western. How can you not be fascinated by them?

Silverado director Lawrence Kasdan
Deauville, 14 September 1985

6 They call me the father of the Spaghetti Western. If so, how many sons of bitches have I spawned?

Sergio Leone (1921–89)
Film Yearbook, 1990

7 The more and more terrified people get of making Westerns, the more I want to do one.

Steven Spielberg
Rolling Stone, 24 October 1985

8 All our Western lore is exaggerated and distorted. The gunmen weren't very good shots. They were fast but their fights were at such close range they could never miss. Audiences think they were daring men. In fact, they were a pretty desperate crowd, not romantic but very cowardly, very dirty and usually, very drunk.

James Stewart
London, January 1966

9 I didn't chose Westerns, they sorta chose me.
James Stewart
Radio Times, 31 August 1972

10 In B-pictures, all we ever did was tell a story. He's gone to Red
Gap! Where's Red Gap? There's Red Gap! Let's git after him to Red
Gap. Here's Red Gap! But in A-pictures, you reacted more to the
situations.
John Wayne (1907–79)
Game, June 1975
(*See also* 166.8)

254 WIVES

1 I kept putting my wife under a pedestal.
Woody Allen
Time, 3 July 1972

255 WOMEN BY MEN

1 Directing is more fun with women – everything is.
Ingmar Bergman
Film Yearbook, 1990

2 What do I look for in women? Clean knickers.
James Caan
London, August 1974

3 In bed, the trouble with women is elbows. They always have an
arm left over – and that arm has an elbow. Women have absolutely
no control of their elbows.
Michael Caine
TV Times, 3 January 1980

4 You know the Canadian definition of the perfect woman? She's
4 ft high, got no teeth and has a flat head so you can rest your drink.
Tommy Chong
Playboy, September 1982

5 I like photographing women because they're aesthetically
interesting.
Brian De Palma
Film Yearbook, 1986
(*See also* 249.1)

6 Women tend to be smarter than men in a lot of areas. You see a lot
of terribly intelligent men with dumb women but you never see
terribly intelligent women with dumb guys.
Clint Eastwood
Playboy, February 1974

7 For years, I was frightened of women. You realize, especially when
you're young, that women are life-givers and they can take it away,
too.
Cary Grant (1904–86)
Daily Mail, 3 October 1974

8 Women who have been sewn into their clothes should never drink
to excess.
Nunnally Johnson
American Film, October 1981

9 Women are the industry's last remnant of optimism. They haven't
been in the business long enough to be battered into animals. They're
not on the phone – on your time – promoting five other deals.
Writer-producer Robert Kaufman
Film Yearbook, 1984

10 When they get a period it's really difficult for them to function
as human beings.
Jerry Lewis hitting headlines in Montreal. (He later 'apologized': 'I wasn't attacking
the female gender by any means – not with the type of sex-drive I have, honey.')
Film Yearbook, 1988

11 Too many women don't realize they're women and that disturbs
me.
Lee Marvin (1924–87)
Sunday Express, 27 March 1966

12   What else is there to live for? Chinese food and women. There is nothing else!

Dudley Moore
Playboy, January 1983

13   I prefer the company of women. I'm buzzed by the female mystique. I always tell young men, there are three rules: they hate us, we hate them; they're stronger, they're smarter; and most important, they don't play fair.

Jack Nicholson
Rolling Stone, 29 March 1984

14   I was scared to death of women for years. I'd have jumped out the window rather than into bed with Bardot.

Anthony Perkins
Photoplay, November 1986

15   Treat every queen like a whore and every whore like a queen.

Anthony Quinn
Sunday Mirror, 1974

16   In most action movies, women are in the way.

Arnold Schwarzenegger
Playboy, January 1988

17   Women are more difficult to handle than men. It's their minds.

Peter Sellers (1925–80)
Sunday Mirror, 19 August 1973

18   The only time I use them [in films], they're either naked or dead.

Producer Joel Silver
Vanity Fair, August 1990

19   I'm supposed to have a PhD on the subject of women. Truth is, I've flunked more often than not. I'm very fond of women. I admire them. But, like all men, I don't understand them.

Frank Sinatra
Life, 17 May 1965

20   The film will have everything women want – men, money, jewellery, castles, caviar, champagne and love, love, love.

Producer Larry Spangler on *Chanel Solitaire*
International Herald Tribune, 6–7 September 1980

21   Behind every successful man you'll find a woman – who has absolutely nothing to wear.

James Stewart
Film Yearbook, 1990

22   I've had three wives, six children, six grandchildren and I still don't understand women.

John Wayne (1907–79)
Weekend, 7 April 1969

256   WOMEN BY WOMEN

1   We do it all! We create the relationships. We hold them together. We maintain the households. We raise the children. We bring in half the income. We are the souls and the nurturers and we don't even give ourselves credit for it. We think: 'What would we do without him?' We don't even *own* the power that we have. Women are so strong and we don't even know it. That's why I love women so much.

Jane Fonda
Cannes, May 1989

2   A woman is exploited *all* the time.

Goldie Hawn
Playboy, January 1985

3   With women it's 'pardon me while I bake a cake or have a child,' they're pulled 60 ways from Sunday. It's hard to know what's woman and what's custom. I find a woman's point of view much grander and finer than a man's.

Katharine Hepburn
Newsweek, 10 November 1969

4   A woman won't insist on marriage. She doesn't depend on the man. In fact, she *does*, but is too brave to show it. Oh, how brave women have to be.

Jeanne Moreau
Evening Standard, 3 August 1962

5   Women are superior to men. I don't even think we're equal.

Barbra Streisand
Playboy, October 1977

257 WOMEN DIRECTORS

1 There does still exist some male resentment over women directors. And it's not only men who're afraid of whatever it is they seem to be afraid of. Women also compound the problem. When they do get into these powerful positions with studios, they don't give their films to women to direct.

Zelda Barron
Photoplay, February 1989

2 There are people in the industry who *cannot* imagine a woman director being in charge of the crew. There's a certain Boys' Club reality to all business, not just film.

Martha Coolidge
Film Yearbook, 1987

3 When I went to work in Universal Studios in 1914, there were five women directors. Lois Weber made the biggest pictures. John Ford and I alternated as prop man for this great director. If women haven't got a directing job now, it's their own fault.

Henry Hathaway (1898–1985)
Deauville, 7 September 1983

4 If this is going to be an article on women directors, I refuse to be part of it.

Diane Kurys
Film Yearbook, 1986

5 Orson Welles said: 'When it becomes painful for you not to be a director – then you do it.' And so I did. And in *L'Adolesence*, you're seeing much more of what I am than when I act.

Jeanne Moreau
International Herald Tribune, 5 October 1982

258 WORK

1 I work to stay alive.

Bette Davis (1908–89)
Films Illustrated, December 1979

2   To work is a noble art.
Catherine Deneuve
L'Express, 1976

3   I don't work – I live!
Gérard Depardieu
Mulhouse (France), 9 September 1976

4   Get the old girl out of the garage, recharge the battery, blow up the tyres, get her simonized and off she goes.
Katharine Hepburn
Panorama (USA), March 1981

5   The President of the United States doesn't know what he's going to be doing March 19 at 9 am – but a movie star does. It doesn't matter if your mother's died or if there's been an earthquake, you're going to be out filming the movie.
Jack Nicholson
Daily Mirror, 30 August 1989

259 WORLD

1   The world was created by a very smart person and it probably took him more than seven days. Probably took him a month. It's that complicated.
Mel Brooks
American Premiere, September 1981

2   I can't help feeling the world is on this terrible roller coaster where nobody can get it up since the atom bomb.
Anjelica Huston
Vanity Fair, July 1990

260 WRITERS

1   Anybody can direct. There are only 11 good writers.
Mel Brooks
New Yorker, 1978

2   Michael Frayn was so flattered to have a film made of his own
script that if we'd done it in Swahili he'd have been perfectly happy.
The thrill of having us mangle his script was all he asked for.

John Cleese (on *Clockwise*)
The Observer magazine, 23 February 1986

3   Umberto Eco's attitude is that of many Italian novelists. He
considers his work finished and doesn't feel like making a statue or
an opera out of it.

Producer Franco Cristaldi
Film Yearbook, 1987

4   Cats gotta scratch. Dogs gotta bite. I gotta write.

James Elroy
Cinéma, Cinémas, No. 40, Antenne 2 (French TV), February 1986

5   In terms of authority, screenwriters rank somewhere between the
man who guards the studio gate and the man who runs the studio
that week.

William Goldman
Film Yearbook, 1984

6   If they treated writers like they treat directors, I wouldn't direct.
But they don't, so I want to direct.

Attributed to *Jaws* scenarist Carl Gottlieb

7   They always say – forget the novel. How could I? I'm a
novelist.

Jerzy Kosinski (1934–91)
Films Illustrated, September 1989

8   Black writers are often measured on a black rage scale. You've
got to be angry. James Baldwin was always seen as being furious or
angry. Saul Bellow didn't have to be angry.

Hanif Kureishi, *My Beautiful Laundrette* scenarist
Film Yearbook, 1987

9   With novelists, I don't *have* to get on well. I buy the rights and
then I create – with another writer. If a novelist wants to have a say
about how his book is translated to the screen, he shouldn't sell it!
The word 'sell' implies giving up his rights.

Otto Preminger (1906–86)
Films Illustrated, January 1980

10   If I write a novel, I'm a god. If I write a screenplay, I'm a minor
deity.

Donald Westlake
Variety, 11 February 1991

261 WRITERS BY STARS

1 I'll make one statement: after reading *Wired*, I believe Nixon was innocent. Does that give you some idea?

James Belushi (on the biography of his brother, John, by Watergate journalist Bob Woodward)
Ritz, March 1987

2 Somerset Maugham said there were three rules for writing – and nobody knows what they are.

Joan Collins
Films Illustrated, August 1978

3 Ian Fleming? A terrific snob but very good company.

Sean Connery
Rolling Stone, 27 October 1981

4 Lillian Hellman is a homely woman, yet she moves as if she were Marilyn Monroe.

Jane Fonda
Newsweek, 10 October 1977

5 Hemingway always rather disconcerted me – by eating the glass after he'd had his drink.

Cary Grant (1904–86)
Sunday Express, 7 June 1964

6 What they think about what *they* write is really not the issue. You're not writing, you're making a film. I never had a conversation with Arthur Miller, on *Death of a Salesman*, apart from a short, unpleasant one, which didn't end well for him.

John Malkovich
Paris, 14 November 1990

7 I'm not just a dumb blonde this time, I'm a crazy dumb blonde. And to think, *Arthur* did this to me. He was supposed to be writing this for me. He could've written *anything* and he came up with *this*.

Marilyn Monroe (1926–62) (on *The Misfits* written by her third husband Arthur Miller)
Lena Pepitone and William Stadiem, *Marilyn Monroe Confidential*, 1979

8 I've got the film rights of *Waiting For Godot* from Samuel Beckett. He said it was impossible. Then, I told him about the talkies. The last film he saw was Buster Keaton.

Peter O'Toole
Scene, 12 December 1962

9 I *respect* writers, for Christ's sake. To an even greater extent than
the director, the writer makes or breaks a picture – certainly not
some smooth-faced, empty-headed actors, strutting and preening.

Robert Redford
Rolling Stone, 15 April 1971

262 WRITERS ON STARS

1 It's certainly no hardship being played by Jack Nicholson or
Dustin Hoffman. I figure that by now those guys have earned about
$8/9 million to play me. It makes me think that next time, I should
play myself.

Watergate journalist Carl Bernstein (on *Heartburn* and *All The President's Men*)
Film Yearbook, 1988

2 I don't think Paul Newman really thinks he's Paul Newman in his
head.

William Goldman
Time, 6 December 1982

3 The public will never see him at his funniest and most intelligent.
Melvin is at his best when he's with friends and in a raging jealousy
over someone more successful.

Joseph Heller (on Mel Brooks)
Newsweek, 17 February 1975

4 Warren Beatty is psychotic about the possibility of overlooking
anything. Easy going is not a quality he has. You know how
presidents age in office? If Beatty were President, either he would be
dead after the first year or the country would be dead – because his
attention to detail is maniacal.

Buck Henry
Time, 3 July 1978

5 Joan Collins' whole career is a testimony to menopausal chic.

Attributed to Erica Jong

6 You'd have to be around him for a year before you saw his ugly
side, assuming he has one. He's very laid back. If you bother him, he
won't bother you. In that sense, he's like the characters in his films.

Norman Mailer (on Clint Eastwood)
Film Comment, October 1984

7 I've interviewed every great sex symbol from Paul Newman to Sting – and Guy the Gorilla before he was stuffed. If you laid their libidoes end to end, they still wouldn't macho up to the sexual impact of Sean Connery – a cross between the Monarch of the Glen and the sharp side of Ben Nevis.

Jean Rook
Sunday Times magazine, 5 November 1989

263 WRITING

1 I'm happy with the typewriter. Heavy and solid, not like these plastic typewriters today. When my mother took me up to buy it, the salesman told me: 'This typewriter will last longer than you will.' Looks like he might have been right.

Woody Allen
Time Out, 1 November 1989

2 Who's ever going to write a film in which I get the girl? Me!

John Cleese
Deauville, September 1988

3 Writing is a lonely job unless you're a drinker, in which case you always have a friend within reach.

Emilio Estevez
Film Yearbook, 1986

4 Sheilagh Delaney and I were working on the script of *Charlie Bubbles*. We didn't know how to end it. One day, she came in: 'I know what happens – they eat him, they cook him!' I didn't think Western film mythology was ready for that.

Albert Finney
Ritz, No. 127, July 1988

5 Most of us so-called stars don't have the discipline to write. Anyway, it's a lot of work for less money.

Richard Gere
New York Daily News, 1979

6 That's something you've got to learn about screenwriting – how to fight for what's written but to know enough about movies to know that things do change.

Mark Peploe
Movieline, December 1990

264 YOUTH

1 Early in life I was visited by the bluebird of anxiety.
Woody Allen
New York Times magazine, 22 April 1979

2 Every kid has to kick his father in the balls.
Michael Douglas
Playboy, February 1986

3 Adolescents turn on you – that's their job.
Attributed to director Ron Howard

INDEX OF AUTHORS

In this index the entries refer to individual quotations rather than pages. Each entry contains two numbers, the first is the number of the topic and the second the actual quotation. For example, under 'Allen, Fred', the reference is 42.1. This refers to the 1st quotation appearing under the 42nd topic, which is 'California'. The numbers and titles of the topics appear at the top of the pages.

Abraham, F. Murray, 179.1, 246.1
Adjani, Isabelle, 82.1, 166.1, 231.1, 232.1, 241.1
Adler, Stella, 243.1
Alda, Alan, 95.1,
Allen, Fred, 42.1
Allen, Woody, 18.1, 19.1, 20.1, 38.1, 60.1, 64.1, 75.1, 80.1, 83.1, 87.1, 89.1, 97.1, 102.1, 108.1–3, 111.1, 140.1, 146.1, 147.1, 156.1, 179.2, 194.1, 202.1, 217.1, 220.1, 226.1, 243.2, 254.1, 263.1, 264.1
Altman, Robert, 104.1, 113.1,
Anderson, Lindsay, 9.1, 40.1,
Andress, Ursula, 36.1, 169.1, 175.1
Andrews, Julie, 229.1
Anger, Kenneth, 20.2, 247.1
Annaud, Jean-Jacques, 98.1
Ann-Margret, 6.1, 82.2, 115.2,
Anonymous, 39.11, 177.1, 186.1
Anspach, Susan, 202.2
Arquette, Rosanna, 82.3, 216.1
Astaire, Fred, 107.1, 220.2, 229.2, 242.1
Autry, Gene, 13.1

Bacall, Lauren, 73.1, 165.1, 173.1
Bach, Barbara, 36.2
Baker, Carroll, 143.1
Baker, Sir Stanley, 5.1
Balaban, Bob, 5.2, 79.1, 86.1
Baldwin, Alec, 149.1, 174.1, 196.1
Baldwin, James, 225.1
Bancroft, Anne, 156.2
Bardot, Brigitte, 17.1
Barker, Clive, 24.1
Barkin, Ellen, 39.1, 156.3
Barron, Zelda, 257.1
Barrymore, Ethel, 131.1

Basinger, Kim, 82.4, 113.2, 137.1, 143.2 (her father: 141.1)
Bates, Alan, 232.2
Beatty, Warren, 6.2, 48.1, 126.1, 131.2, 138.1, 151.1, 156.4, 167.1, 183.1, 188.1, 190.1, 220.3
Bedelia, Bonnie, 218.1
Begley Jr, Ed, 94.1
Belushi, James, 261.1
Belushi, John, 90.1, 146.2
Benazeraf, José, 233.11
Bennett, Hywel, 197.1
Benson, Robby, 200.1
Benton, Robert, 237.1
Berenger, Tom, 7.1, 223.2
Bergen, Candice, 3.1, 75.2, 104.2, 152.1, 175.2, 223.1
Bergman, Ingmar, 79.2, 204.1, 255.1
Bergman, Ingrid, 4.1, 47.1, 63.1, 127.2, 138.2, 150.1, 157.2, 208.1
Bernstein, Carl, 262.1
Berry, John, 80.2
Bertolucci, Bernardo, 114.1, 179.2, 244.1
Birkin, Jane, 117.1
Bisset, Jacqueline, 137.2, 208.2
Black, Karen, 112.1, 130.1, 141.2, 221.1
Bogarde, Dirk, 6.3, 22.1, 43.1, 44.1, 59.1, 105.1, 106.1, 112.2, 132.1, 148.1, 170.1, 244.2
Bogart, Humphrey, 2.1, 11.1
Bogdanovich, Peter, 88.1, 133.1
Bonnaire, Sandrine, 103.1
Boorman, John, 23.1, 45.1, 47.2, 171.1, 209.1
Borgnine, Ernest, 112.3
Bowie, David, 65.1, 74.1, 81.1, 183.2, 194.2, 220.4
Boyle, Peter, 65.2

Index of Authors

Braga, Sonia, 94.2, 181.1, 219.1, 223.3
Branagh, Kenneth, 138.3
Brando, Marlon, 2.2, 4.2, 5.3–4, 14.1, 19.2, 21.1, 26.1, 30.1, 60.2, 62.1, 64.2, 100.1, 106.2, 116.1, 125.1, 128.2, 131.3, 139.1, 141.3, 146.3, 167.2, 171.2, 181.2, 184.1, 197.2, 200.2, 220.5, 232.3, 234.1, 236.1, 240.1
Brasseur, Claude, 81.2
Brest, Martin, 80.3
Brickman, Marshall, 12.1, 60.3, 113.3
Broccoli, Cubby, 35.10
Bronson, Charles, 48.2, 69.1, 101.2, 174.2, 251.1
Brooks, Albert, 22.2, 101.1, 189.1, 205.1, 238.1
Brooks, James L., 238.2
Brooks, Mel, 28.1, 42.2, 54.1, 57.1, 64.3, 69.2, 86.2, 88.2, 90.2, 96.1, 116.2, 128.3, 129.1, 140.2, 147.2, 149.2, 167.3, 181.3, 184.2, 200.3, 236.2, 240.2, 250.1, 259.1, 260.1
Brooks, Richard, 151.2
Brown, Reb, 10.1
Buñuel, Luis, 178.1
Burns, George, 8.1, 9.2, 72.1, 181.4, 220.6, 234.2
Burstyn, Ellen, 38.2
Burton, Richard, 8.2, 11.2, 13.2, 89.2, 112.4, 118.1, 138.4, 141.4, 148.2, 158.1, 166.2, 167.4, 185.1, 199.1, 202.3, 217.2, 235.1, 236.3
Burton, Tim, 77.1
Busey, Gary, 131.4
Buttons, Red, 10.2
Byrne, Gabriel, 187.1, 236.4

Caan, James, 10.3, 11.3, 27.1, 38.3, 117.2, 142.1, 148.3, 255.2
Cage, Nicolas, 147.3, 172.1, 214.1, 224.1
Cagney, James, 46.1, 112.5, 167.5, 229.3
Cain, Chris, 215.1
Caine, Michael, 7.2, 8.3, 40.2, 46.2, 56.1, 61.1, 76.1, 90.3, 93.1, 117.3, 119.2, 122.2, 126.2, 132.2, 134.1, 138.5, 141.5, 149.3, 150.2, 167.6, 181.5, 184.3, 185.2, 190.2, 194.3, 209.2, 211.1, 220.7, 225.2, 240.3, 243.3, 250.2, 255.3

Cameron, James, 136.1
Cannon, Dyan, 82.5
Capra, Frank, 87.2
Cardinale, Claudia, 7.3, 40.3
Caron, Leslie, 229.4
Carr, Allan, 42.3, 133.2
Carradine, David, 154.1
Carradine, John, 46.3, 181.6
Carradine, Keith, 26.2
Carson, Johnny, 177.2
Carson, Kit, 149.4
Cassavetes, John, 79.3, 97.2
Cassavetes, Nick, 215.2
Chabrol, Claude, 95.2
Chambers, Marilyn, 34.1, 186.2, 203.1, 221.2
Chaplin, Sir Charles, 2.3, 88.3, 116.3, 166.3, 174.3, 179.4
Chaplin, Geraldine, 161.1, 215.3
Chase, Chevy, 62.2, 90.4, 103.2, 220.8
Cher, 3.2, 90.5, 103.3, 117.4, 148.4, 182.1, 203.2, 216.2, 221.3, 237.2
Chong, Rae Dawn, 33.1, 148.5, 175.3, 187.2, 216.3
Chong, Tommy, 22.3, 57.2, 64.4, 69.3, 147.4, 205.2, 255.4
Christie, Julie, 3.3, 9.3, 103.4, 156.5, 216.4, 234.3
Cimino, Michael, 78.1, 116.4, 129.2
Clarke, Frank, 44.2
Clayburgh, Jill, 39.2
Cleese, John, 12.2, 14.2, 37.1, 61.2, 64.5, 65.3, 73.2, 75.3, 76.2, 125.2, 156.6, 174.4, 181.7, 229.5, 260.2, 263.2 – plus Introduction.
Clemons, Clarence, 207.1
Close, Glenn, 57.3, 161.2, 165.2
Cohen, Larry, 214.2
Collins, Joan, 8.4, 9.4, 12.3, 32.1, 38.4, 39.3, 69.4, 74.2, 90.6, 103.5, 117.5, 138.6, 151.3, 157.3, 182.2, 186.3, 194.4, 199.2, 205.3, 221.4, 222.1, 224.2, 226.2, 232.4, 235.2, 236.5, 261.2
Connery, Sean, 1.1, 9.5, 14.3, 35.1, 35.4, 35.8, 35.12, 75.4, 115.3, 142.2, 146.4, 167.7, 194.5, 203.3, 204.2, 209.3, 224.3, 261.3
Conti, Tom, 40.4, 78.2, 81.3, 114.5.
Coolidge, Martha, 257.2

Coppola, Francis, 17.2, 60.4, 75.5, 87.3, 102.3, 120.1, 146.5, 188.2, 233.2, 243.4

Cort, Bud, 227.1

Costner, Kevin, 2.4, 4.3, 5.5, 46.4, 48.3, 93.2, 131.5, 146.6, 207.2, 231.2

Cotton, Joseph, 60.5, 252.1

Coward, Sir Noël, 29.1

Cox, Brian, 59.2

Coyote, Peter, 90.7, 202.4

Crawford, Joan, 32.2, 43.2, 235.3

Cristaldi, Franco, 260.3

Cronenberg, David, 1.2, 67.1, 153.1, 169.2

Crosby, Bing, 229.6

Cruise, Tom, 65.4, 103.6, 149.5, 210.1, 231.3, 234.4

Cukor, George, 233.3

Curtis, Jamie Lee, 34.2, 39.4, 109.1, 151.4, 175.4

Curtis, Tony, 9.6, 22.4, 64.6, 68.1, 94.3, 146.7, 168.1, 181.8, 205.4, 239.1

Cushing, Peter, 6.4, 125.3, 226.3

d'Abo, Maryam, 36.3

Dafoe, Willem, 6.5

Dalle, Béatrice, 148.6, 175.5, 214.3

Dalton, Timothy, 35.13, 142.3, 209.4

Dance, Charles, 232.5

D'Angelo, Beverly, 231.4

Danning, Sybil, 251.2

Danson, Ted, 4.4, 106.3

Davis, Bette, 3.4, 9.7, 31.1, 38.5, 50.1, 56.2, 117.6, 122.3, 147.5, 148.7, 151.5, 155.1, 163.1, 165.3, 178.2, 194.6, 204.3, 221.5, 231.5, 258.1

Davis, Brad, 9.8, 13.3

Davis Jnr, Sammy, 25.1

Davis, William, 188.3

Day, Doris, 204.4

Day Lewis, Daniel, 141.6, 207.3

Dean, James, 75.6, 245.11

Delon, Alain, 67.2, 80.4, 101.3, 143.3, 180.1, 193.1, 217.3

Deneuve, Catherine, 65.5, 89.3, 156.7, 163.2, 232.6, 258.2

De Niro, Robert, 2.5, 4.5, 5.6, 17.3, 27.2, 44.3, 78.3, 96.2, 138.7,

141.7, 146.8, 170.2, 207.4, 217.4, 226.4, 231.6, 251.3

Dennehy, Brian, 10.4

De Palma, Brian, 249.1, 255.5

Depardieu, Gérard, 2.6, 4.6, 6.6, 26.3, 55.1, 57.4, 59.3, 75.7, 78.4, 80.5, 111.2, 112.6, 122.4, 139.2, 148.8, 152.2, 153.2, 174.5, 194.7, 195.1, 207.5, 217.5, 224.4, 235.4, 240.4, 243.5, 258.3

Derek, Bo, 48.4, 141.8, 172.2, 175.6

Derek, John, 15.1, 74.3, 81.4, 122.5, 143.4, 151.6, 175.6

Dern, Bruce, 4.7, 74.3, 81.5, 94.4, 248.1

Dern, Laura, 202.5, 212.1, 215.4

Dickinson, Angie, 7.4, 151.7, 187.3

Dietrich, Marlene, 7.5, 60.6, 115.6, 171.3, 252.2

Divine, 138.8

Donahue, Troy, 246.2

Dors, Diana, 8.5, 39.5, 148.9, 224.5

Douglas, Kirk, 2.7, 6.7, 54.3, 215.5, 217.6, 248.2, 251.4

Douglas, Michael, 2.8, 6.8, 7.6, 43.3, 54.4, 113.4, 152.3, 164.1, 215.6, 246.3, 264.2

Dreyfuss, Richard, 8.6, 68.2, 94.5, 103.7, 185.3

Dunaway, Faye, 150.3, 232.7, 236.6

Duncan, Patrick, 250.3

Duvall, Robert, 10.5, 69.5, 81.6

Eastwood, Clint, 2.9, 4.8, 5.7, 19.3, 20.3, 22.5, 27.3, 41.1, 43.4, 44.4, 50.2, 54.2, 55.2, 56.3, 57.5, 60.7, 67.3, 69.6, 94.6, 103.8, 112.7, 116.5, 125.4, 128.4, 141.9, 147.6, 148.10, 170.3, 181.9, 183.3, 185.4, 186.4, 193.2, 202.6, 204.5, 207.6, 226.5, 239.2, 249.2, 249.3, 253.1, 253.2–3, 255.6

Edwards, Blake, 121.1, 240.5

Ekberg, Anita, 39.6, 251.5

Ekland, Britt, 36.4, 245.2

Eisner, Michael, 167.8

Elroy, James, 260.4

Epstein, Julius J., 47.3

Estevez, Emilio, 6.9, 263.3

Evans, Peter, 38.6

Evans, Robert, 89.4

Fairbanks Jr, Douglas, 203.4

Index of Authors

Farrow, Mia, 12.4
Feldman, Marty, 5.8, 64.7, 112.8, 148.11
Fellini, Federico, 210.2
Ferreri, Marco, 110.1
Field, Sally, 10.6, 46.5, 97.3, 104.3, 118.2, 179.5–6
Fields, W.C., 202.7
Fierstein, Harvey, 134.2–3, 220.9
Finch, Peter, 132.3, 240.6
Finney, Albert, 38.7, 116.6, 162.1, 185.5, 263.4
Finney, Alice, 172.3
Fisher, Carrie, 3.5, 9.9, 39.7, 52.1, 90.8, 117.7, 143.5, 241.2
Fletcher, Louise, 26.4, 82.6
Fonda, Henry, 4.9, 6.10, 38.8, 117.8, 157.7, 174.7, 178.3, 183.4, 184.4, 202.8, 215.7, 234.5, 253.4
Fonda, Jane, 3.6, 9.10, 14.4, 18.2, 34.3, 39.8, 51.1, 110.2, 115.7, 116.7, 146.9, 148.12, 150.4, 156.8, 173.2, 225.3, 236.7, 238.3, 256.1, 261.4
Fonda, Peter, 90.9, 98.2, 128.5
Ford, Glenn, Introduction
Ford, Harrison, 42.4, 77.2, 102.4, 103.9, 149.6, 167.9, 172.4, 211.2, 214.4, 217.7, 239.3
Ford, John, 233.4
Forrest, Frederic, 131.6
Forsyth, Bill, 140.3
Fosse, Bob, 80.6, 95.3
Foster, Jodie, 112.9, 139.3
Fox, Michael J., 91.1, 127.3, 154.2, 240.7
Frears, Stephen, 32.3, 88.4
Friedkin, William, 88.5
Friedman, David F., 186.5
Fuller, Sam, 116.8

Gabin, Jean, 153.3
Gable, Clark, 168.2
Gabor, Zsa Zsa, 199.3
Gainsbourg, Serge, 150.5
Garcia, Andy, 246.4
Garner, James, 57.6, 143.6
Garr, Teri, 61.3, 65.6, 94.7
Gassman, Vittorio, 163.3
Gazzara, Ben, 80.7
Gere, Richard, 170.4, 180.2, 263.5
Gibson, Mel, 43.5, 67.4, 141.10, 195.2, 217.8, 226.6

Gielgud, Sir John, 9.11, 14.5, 66.1, 116.9, 207.7
Gilliam, Terry, 137.3, 238.4
Giroux, Jackelyn, 168.3
Gish, Lillian, 9.12
Gleason, Jackie, 11.4, 96.3, 145.1, 220.10
Glenn, Scott, 6.11
Godard, Jean-Luc, 17.4, 22.6, 23.2, 35.3, 86.3, 90.10, 115.8, 116.10, 132.4, 141.11, 185.6, 206.1, 245.3
Goering, Dr Gerd, 77.3
Golan, Menahem, 113.5, 167.10, 170.5, 192.1, 226.7
Goldberg, Whoopi, 33.2, 161.3, 200.4
Goldman, William, 10.7, 160.1, 262.2, 262.2
Goodman, John, 244.3
Gottlieb, Carl, 260.6
Gould, Elliott, 81.7, 181.10, 204.6
Granger, Stewart, 46.6, 118.3, 204.7
Grant, Cary, 25.2, 46.7, 75.8, 90.11, 107.2, 124.1, 130.2, 138.9, 193.3, 235.5, 255.7, 261.5
Grey, Jennifer, 229.7
Guinness, Sir Alec, 121.2, 207.8, 213.1

Hackman, Gene, 4.10, 5.9, 93.3, 115.9, 139.4, 173.3, 211.3, 231.7, 236.8
Hall, David, 168.4
Hall, Jerry, 165.4
Hamill, Mark, 161.4
Hamilton, George, 72.2, 90.12, 107.3, 120.2
Hamilton, Guy, 36.5, 48.5
Hanks, Tom, 57.7, 226.8
Hare, David, 233.5
Hargreaves, John, 105.2
Harvey, Laurence, 60.8, 167.11, 174.8
Hathaway, Henry, 257.3
Hawn, Goldie, 8.7, 62.3, 64.8, 101.4, 110.3, 113.6, 157.4, 206.2, 229.8, 235.6, 256.2
Hayden, Sterling, 46.8, 109.2, 176.1
Heller, Joseph, 262.3
Hemingway, Mariel, 54.5
Hemmings, David, 25.4, 67.5, 113.7, 174.9, 193.4

— 290 —

Hendra, Tony, 33.3, 62.4
Henry, Buck, 262.4
Hepburn, Audrey, 46.9
Hepburn, Katharine, 1.3, 3.7, 25.3,
    26.5, 37.2, 46.10, 51.2, 54.6, 75.9,
    78.5, 107.4, 156.9, 165.5, 167.12,
    180.3, 205.6, 208.3, 221.6, 223.4,
    234.6, 236.9, 256.3, 258.4
Herman, Pee Wee, 155.2
Hershey, Barbara, 12.5, 150.6,
    210.3
Herzog, Werner, 26.6
Heston, Charlton, 101.5, 115.9,
    138.10, 161.5, 207.9, 252.3
Hill, George Roy, 88.6
Hill, Walter, 101.2
Hines, Gregory, 200.5
Hitchcock, Sir Alfred, 22.7, 35.2,
    48.6, 125.5, 130.3–4, 174.10
Hoffman, Dustin, 6.12, 27.4, 56.4,
    93.4, 102.5, 110.4, 113.8, 131.7,
    158.2, 161.6, 170.6, 172.5, 184.5,
    191.1, 194.8, 207.10, 231.8,
    236.10, 237.3
Hogan, Paul, 69.7
Holden, William, 39.9, 48.7, 54.7,
    211.4
Holm, Ian, 147.7
Hooper, Tobe, 135.2
Hope, Bob, 167.13, 186.6
Hopkins, Anthony, 4.11, 20.4, 38.9,
    74.4, 93.5, 138.11, 166.4
Hopper, Dennis, 74.5
Hoskins, Bob, 5.10, 46.11, 81.8,
    86.4, 199.4, 230.1
Howard, Ron, 264.3
Huppert, Isabelle, 3.8
Hudson, Hugh, 40.5
Hudson, Rock, 142.4, 172.6
Hurt, John, 11.5, 14.6, 80.8, 132.5
Hurt, William, 2.10, 52.2, 56.5,
    75.10, 181.11
Huston, Anjelica, 61.4, 90.13,
    126.3, 259.2
Huston, John, 37.3, 38.10, 54.8,
    79.4, 86.5, 88.7, 120.3, 154.3,
    157.8, 168.5, 183.5, 201.1, 203.5,
    222.2, 226.9, 252.4, plus
    Introduction
Hutton, Lauren, 175.7, 221.7

Idle, Eric, 136.1

Independent, 168.footnote
Irons, Jeremy, 2.11, 100.2, 101.6,
Irving, John, 24.3

Jackson, Glenda, 3.9, 4.12, 39.10,
    40.6, 57.8, 69.8, 93.6, 155.3,
    165.6, 167.14, 169.3, 179.7,
    182.3, 219.2, 226.10
Jaffe, Stanley, 101.7
Jaglom, Henry, 12.6, 170.7
Jarmusch, Jim, 209.5
Joffe, Charles, 12.7
Johnson, Don, 52.3
Johnson, Nunally, 168.6–7, 255.8
Jones, Terry, 45.2
Jong, Erica, 262.5
Jordan, Neil, 15.2

Kael, Pauline, 131.8
Kahn, Madeline, 7.7, 62.5, 82.7
Kaprisky, Valerie, 65.7
Kasdan, Lawrence, 253.5
Katzenberg, Jeffrey, 137.4
Kaufman, Lloyd, 198.1
Kaufman, Robert, 64.9, 255.9
Kazan, Elia, 38.11, 74.6, 166.5
Keaton, Buster, 116.11
Keaton, Diane, 12.8, 103.10
Keller, Marthe, 14.7, 133.3
Kellerman, Sally, 7.8
Kelly, Gene, 229.9, 233.6
Kennedy, Kathleen, 84.1
Kernan, Margot, 205.5
Kidder, Margot, 118.4, 175.8
Kieslowski, Krzysztof, 115.10,
    140.4
Kingsley, Ben, 40.7, 199.5
Kinski, Klaus, 5.11, 58.1, 96.4,
    97.4, 129.3, 167.15, 170.8
Kinski, Nastassja, 3.10, 13.4,
    115.11, 168.8, 242.2
Kline, Kevin, 69.9, 178.4
Konchalovsky, Andrei, 42.5, 113.9,
    132.6, 241.3
Kosinski, Jerzy, 260.7
Kristel, Sylvia, 141.12, 161.7, 165.7,
    224.6
Kubrick, Stanley, 83.2, 141.13
Kureishi, Hanif, 260.8
Kurosawa, Akira, 87.4
Kurtz, Swoosie, 7.9, 172.7
Kurys, Diane, 257.4

Index of Authors

Lahti, Christine, 232.8
Lancaster, Burt, 222.3, 236.11
Landis, John, 79.5
Lange, Jessica, 141.14, 148.13, 230.2
Laughton, Charles, 166.6, 226.11
Lauper, Cyndie, 9.13
Lavi, Daliah, 159.1
Lean, Sir David, 87.5, 95.4
Lee, Brandon, 106.4
Lee, Christopher, 113.10, 135.3, 240.8
Lee, Spike, 12.9, 200.6, 225.4
Leigh, Janet, 130.5
Lelouch, Claude, 13.5, 98.3, 115.12, 185.7, 232.9
Lemmon, Chris, 215.8
Lemmon, Jack, 234.7
Leone, Sergio, 253.6
Levant, Oscar, 131.9
Levinson, Barry, 233.7
Lewis, Charlotte, 196.2
Lewis, Jerry, 44.5, 255.10
Lithgow, John, 231.9
Little Richard, 182.4
Lloyd, Emily, 123.1
Locke, Peter, 241.4
Logan, Josh, 168.7–8, 233.8
Loren, Sophia, 8.8, 57.9, 100.3, 175.9, 204.8, 216.5, 221.8, 224.7
Lovelace, Linda, 186.7–8
Lucas, George, 96.5, 240.9
Lumet, Sidney, 127.4, 233.9
Lynch, David, 213.2

McDowell, Malcolm, 144.1, 214.5
McGillis, Kelly, 138.12, 150.7, 210.4
MacLaine, Shirley, 43.6, 75.11, 122.6, 178.5, 179.8, 183.6, 199.6, 216.6, 221.9, 234.8, 235.7, 236.12
MacMurray, Fred, 242.3, 245.4
MacNee, Patrick, 73.3
Madigan, Amy, 170.9, 208.4
Madonna, 66.2, 90.14, 117.9, 128.6, 191.2, 219.3, 221.10
Mailer, Norman, 24.3, 37.4, 46.6, 80.9, 112.10, 262.6
Makavejev, Dusan, 88.8
Malden, Karl, 93.7
Malkovich, John, 4.13, 115.13, 116.12, 147.8, 261.6

Malle, Louis, 12.10, 79.6, 88.9, 203.6
Mankiewicz, Joseph L., 127.5, 209.6
Marchiano (ex-Lovelace), Linda, 186.8
Marcovicci, Andrea, 143.7
Marin, Cheech, 159.2, 170.10, 212.2
Marshall, Alan, 192.2
Marshall, Garry, 233.10
Martin, Dean, 46.12
Martin, Steve, 52.4, 62.6, 102.6
Marvin, Lee, 11.6, 38.12, 116.13, 188.4, 203.7, 218.2, 248.3, 249.4, 255.11
Marx, Groucho, 12.11, 168.9
Masina, Guilietta, 120.4
Mastroianni, Marcello, 4.14, 13.6, 15.3, 104.4, 122.7, 150.8, 152.4, 164.2, 195.3, 217.9, 234.9
Mathison, Melissa, 131.10
Matthau, Walter, 161.8, 235.8, 240.10
Mercouri, Melina, 194.9, 209.7
Meyer, Russ, 39.11
Midler, Bette, 11.7, 93.8, 175.10, 216.7, 226.12
Milchan, Arnon, 102.7
Miles, Sarah, 156.10, 223.5
Milius, John, 13.7
Miller, George, 86.6
Mills, Hayley, 3.11, 150.9
Mimieux, Yvette, 231.10
Minnelli, Liza, 57.10, 196.3
Miou-Miou, 232.10
Mitchum, Robert, 6.13, 19.4, 25.5, 27.5, 46.13, 60.9, 105.3, 106.5, 115.14, 136.2, 156.11, 168.10, 192.3, 204.9, 207.11, 210.5, 234.10, 236.13
Monroe, Marilyn, 146.10, 163.4, 219.4, 235.9, 261.7
Montand, Yves, 236.14
Moore, Dudley, 55.3, 90.15, 151.8, 220.11, 225.5, 255.12
Moore, Roger, 35.5–7, 35.9, 132.7, 147.9, 155.4, 205.7, 232.11, 246.5
Moreau, Jeanne, 3.12, 29.2, 112.11, 141.15, 256.4, 257.5
Morrell, David, 201.2
Murphy, Audie, 243.6

Murphy, Eddie, 13.8, 27.6, 33.4, 62.7, 181.12, 200.7, 227.2, 242.4
Murray, Bill, 144.2, 191.3

Neal, Patricia, 183.7
Neame, Ronald, 83.3
Newley, Anthony, 132.8
Newman, Paul, 2.12, 8.9, 14.8, 25.6, 38.13, 44.7, 46.14, 65.8, 100.4–5, 103.10, 109.3, 119.4, 145.2, 156.12, 158.3, 179.9, 181.13, 183.8, 184.6, 191.4, 194.10, 195.4, 197.3, 231.11, 233,11–12, 234.11, 236.15, 240.11, 241.5, 242.5
Newmar, Julie, 76.3
Nichols, Mike, 233.11–12
Nicholson, Jack, 4.15, 5.12, 20.5, 22.8, 37.5, 38.footnote, 54.9, 55.4, 75.12, 90.16, 112.11, 128.7, 131.11, 144.3–4, 145.3, 148.14, 166.7, 179.10, 194.11, 199.7, 214.6, 217.10, 220.12, 222.4, 225.6, 227.3, 230.3, 231.12, 232.12, 234.12, 235.10, 239.4, 241.6, 251.6, 255.13, 258.5
Niven, David, 13.9, 67.6, 99.1, 204.10, 235.11
Novak, Kim, 239.5

O'Connor, Pat, 133.4
Olivier, Lord Laurence, 2.13, 4.16, 22.9, 27.7, 75.13, 120.5, 164.3, 168.11, 195.5, 226.13
Oshima, Nagisa, 206.3
O'Toole, Peter, 2.14, 43.7, 63.2, 102.8, 105.4, 112.12, 117.10, 132.9, 135.4, 138.13, 141.16, 146.11, 155.5, 161.9, 176.2, 181.14, 193.5, 194.12, 202.9, 222.5, 228.1, 232.13, 261.8
Ovitz, Mike, 188.5

Pacino, Al, 10.8, 38.14, 74.7, 91.2, 178.6, 217.11
Palance, Jack, 141.17
Paluzzi, Luciana, 36.6
Pantoliano, Joe, 6.14
Parker, Alan, 44.8, 68.3, 69.10, 79.7, 83.4
Parker, Dorothy, 205.6
Parry, Natasha, 235.12

Parton, Dolly, 39.12, 57.11, 182.5, 188.6, 212.3
Pasternak, Joe, 7.10
Peck, Gregory, 159.3, 183.9
Peckinpah, Sam, 18.3
Penn, Arthur, 233.13
Peploe, Mark, 263.6
Perkins, Anthony, 130.6–7, 135.5, 255.14
Pfeiffer, Michele, 48.8, 115.15, 189.2, 205.8
Pflug, Jo Anne, 172.8
Phillips, Lou Diamond, 187.4
Pialat, Maurice, 45.3
Piccoli, Michel, 143.8
Pickins, Slim, 166.8
Pierson, Frank, 115.16
Pleasence, Donald, 6.15
Poitier, Sidney, 33.5, 200.8
Polanski, Roman, 233.14, 244.4
Pollack, Sydney, 237.4
Pollard, Michael J., 249.5
Pollock, Tom, 238.5
Porizkova, Paulina, 221.11
Powell, Michael, 86.7
Preminger, Otto, 46.15, 113.11, 168.12, 260.9
Presley, Elvis, 27.8, 107.5
Presley, Priscilla, 162.2
Price, Vincent, 6.16, 27.9, 166.9, 167.16
Pryor, Richard, 33.6, 61.5, 62.3, 90.17
Puttnam, David, 16.1, 59.4, 78.6, 102.9, 119.5, 192.4

Quaid, Dennis, 93.9, 162.3, 174.11, 196.4
Quinn, Anthony, 21.2, 38.15, 53.1, 57.12, 93.10, 128.8, 146.12, 164.4, 169.4, 243.7, 254.15

Rampling, Charlotte, 17.5
Reagan, Nancy, 116.footnote
Reagan, Ronald, 4.17, 131.12
Redford, Robert, 5.13, 68.4, 69.11, 71.1, 94.8, 103.11, 112.13, 113.12, 123, 2, 128.9, 131.13, 138.14, 141.18, 156.13, 178.7, 184.7, 185.8, 194.13, 204.11, 220.13, 224.8, 236.16, 261.9
Redgrave, Lynn, 150.10, 185.9

Index of Authors

Redgrave, Vanessa, 3.13, 179.11,
185.10, 187.5, 208.5
Reed, Oliver, 19.5, 81.9
Reeve, Christopher, 58.2, 106.6,
Reguerio, Francisco, 116.14
Remick, Lee, 175.11
Rey, Fernando, 48.9, 81.10, 99.2,
252.5
Reynolds, Burt, 2.15, 5.14, 13.10,
22.10, 27.10, 37.6, 38.16, 63.4,
79.8, 80.10, 86.8, 105.5, 117.11,
128.10, 154.4, 211.5, 219.5,
229.10, 231.13, 232.14
Riazanov, Eldar, 44.9
Richardson, Sir Ralph, 80.11
Rifkind, Malcolm, 41.2
Ritt, Martin, 12.12, 20.6, 31.2, 79.9,
88.10, 115.17,
Rivers, Joan, 34.4
Roberts, Julia, 55.5, 103.12, 127.6,
167.17
Robinson, Bruce, 133.5
Robinson, Phil Alden, 97.5, 233.15
Roddam, Franc, 238.6, 247.2
Roeg, Nicolas, 68.5, 79.10, 87.6,
206.4
Rogers, Roy, 2.16
Romero, George, 135.6
Rook, Jean, 262.7
Rooney, Mickey, 9.14, 22.11,
46.16, 80.11, 150.11, 157.10
Ross, Katharine, 48.10
Rourke, Mickey, 6.17, 58.3, 161.10,
178.8, 203.8, 220.14, 234.13
Russell, Jane, 39.13, 197.4
Russell, Ken, 69.12
Russell, Theresa, 165.8, 225.7

St John, Jill, 157.6
Sampson, Will, 200.9
San Giacomo, Laura, 161.11
Sarandon, Susan, 39.14
Scacchi, Greta, 7.11, 175.12
Schatzberg, Jerry, 87.8
Scheider, Roy, 38.17, 41.3, 111.3,
133.6, 196.5, 218.3, 220.15,
226.14
Schlesinger, John, 48.11, 166.10
Schneider, Maria, 30.2, 60.10,
138.15
Schneider, Romy, 234.14, plus
Introduction

Schrader, Paul, 22.12, 115.18
Schumacher, Joel, 214.7
Schwarzenegger, Arnold, 120.6,
124.2, 150.12, 254.16
Schygulla, Hanna, 82.8
Scorsese, Martin, 70.1, 88.11,
114.2, 115.19
Scott, George C., 26.7, 38.19, 78.7,
144.5, 177.3, 178.9, 194.14,
235.13
Seberg, Jean, 7.12, 157.1
Selleck, Tom, 174.12
Sellers, Peter, 62.8, 92.1–2, 132.10,
138.16, 161.12, 207.12, 217.12,
254.17
Serious, Yahoo, 218.4
Seyrig, Delphine, 134.4
Sharif, Omar, 27.11, 226.15
Shaver, Helen, 3.14
Shaw, Robert, 38.18
Sheen, Charlie, 53.2, 112.15
Sheen, Martin, 74.8, 104.5
Shepard, Sam, 21.3, 90.18, 112.14,
180.4, 191.5
Shepherd, Cybill, 26.8, 141.19
Shields, Brooke, 25.7, 167.18,
208.6, 221.12
Shimkus, Joanna, 65.9
Shire, Talia, 85.1
Short, Robert, 39.15
Sidney, Sylvia, 130.8
Siegel, Don, 23.3, 233.26
Signoret, Simone, 3.15, 7.13, 27.12,
99.3, 185.11, 208.7
Silberman, Serge, 44.10
Silver, Joel, 13.11, 20.7, 255.18
Sinatra, Frank, 151.9, 188.7, 197.5,
202.10, 204.12, 235.14, 155.19
Smith, Madeline, 39.16
Soderbergh, Steven, 12.13, 45.4,
174.13
Spacek, Sissy, 162.4, 172.9
Spangler, Larry, 255.20
Spielberg, Anne, 85.2
Spielberg, Steven, 22.13, 46.17,
60.11, 83.5, 88.12, 90.19, 102.10,
131.14, 176.3, 185.12, 193.6,
194.15, 201.3, 253.7, plus
Introduction
Stallone, Jackie, 7.14
Stallone, Sylvester, 8.10, 9.15, 20.8,
34.5, 69.13, 127.7, 148.15, 159.4,
201.4–6, 203.9, 210.6, 245.5

— 294 —

Stamp, Terence, 75.14
Stanwyck, Barbara 6.18, 100.6
Stapleton, Maureen, 3.16, 228.2
Stark, Ray, 16.2
Steele, Barbara, 70.2
Steiger, Rod, 2.17, 21.4, 103.14, 104.6, 137.5
Stewart, James, 17.6, 60.12, 107.6, 112.15, 130.9, 143.9, 250.4, 253.8–9, 255.21
Stone, Oliver, 61.6, 113.13
Strasberg, Susan, 166.11
Streep, Meryl, 101.8, 103.13, 104.6, 137.5, 141.20, 158.4, 166.12, 172.10, 211.6, 212.4, 235.15
Streisand, Barbra, 22.14, 26.9, 32.4, 38.20, 67.7, 69.14, 96.6, 103.14, 143.10, 161.13, 171.4, 182.6, 188.8–9, 196.6, 205.9, 216.8, 229.11, 232.15, 240.12, 241.7, 256.5
Sutherland, Donald, 48.12, 68.6, 80.12, 127.8, 159.5
Sutherland, Kiefer, 172.11

Tannen, Ned, 22.15, 113.14
Tavoularis, Dean, 160.2, 214.8
Taylor, Don, 139.5
Taylor, Elizabeth, 9.16, 11.8. 60.13, 76.4, 92.3, 115.20, 118.5, 156.14, 157.9, 159.6, 161.14, 172.12, 216.9, 225.8, 229.12, 236.17
Tompkins, Angel, 39.17
Torn, Rip, 172.13
Tracy, Spencer, 4.18, 11.9, 73.4
Travolta, John, 154.5
Trintignant, Jean-Louis, 4.19, 14.9, 75.15, 111.4, 214.9, 226.16, 234.15, 243.8
Truffaut, François, 74.9
Trumbull, Douglas, 230.4, 238.7
Turner, Kathleen, 9.17, 101.9, 152.5, 165.9, 223.6, 251.7
Tyson, Cicley, 200.10

Ullmann, Liv, 234.16
Ustinov, Sir Peter, 64.10, 83.6, 248.4

Vadim, Roger, 29.3, 150.13, 151.10
Valenti, Jack, 247.3
Van der Kamp, John, 168.13

Voight, Jon, 116.19

Walters, Julie, 1.4, 226.17
Wambaugh, Joseph, 238.8
Warhol, Andy, 34.6, 73.5, 90.20
Waters, John, 83.7, 244.5
Wayne, John, 11.10, 38.21, 93.11, 112.16. 113.15, 116.15, 141.21, 147.10, 158.5, 161.15, 173.4, 177.4, 180.5, 194.16, 207.13, 231.14, 234.17, 238.9, 253.10, 255.22
Weaver, Sigourney, 3.17, 7.15, 17.7, 208.8
Weinstein, Henry T., 168.14
Welch, Raquel, 8.11, 21.5, 29.4, 34.7, 39.18, 101.10, 151.11, 157.5, 165.10, 175.13, 178.10, 189.3, 203.10, 221.13, 224.9
Weld, Tuesday, 58.4, 78.8
Welles, Orson, 83.8, 83.9, 86.9, 88.13, 131.15, 137.6, 187.6, 251.8
West, Mae, 39.19, 50.3, 53.3, 54.10, 117.12, 150.14, 151.12, 156.15–16, 175.14, 209.8, 214.10, 219.6, 221.14, 224.10, 232.16, 235.16
Westlake, Donald, 260.10
Widmark, Richard, 248.5
Wiest, Dianne, 12.14, 156.15–16, 179.12
Wilder, Billy, 83.10, 168.15
Wilder, Gene, 12.15, 120.7
Williams, Edy, 44.11, 53.4, 197.6
Williams, Robin, 41.4, 61.7, 64.11, 96.7, 136.3, 240.13
Willis, Bruce, 237.5
Wilson, Michael, 35.11
Winger, Debra, 30.3, 31.3, 65.10
Winner, Michael, 113.16, 190.3
Winters, Shelley, 39.20, 40.8, 49.1, 152.6, 155.6, 175.15, 180.6, .181.15
Winwood, Estelle, 9.18, 73.6
Wise, Robert, 252.6
Woods, James, 26.10, 81.12, 128.11, 131.16, 178.11, 190.4, 223.7, 237.6, 245.6
Woodward, Joanne, 3.18, 25.8

Yakovleva, Elena, 241.8
Yanne, Jean, 28.2
Young, Sean, 13.12, 148.16

Young, Terence, 233.17

Zeffirelli, Franco, 96.8

Zetterling, Mai, 106.7
Zimmerman, Paul, 25.9, 71.2
Zwick, Edward, 95.5

DISTRIBUTORS
for the Wordsworth Reference Series

**AUSTRALIA, BRUNEI,
MALAYSIA & SINGAPORE**

Reed Editions
22 Salmon Street
Port Melbourne
Vic 3207
Australia

Tel: (03) 646 6716
Fax: (03) 646 6925

**GERMANY, AUSTRIA
& SWITZERLAND**

Swan Buch-Marketing GmbH
Goldscheuerstraße 16
D-7640 Kehl am Rhein
Germany

GREAT BRITAIN & IRELAND

Wordsworth Editions Ltd
Cumberland House
Crib Street
Ware
Hertfordshire SG12 9ET

INDIA

Om Book Service
1690 First Floor
Nai Sarak, Delhi - 110006

Tel: 3279823/3265303
Fax: 3278091

ITALY

Magis Books
Piazza della Vittoria 1/C
42100 Reggio Emilia

Tel: 0522-452303
Fax: 0522-452845

NEW ZEALAND

Whitcoulls Limited
Private Bag 92098, Auckland

USA, CANADA & MEXICO

Universal Sales & Marketing
230 Fifth Avenue
Suite 1212
New York, NY 10001 USA

Tel: 212-481-3500
Fax: 212-481-3534